Fat Rights

Fat Rights

*Dilemmas of Difference
and Personhood*

Anna Kirkland

NEW YORK UNIVERSITY PRESS
New York and London

NEW YORK UNIVERSITY PRESS
New York and London
www.nyupress.org

Library of Congress Cataloging-in-Publication Data
Kirkland, Anna Rutherford.
Fat rights : dilemmas of difference and personhood / Anna
Kirkland.
p. cm.
Includes bibliographical references and index.
ISBN-13: 978-0-8147-4807-7 (cl : alk. paper)
ISBN-10: 0-8147-4807-4 (cl : alk. paper)
ISBN-13: 978-0-8147-4813-8 (pb : alk. paper)
ISBN-10: 0-8147-4813-9 (pb : alk. paper)
1. Discrimination against overweight persons—Law and legislation
—United States. 2. Overweight persons—Civil rights—United
States. 3. Discrimination—Law and legislation—United States.
4. Overweight persons—Social aspects—United States. I. Title.
KF4757.5.O94K57 2008
342.7308'7—dc22   2007043256

New York University Press books are printed on acid-free paper,
and their binding materials are chosen for strength and durability.

Manufactured in the United States of America

c 10 9 8 7 6 5 4 3 2 1
p 10 9 8 7 6 5 4 3 2 1

for Ben

Contents

Preface   ix

Introduction: The Challenge of Difference   1

1   Imagining Legal Protections for Fatness   30

2   Shifting the Blame   55

3   Balancing Functional Individuals and
Embedded Selves   75

4   Governing Risk: Medicalization and Normalization   97

5   Accommodating Fatness   126

Conclusion: What Is Worth Wanting in American
Antidiscrimination Law?   147

Notes   161
Index   191
About the Author   196

Preface

This is a book about fat rights. To be more precise, this is a book about what makes fat rights possible or impossible, credible or incredible, reasonable or untenable in contemporary American law and society. It must then also be a book about rights in general, about who properly possesses rights, and about how rights work. It must be about the society we actually live in and the tools we regularly use to make sense of what different people deserve in their ordinary quests to get by and get ahead. As anyone who has even glanced at the news in the last few years well knows, we are alleged to be in the midst of what has been called an "obesity epidemic." (Throughout this book I use the straightforward descriptor "fat"; I avoid the language of "overweight" and "obesity" because I do not endorse the medical and pejorative view of fat people those terms suggest.) As soon as a new social problem emerges in our society, it is never too long before we begin debating the issue in terms of rights. Are fat citizens a new rights group on their way to being seen as objects of unfair discrimination? If so, how will we talk about what they deserve? Being fat is surely quite stigmatizing. Media coverage of the trend has been sensationalist and misleading, feeding a national and even international fat panic. U.S. Surgeon General Richard Carmona said in a 2006 speech that rising weights would "dwarf" the terrorist attacks of September 11, 2001, calling it "the terror within." Blame has been pinned on "feminist careerism" because women now work rather than stay home and cook healthy meals for their families. The tone of public debate may now be turning back toward greater calm, however, and it is my hope that this book will contribute to a discussion about what our antidiscrimination traditions can and cannot offer us to help puzzle through the relationship between the reality of our differences in body sizes and what justice requires for all of us.

This book places fat citizens within our antidiscrimination traditions in order to show how those traditions will decipher fat citizens' claims to rights. Its aim is to promote deeper understanding of the languages we have to use to defend new rights claims. So this book is about black civil rights and women's rights, too, since the categories of race and sex have most deeply shaped the ways we think and talk about who deserves to be covered in the law. It is a book about disability rights as well, because disability is the newest, and in many ways most fraught, category for legal protections in American law. Protection against transgender discrimination is even more unfamiliar to many Americans than protection against weight discrimination, but it is also a new idea beginning to have its day in court. To understand what we will get out of gaining new legal protections, we must understand all the categories that are already there.

This book is more like a field guide to the underlying presumptions of antidiscrimination laws than a plan for adding "weight" to the list of protected traits. It has seemed to me that arguments straightforwardly advocating for an end to weight-based discrimination miss an opportunity to take stock of why we must use the terms that we do. Why must arguments for employment rights begin from the (usually unquestioned) presumption that the deserving worker is a fully normal and functional individual just like everyone else? This starting point is so obvious that it is rarely discussed. And yet it closes off discussion of the place of difference in antidiscrimination rules, or at least puts difference on the defensive: "Well, yes, I guess my body is a little different, but don't worry, not in a way that matters for doing the job."

There are many ways to read this book. Readers interested in the politics of the obesity epidemic should read this book for the legal angles it supplies. Many of the same arguments about fat (health issue or civil rights issue, under the control of individuals or the fault of food companies?) play over again in legal cases. Readers interested in antidiscrimination theories should read this book for its technique: it uses the trait of fatness as a lever to pry into the deep theoretical presumptions about personhood that determine what arguments are possible. Readers interested in identity and law may appreciate its inside-out construction, by which I mean its use of largely unrecognized traits like fatness to unfold the interior presumptions of the "classic" traits of race and gender. Readers keen on normative arguments defending the dignity of persons (as in human rights law, for example) will find a thickly descriptive account of persons in the law, which in turn can tell them what is likely to happen when this or that argument is made. Fat advocates will gain insights into how their arguments will resonate or fail to resonate as justice claims, and receive an account of how we still do not have an adequate place in the law to receive their claims. Many advocates realize this inadequacy all too well. They also realize they must keep pressing those claims. *Fat Rights* offers a way to keep doing that in an eyes-wide-open, strategic, and supple way.

Readers who love stories—and I think that is most everyone—will meet ordinary people in this book whose struggles for rights reveal much beyond their individual struggles. Arazella Manuel, a fat woman who applied to drive an airport shuttle bus in Houston, went to court when a doctor's view of her waddling gait lost her the job. Darlene Jespersen worked at Harrah's Casino in Reno for many years before being fired for refusing to comply with a new makeup and hairstyle policy. Deborah Marks was an award-winning telemarketer who couldn't get promoted to a face-to-face sales position because management didn't want people to see how fat she was. Romell Carter worked unloading baggage at Chicago O'Hare airport until he smashed his foot in a machine, and then was not able to work out a transfer to another job that could accommodate his new disability. We often think of law as a lofty set of rules that only professionals like judges and lawyers understand. But law is also just one way of trying to make sense of what all these things we do—walking around, appearing at work, trying to perform tasks—mean for what we deserve to get out of life.

Seeing one's work through the eyes of others and rethinking it is one of the great joys of scholarship. I am deeply grateful to many supportive colleagues whose thoughts I have ingested in writing this book. They have not vanquished all the errors, though not for lack of trying. Naomi Andre, Kristin Bumiller, Paul Campos, Elizabeth Cole, Marianne Constable, Jonathan Goldberg-Hiller, Dena Goodman, Don Herzog, Deborah Keller-Cohen, Mika Lavaque-Manty, Peggy McCracken, Abigail Saguy, Tobin Siebers, Peggy Somers, Abigail Stewart, Miriam Ticktin, Valerie Traub, James Boyd White, Christina Whitman, and Elizabeth Wingrove provided rich feedback, in many cases over and over again. Wendy Brown, Kristin Luker, Robert Post, Samuel Scheffler, and Jonathan Simon at the University of California, Berkeley nurtured this project in its earliest stages. I received timely and exacting research support from the University of Michigan School of Law librarians, particularly Aimee Mangan and her staff of student researchers.

I also thankfully acknowledge permissions by the University of California Press, the University of Chicago Press, and the Society for Disability Studies to use material from my previously published work. Sections of the Introduction, chapter 1, and chapter 4 originally appeared as "Representations of Fatness and Personhood: Pro-Fat Advocacy and the Limits and Uses of Law," *Representations,* No. 82 (Spring 2003): 24–51. Parts of chapter 3 first lived as "What's at Stake in Transgender Discrimination as Sex Discrimination?" *Signs: Journal of Women in Culture and Society,* Vol. 32, No. 1 (Autumn 2006): 83–111, and chapter 5 is based on "What's at Stake in Fatness as a Disability?" *Disability Studies Quarterly,* Vol. 26, No. 1 (Winter 2006).

Introduction
The Challenge of Difference

A prominent idea in American law is that similarly situated people ought to be treated similarly. Equality, in this view, is not about treating each and every person in exactly the same way. Instead, it is about knowing which differences among persons really matter. If persons differ in some meaningful way, they are not similarly situated, and thus may be treated differently. Children are not similarly situated to adults with respect to responsibility, for example, so they are held to a more lenient legal standard and given duties like attending school that do not apply to adults. It is not discrimination to tell a twelve-year-old that she cannot drive the family car while her twenty-year-old sibling can.

Contemporary American antidiscrimination law attempts to draw these distinctions by constructing categories that then are presumptively off limits for judging persons.[1] Race, sex, pregnancy, ethnic background, national origin, disability, age (but only for workers over forty), and religion are the most commonly protected, but some jurisdictions also include sexual orientation, Vietnam veteran status, or marital status. In a few places, what is called gender identity (usually meaning transsexual or transgender identity), weight and height, and other aspects of personal appearance are included as well. The basic challenge of this system of antidiscrimination law is to know which differences matter, which ones are incidental, and how to tell between them. The challenge of establishing which differences really matter is often framed as a debate over which traits belong on these lists. Some of these categories are acceptably salient axes of identities that most people recognize and accept as part of our civil rights law, such as race and gender, while coverage for others, like weight or transgender status, is highly contentious.[2] Legislatures or city councils may add new categories to civil rights statutes, and judges may interpret existing guarantees to include new identity traits (such as interpreting the ban on sex discrimination to include transgender discrimination or classifying obesity as a disability).

Inclusion of a trait in these protected categories is one effect of law's approach to difference. The extension of antidiscrimination rights is a political conclusion, marking the fact that a trait has garnered sufficient support from either politicians or judges to be ushered onto the list of protected traits.[3] But what logics justify these conclusions? I want to shift attention from the construction of categories to the underlying presuppositions that help us recognize some persons as different in such a way that justifies legal protection. Just the knowledge that a trait has been granted legal protection does not tell us what its meaning is. Political arguments and judicial rhetoric appear to be the primary grounds upon which debates about civil rights protections take place. But these dispute resolution processes (lawsuits or legislation, as we know them formally) do not supply the grounds for understanding difference in the first place. They supply, but do not explain, the institutions and practices for resolving conflict about difference.

Debates about difference are actually comprised of competing descriptions of what persons are, how they function, how their merit is to be determined, how they exist within communities, and what they deserve as a result. Logics, after all, always rely on underlying premises, and these descriptions constitute those underlying premises. These competing descriptions then create dilemmas for advocates because they conflict with each other, but they are required for each logic to make sense on its own. In this book I argue that logics of personhood can explain the complex, shifting, and often muddy terrain of our antidiscrimination laws. Logics of personhood are forms of reasoning about what persons are—specifically, ways we explain to each other how and why someone's traits should or should not matter for judging what is really important about her. There are competing and incommensurable logics of personhood that undergird law's conclusions about whether or not difference matters, and in what ways that matters. What we often think of as identity politics or multiculturalism, then, turns out to be more fruitfully understood as the effect of logics of personhood. It is no surprise that antidiscrimination, an area of law that includes so many of the most basic and contentious problems of judgment, equality, and fairness, would back up to equally fundamental questions about personhood. The abiding ambiguities and conflicts in these areas are dilemmas deeply rooted in the ways we reason through problems of difference in the law. Deeply rooted ways of thinking are not deterministic, however; these logics of personhood are contingent and historically situated, and of late they have exhibited some interesting shifts that I will discuss in detail. Nonetheless, I examine them here not for their full arc of history, but for their appearance in the present. The focus on fatness situates this work in a very particular moment (because, of course, cultural conceptions of fatness even in our own society have at other times been quite different than they are now).

There is always an account (or more often, multiple accounts) about a person's difference in the law: what caused it; whether it prevents her from functioning in a role; whether its significance is part of a shameful historical legacy of state-sponsored discrimination; whether the person brought it on herself; whether it is relevant because it is a trait that creates risk for others or only because it is a health problem; whether it places her within a group or whether the difference is understood to be individually variable; whether it is something to be protected as a tie to her community; or whether it is a lamentably incurable affliction that merits accommodation. These stories rest on different logics of personhood that link together identity, personal traits, moral responsibility, governmental response, and legal protections. I call them functional personhood; embedded personhood; the blame shifting account of personhood; diverse personhood; actuarial personhood; and managerial individualism (and explain them each fully below). These logics, their interrelationships, and their implications for law and politics are the subject of *Fat Rights*. By insisting upon the accessibility of these logics in our ordinary language, as well as their deep significance in the formal law, *Fat Rights* offers a new framework for, first, explaining what we do when we make choices about difference, and second, evaluating and anticipating what those choices, as they are expressed in the law, are likely to mean for persons.

Logics of personhood are ordinary, commonsense ways of talking about difference and how it matters. They are also the basis of legal rules and judicial decision making. Logics of personhood are institutions in the sense of providing stable, useable patterns of "rhetorical legitimation characteristic of certain traditions of political discourse," as Rogers Smith describes in his influential essay on the future of public law in political science.[4] They provide justifications for legal outcomes: one person's firing is held to have been illegal, another's legal. These logics give us boundaries for seeing injustice, and they tell us what kinds of justice to hope for.[5] They are not radical ways of thinking. These logics hold up and fortify our legal and political system in its current form, with some shifting and contestation at the margins. There are multiple logics of personhood to invoke, and they sometimes conflict. But even so, they relate back to ways of understanding ourselves and each other that seem obviously correct to many people. Their power thus derives from their roots in overlapping domains of ordinary life, legal rules, and governmental practices. My analysis suggests that there is no unified moral approach that will tell us who deserves legal protection based on their traits. That is why this book cannot be a unified moral argument for extending fat rights. My aim is to make clear the ways we talk through and justify various legal protections (or the lack of them) and to draw out their sometimes counter-intuitive implications. This approach is helpful because it shows anyone interested in the extensions of rights protections—for any group, not just fat people—the possible effects their justifications will have, giving them the tools to deploy their reason-giving in much more sophisticated ways.

Why call these ways of talking about difference "logics," though? Logic suggests a tidy reasoning process, whereas what I will describe in this book is often quite messy and contradictory. What I mean to stress in the term "logic" is its bounded nature, in which one sets out the premises that will be part of the progression and uses them to generate an outcome that is consistent with those starting premises. Each logic has its own bounded area in which it can spin an account of difference and reveal how to handle it in antidiscrimination law. Each logic has starting premises that guide its account of persons and their difference. If the premise is that functional capacity is the most important thing about a worker and that traits of appearance have nothing to do with performing a job, then we may mandate that employers disregard race and gender while hiring and measure only, say, the speed of typing without errors in interviewing a secretary. The logic would yield a certain set of practices based on the premise that appearance is not a difference that matters. Suppose then an employee who uses a wheelchair appears. The logic, if we stick to it, would dictate that we simply ignore that feature of her appearance. In such a world—of staircases, big heavy doors, cramped toilet stalls, and high shelving—people in wheelchairs will simply be excluded much of the time. The logic simply cannot devise an approach to their differences. Antidiscrimination law can then generate a new logic to justify making some accommodations. It may maintain the value of functional capacity while adding ramps and elevators, for example, or it may revisit the idea that functional capacity is indeed a neutral measure of merit in the first place. It is not that we are simply stuck with confining and unimaginative ways of thinking; rather, we draw on a set of logics that are on their own quite rich and which seem perfectly suitable for resolving many questions, but which co-exist in tension with others that are equally compelling.

So I do not mean to use the term "logic" in a formal or lofty way; rather, I simply think it captures well the ways that we begin with seemingly uncontroversial premises and then generate conclusions about to how to treat difference. Then when we bump into an unpalatable outcome, we must back up and revise our starting premises about what is really important about persons after all. This bumping about and revising may take place in one person's mind, in a judicial opinion, or within a legislative body. It is this process of bumping about, realizing what our premises really are, and seeing the dilemmas they produce that I draw out in *Fat Rights*. I could have chosen other terms like "frameworks" or "grammars" of personhood, but I want to emphasize the process of reasoning, prioritizing, and line drawing that logical thinking involves (even if it only looks quasi-logical in application).

I have not drawn these logics that I name and use out of thin air, of course. They derive their meaning and usefulness from roots within post-Enlightenment cultures of the modern industrialized West. The functional individual is a liberal citizen who asks that others suspend their prejudices in the public sphere of work and citizenship. She is a figure of Weberian rationalization as well, in as much as she must be managed and incorporated successfully into organizations. Diversity has been a means of making the organizational man cosmopolitan and tolerant in the perfect blend of the two. Embedded personhood pushes back against the individualism of liberal legalism with a call to community, asking us to remember the constitution of the self within culture. To shift the blame away from supposed dysfunction to the basic arrangement of goods and opportunities can be derived from a mild form of social welfare liberalism, but it also shares roots with more radical Marxist-flavored critiques of bourgeois individualism. The techniques of actuarial governance debated in antidiscrimination cases are the same ones traced in Michel Foucault's work on governmentality. I have elected to go directly to contemporary legal justifications rather than to texts in the canon of Western thought in which these same disputes about the person are foregrounded because I've found that the details of legal thought are sufficiently demanding and exciting to stand without annotation and the roots are clear enough and traced well by others.[6] So while this book is not a work of political or social theory in the usual sense, I invite readers to see these debates within antidiscrimination law as examples of many of the same perennial questions treated in those fields.

If antidiscrimination protections are markers of conclusions, the meanings of which require explanation, then their boundaries require explanation. Why do some traits seem paradigmatically to deserve antidiscrimination protections, while for other traits the same protections seem absurd? To better see the boundaries, I examine rights protections based on race, gender, and disability which have already been clearly established, as well as claims based on weight and transgender identity, which exist on the fringes of legal protection.[7] Fat discrimination will be my primary lever for exposing the fascinating details of these claims. Examining antidiscrimination law from both the center and the edges helps me to ignore what I'm supposed to take for granted about rights and to examine their boundaries with fresh eyes. For instance, the assertion that one cannot change one's trait (that it is immutable) has often been assumed to be the primary way one defends oneself against prejudice. But revisiting the whole field of legal protections leads me to downgrade it in relative importance compared to claims about functional capacities.

This is not a study about, for example, whether fat people *should* have more rights, although it will undoubtedly assist arguments that they should. Rather, *Fat Rights* is a study about what it means when they do or do not have rights. I'm interested in what these liminal cases tell us about boundaries in our reasoning about justice. In watching how law extends or retracts rights to these persons, we can observe the properties of the boundaries and how they move. Austin Sarat and Thomas Kearns explain that "[e]xamining . . . constitutive effects [of rights] means inquiring into the way rights call into being, and enable, particular forms and expressions of personhood, as well as the way they disable others."[8] My approach shares this same constitutive orientation but argues that "forms and expressions" of personhood need much more elaboration than they have hitherto received.

In the following chapters I both explain the various logics of personhood that currently traffic across and within antidiscrimination law, and draw out their implications for the persons who find themselves explained by them. I do not presume that personhood is something always present, inherently dignified, and often unrecognized. Reasoning about persons is something we all do all the time and which law relies upon to generate its own particular forms of justification in legal opinions, statutes, and constitutional interpretation. Rather than constructing a primarily normative argument about which differences really ought to matter, I ask how it is that we come to know and justify the meaning of differences in the first place.

Logics of Personhood

The Logic of Functional Individualism

Consider the following common arguments. Bonnie Cook, a victorious plaintiff in a fat discrimination lawsuit: "I guess all I can say is that people shouldn't judge others because of how they look. What's important is whether or not they can do the job."[9] "You're making a determination of people's capability and their health based on how they look, and that's not fair," said Jeannette DePatie, a spokeswoman for the National Association for the Advancement of Fat Acceptance (NAAFA). An attorney for a 420-pound man who did not get a job at McDonald's as a cook argued that "[t]he only thing that should matter to McDonald's was how he cooks, not how he looks."[10] The logic of personhood working here is what I call functional individualism: a person should be judged by her ability to perform, not by her appearance. The differences that matter are differences in merit, talent, and capabilities. Capacities are features of persons that ought to be separated from outwardly appearing traits, the argument goes, and being fat ought not to count as evidence that a person is unhealthy or lazy. This functional individualist logic ignores some traits—above, it's proposed that fatness ("how he looks") be ignored—but only if they are understood to be disconnected from the individual's merit ("how he cooks").[11]

Plaintiffs use this logic when filing antidiscrimination cases. Their goal is to convince judges and juries that they were unfairly disadvantaged because their difference should not have made a difference, and they articulate their claims in terms of functional individualism. On March 2, 1994, Arazella Manuel applied for a job as a bus driver with

Texas Bus Lines, which operated a shuttle service in Houston between area hotels and the airports. She passed all the qualifying tests, and then had to go for a physical exam. She was five feet seven inches tall and weighed 345 pounds, but the doctor who examined her, Dr. James Frierson, found that her blood pressure was normal and that she had no health problems. Nonetheless, he declined to certify Ms. Manuel to drive because of her weight, citing concerns that her size would prevent her from helping passengers in an emergency. Even though obesity is not an automatic disqualification for the job under the federal rules, Texas Bus Lines withdrew its conditional offer to hire her.[12] Ms. Manuel sued, claiming that she had been discriminated against when the company wrongly assumed that her weight was disabling. The logic she was invoking was functional individualism.

Catherine McDermott, another fat woman, applied to Xerox for a job as a business systems consultant. She also had to undergo a medical exam as part of the hiring process. The Director of Health Services for Xerox who reviewed the results of her pre-employment medical examination told her would-be manager that she posed a financial risk to the company.[13] According to this doctor, obesity would probably not have any short term effect on her job performance, but "over the long term the obese group will have a higher absenteeism rate, higher utilization of long-term and disability benefits, medical care plans, [and] life insurance."[14] Because health care in the United States is tied to employment, companies often screen prospective employees in this way or promote among current employees health habits that are meant to lower the company's health care costs. Xerox refused to hire Ms. McDermott based entirely on these actuarial concerns. She sued under New York's state human rights law. Again, her claim is based on functional individualism, brought to bear against the company's actuarial reasoning, which neither treated her as an individual nor cared much about her levels of functioning in the present moment.

Both Ms. Manuel and Ms. McDermott thought of themselves as perfectly well-functioning people who were qualified for these jobs. As it turned out, the judges in their cases agreed with them. Both women won their lawsuits. The judges ruled that it was unfair for the companies to have made assumptions about their risk on the job, health and fitness, and job performances just because they were fat. The employers had assumed the women were disabled when they were not, and that assumption is equivalent to disability discrimination. But in another

case, a fat woman's appearance was understood to be part of job performance. Deborah Marks, who weighed 270 pounds, had been named
"Telemarketer of the Year" but was passed over for a face-to-face
sales job.[15] When she complained, her supervisor told her "to lose the
weight and that was important for outside sales because you were—you
weren't just on the telephone, you were going around from person to
person and therefore presentation was extremely important."[16] Ms.
Marks lost her case because weight is not included in Title VII of the
1964 Civil Rights Act, making it perfectly legal for her employer to decide that she was just too fat to put forth the right image.[17] Ms. Marks
tried to invoke functional individualism based on her past success in
telemarketing, but was thwarted because antidiscrimination law often
permits fatness to count as a meaningful difference between persons.
The critical features of functional individualism for us to watch are its
ability to thwart unjust assessments of many people, but also its ten-
dency to collapse when someone really does function differently from
the norm, as well as its uselessness when the norm itself should be inter-
rogated. It seems stunningly obvious to talk about functional capacity
when parsing job discrimination, but what's fascinating is how quickly
this logic—to which we all turn so readily—reaches its limit.

The Logic of Embedded Personhood

Functional individualism reaches its limit when there is not a clear
functionalist account of what a person should be doing to fill a given
position. Functionalist logic works best when there is a clear description
of a task, like typing a certain number of words per minute. But filling
many positions involves filling a social role, not just performing a set of
movements. What I call embedded personhood tells us that some aspects of a person cannot simply be ignored because they supply valuable
information about what kind of person she is and how we can understand and judge her within a particular context. Embedded personhood
is not just the way a person looks—gender, age, or social status—although looks are often the primary means of conveying the information
necessary to draw on its logic. It is also made up by the social meanings
that our differences convey to others and to ourselves. On the phone,
Ms. Marks did not need to worry about any of the social meanings of
her appearance. It turned out that the company did not hire or promote
any fat people into face-to-face sales positions because of the impression

these sales people would make on customers. Customer preferences in employment law are often the site of legal disputes: shall a company be required to define the job in a functional individualist way without consideration of the social meanings of appearance, or shall the company be allowed to hew to social norms—including employee appearance—that result in some people not being hired just because of the way they look?

If the judgment in Ms. Mark's case seems heartless, that is probably because one can imagine a social policy that has as its aim changing the social meaning of fatness. Fatness, in other words, would no longer mean laziness or the inability to care for the self. It might be accepted as something largely determined by a person's genes, with no necessary link to character or habits. However, if the outcome of Ms. Mark's case seems reasonable, that is because one is comfortable with these negative social meanings for fatness. Maintaining the negative social meaning of a trait is often justified in terms of deterrence. If fatness is unhealthy and comes from eating too much, then it is a behavior that could be deterred and we would all be better off. Legal protection then looks like misguided sympathy that makes it easier for people to keep on indulging themselves. The logic of embedded personhood recognizes ordinary experiences as embodied selves, but in a much more complex way than the mechanized view of functional individualism. Overeating, trying to lose weight and succeeding, trying and failing (or both over and over again), and monitoring our physical health are things many of us do. Our familiarity gives us knowledge about these things, and this knowledge is hard to force aside in favor of a simple prescription of functional individualism. Though we disagree with each other about what we learn from our embedded, embodied lives, it is clear that the experiences teach us ways of reasoning about the differences between people that we see arrayed in the world. Jurors use this same logic when they decide, for example, whether a fat plaintiff has done all she could to lose weight and heal faster after an injury. If she should have tried harder and lost more weight, then perhaps the business owner she's suing cannot be wholly liable for the injury.[18]

The antidote to embedded personhood is usually functional individualism: ignore the social meaning of the person's difference, and only measure whether she can perform the job. It would seem that those who want to extend antidiscrimination protections would want to use the

logic of functional individualism and reject embedded personhood altogether. But that cannot be right. What about the meaning of difference
for strip club owners and customers? Is erotic dancing just choreo-
graphed moves to music, or does it require a sexualized presentation of
a person of a certain gender (depending on the type of establishment)?
Don't most people select their sexual partners based on gender, and is
that such a bad thing? The point is that whatever our preferences in any
given case, the vast majority of us would not really want to live in a
world in which the only way to judge others was functional individualism. Such a world would lack many of the cues about other people
that sustain our most important relationships, both legal and personal.
It is not even possible to keep embedded personhood for our private
lives and promote functional individualism in employment or the public
sphere.

That's the rub with embedded personhood: it is simultaneously the
site of our most base prejudices, and also grounds the construction of
an everyday life that has meaning and order. "Just because of how I
look" is an oddly dismissive way to talk about ourselves. What we see
in the mirror every day is a race, a gender, an able body or a disabled
body, fatness or thinness, age or youth. These traits anchor us within
communities and render us recognizably ourselves to others. Occa-
sionally I have dreams that I wake up looking completely physically
changed, and in those dreams I cannot help but feel that I've become
someone else, or that I have lost my friends at least for a while. Perhaps
someone bearing a highly stigmatized trait would be delighted if it
would disappear in the night (fat would be a likely candidate). But I
suspect most of us would be traumatized by the loss or transformation
of even our most ordinary features. That is because both the traits that
make us different and the practices associated with them tell us what it
is to be a person like us. Even most transgender people who seek sex reassignment surgeries, perhaps the most dramatic shift one could imagine, are pursuing a switch from one recognizable community to another
rather than casting off gender altogether. The crucial question will be
how antidiscrimination law makes sense of these conflicting logics of
personhood, one pulling away from embeddedness and toward measuring the ability to function, and the other insisting that embeddedness offers us a vision of ourselves that is worth preserving even though it has
its cruelties.

The Blame-Shifting Tradition in American Antidiscrimination Law

There is no denying the power of American law's entanglements with racial discrimination in building up our history of talking about difference. Nearly all the legal formulations of why discrimination is wrong were born from racial conflict, specifically the dismantling of slavery and its effects. Color blindness is a popular formulation of the impulse to ignore racial difference. But antidiscrimination laws have not always hewn to the presumption that as a society once we blind ourselves to race (leaving aside the difficulties of actually doing that), persons' functional capacities would reveal themselves and everyone would have an equal opportunity to succeed based on a fair assessment of their merits. I shall argue that racial discrimination has at times been answered with a transformative logic that disrupts functional individualism, but in more recent years has been reconfigured as something to be addressed by diversity management.

Both the initial justifications for enacting the 1964 Civil Rights Act and its subsequent interpretations in the courts rested upon the idea that black Americans had not simply been misjudged, but rather that social structures of American society in fact created them to be dysfunctional (to echo the language of functional individualism) and operated to keep them that way as a group: lacking educational opportunities and shut out of good jobs. This logic suggests that it is deeply unfair to run a segregated school system, expect the group shunted into the inferior schools to compete with the dominant group, and then blame their lower rates of success on their moral inferiority, backward culture, or innate lack of capacity. It is a logic that transforms what would otherwise look like personal dysfunction into social debt. It shifts the blame for differential outcomes away from the people who come out looking inferior, and onto the institutions and structures that are understood to have made them that way. Solutions involve not only dismantling structures that create dysfunction, but also an intolerance for imbalances that preserve the disadvantaged groups' inferior positions. In one sense it is strange to call the blame-shifting response a logic of personhood since it removes the focus from the individual and places it back on history, institutions, and state practices. But it still works in the same way as the other logics I've outlined here: it justifies a certain treatment of difference by explaining the connections between the person, her trait, and what justice requires for her.

American antidiscrimination law has at times embraced the blame-shifting logic. Consider this classic case in which the Supreme Court had to decide who was to blame for racial disparities in jobs. Jobs at the Duke Power Company's Dan River Steam Station in Draper, North Carolina were organized into five categories: Labor, Coal Handling, Operations, Maintenance, and Laboratory and Test. Prior to 1965, African Americans could only get jobs in Labor (which paid less than the other four categories). All remaining departments were filled with white employees. In 1965, Duke Power instituted a high school graduation requirement for transfer from Labor to any other department, though white employees working in other areas who did not have high school diplomas kept their jobs and continued to achieve promotions within the other four departments. On the day the Civil Rights Act of 1964 went into effect, outlawing discrimination on the basis of race in employment and public accommodations, the company instituted an additional requirement for a job in any department except for Labor: successful completion of two aptitude tests. The tests screened out vastly greater numbers of black employees than white. There was no proof that Duke Power had instituted the test hoping for such an outcome, but it effectively preserved the racial divisions at the company.

Black employees at the Dan River Steam Station filed a class action lawsuit under Title VII of the newly enacted Civil Rights Act of 1964 alleging discrimination on the basis of race.[19] The Supreme Court held that the tests, ostensibly to measure individual functional capacities, could not be justified as necessary to the business, and thus could not be allowed to have their racially disparate effects. Duke Power may have instituted the tests just so they would maintain *de facto* segregation of the workforce, but the Court held that the company's intent to discriminate did not matter. This theory of discrimination, called disparate impact, applies to situations in which a workplace rule creates group-level disparities along the lines of protected traits (race, color, sex, religion, or national origin). Disparate impact theory has been used subsequently to dismantle height requirements for police officers that keep out women and Asians, for example, and to force fire departments to justify the tests they give to recruits as being necessary to the job of being a fire fighter, and not just the usual practices of an all-male profession.

The job tests at issue measure something, of course, and litigation is based on the fact that women and minorities fail to measure up. Why, though? What is being measured? Functional individualism would make it possible for an employer to say that there is not anything wrong with being black or a woman, but that those folks simply do not have the necessary qualifications. The tests could be given with race and sex screened out, so that prejudices would not influence the outcome. Indeed, many conservatives espouse this position, condemning racial prejudice while insisting that individuals be judged against each other without any special dispensations for members of any group.[20] Disparate impact discrimination suits prompt employers to undo certain practices in order to increase numbers of women or minorities who will succeed, and thus shares much in common with affirmative action programs. The essential core of the disagreement between liberals and conservatives about both disparate impact and affirmative action is this choice between sticking with functional individualism and letting the chips fall where they may versus intervening to shift the blame for the out-groups' lower levels of success and then changing the rules of the game so that more of them will succeed. Though this dichotomy sacrifices nuanced views across the political spectrum, it is still useful to trace the basic disagreement to this simple choice, since it is so vastly meaningful for so many social policies and legal judgments. Liberals emphasize the never-neutral history of our society's treatment of women and racial minorities, arguing that men and whites have always rigged the game to their advantage. Conservatives maintain that true functional merit really does exist and that fairness requires applying the same standards to everyone, even if racial or sex disparities appear in the final distribution.

Diversity: When Difference Is Good

In the heyday of the Great Society era when these legal rules appeared, they were justified using this blame-shifting logic of personhood. Much has changed, however. President Ronald Reagan's Justice Department was largely hostile to race-conscious remedies in the form of affirmative action, quotas, or disparate impact lawsuits, and thus sharply scaled back these efforts through non-enforcement, direct criticism, and the appointment of conservatives like future Supreme Court Justice Clarence Thomas to run the Equal Employment Opportunity Commission (EEOC).[21] The Supreme Court continued to uphold the disparate impact interpretation of Title VII for the private sector, but began to interpret the equal protection clause of the 14th Amendment to ban nearly all governmental use of race to classify citizens, even when the intent was benign assistance to racial minorities through affirmative action programs. Diversity in education remained a possible justification for race-conscious admissions after the Supreme Court's 1978 decision in *Regents of the University of California v. Bakke,* recently affirmed in the 2003 University of Michigan affirmative action cases. The idea of diversity took hold in business and managerial circles with the 1987 publication of a report called *Workforce 2000,* projecting that the American workplace would soon become dominated by non-white workers (projections that turned out to be misstated but nonetheless took on a life of their own).[22] Diversity management came to be understood as crucial to business success in a multicultural, globalized world at the same time as affirmative action supporters realized that diversity was their last hope for maintaining any kind of race-conscious policies under the 14th Amendment.[23]

Diversity is a way of conceptualizing what difference is and why it matters, and it also proposes a logic of personhood and a meaning for difference. Under diversity management, persons are understood to come in different races, sexes, and nationalities, but also to have different perspectives, talents, backgrounds, approaches to problem-solving, ideologies, and personalities. Variations in personality, for instance, are just as important as racial differences because they have the same potential to contribute to group dynamics. The logic of diverse personhood does not make use of the classic divisions of group-based identity politics, but rather promiscuously counts as "diversity" pretty much anything that contributes to noticeable variation among persons and which could either assist or inhibit the organizations' pursuit of its goals. Personhood in this view is infinitely variable but always located within the individual and her unique combinations of experiences, outlook, training, background, and traits. Indeed, because no one person has had exactly the same life as another person, the logic of diversity suggests that each of us is primarily unique, not primarily located in social subgroups. Of course persons can be diverse in ways that damage organizations, but generally this kind of talk represents difference as useful variation that just requires a deft touch to manage. Diversity management is a way of making meaning from all kinds of human differences, but for the purposes of achieving success in group undertakings at work or in a college learning environment. Managerial techniques tend to focus on group processes rather than group status, moving notions of racial justice away from their early roots in antidiscrimination law.

Some supporters of affirmative action use the term diversity as code for racial preferences. Conservatives, sniffing this out, suspect that diversity is a canard. But both sides have missed the transformation of diversity in recent years from an *ad hoc* gesture toward group-based differences to a profoundly individualistic logic of personal difference. Tracing the logics of personhood through our society's debates about racial difference shows what is at stake as one form of reasoning loses ground and another replaces it. It also confirms yet again that ideas circulate from the law (the *Bakke* case's defense of diversity) though other institutions with their own aims (companies' responses to *Workplace 2000*) all the while becoming more and more ordinary ways of talking in more and more settings.

Stereotyping: What to Call the Wrong Attention to Difference

The salience of race in American antidiscrimination law has also had profound effects on understandings of sex discrimination. From the moment of the amendment adding "sex" to the list of protected categories in Title VII, gender difference has borne an unsteady and derivative relationship to racial difference.[24] Antidiscrimination law permits employers to discriminate on the basis of gender if it is crucial to the business (as with my strip club example), but there is no such excuse for race-based hiring (at an inner city club for boys where a black male role model might be needed, for example). Gender has never really made a good analogy to race, and as a result judges have had to come up with somewhat awkward ways of talking about when it should and should not be allowed to make a difference. I will argue that the intertwined histories of race and gender can help us better understand intersectional identities and their lack of recognition in the law, as well as the hackneyed path of gender discrimination doctrine.

Gender is a fascinating lens on questions of personhood because, as I've already implied, gender differences organize our social world so deeply that they cannot realistically be ignored and unlike racial difference, law has never really aimed to fully suppress the social meanings of gender. Gender differences can be recast as simple biological realities that many people accept as obvious. Perhaps men and women just have different roles and skills, and that difference does not imply inferiority but rather complementarity. Then we would not want to ban all considerations of gender difference, just to choose which ones are to be preserved and which ones discarded. Robert Post concludes that indeed, "so long as gender conventions remain salient within our culture, Title VII must be understood as marking a frontier between those gender conventions subject to legal transformation and those left untouched or actually reproduced within the law."[25]

This range of possibilities for gender in the law—transformation, reproduction, or disinterest—are produced and justified by different logics of personhood, drawing on embedded personhood, functional individualism, and blame-shifting. These logics emerge and are contested most often through the concept of the illegal sex stereotype. Sex stereotyping is a legal concept that is foundational to contemporary sex discrimination law, but which I shall argue is a deeply unsettled idea. The word stereotype is also our most common way to talk about an unfair generalization about a person because of her group membership. It is a way of ascribing meaning to difference: "Because you're an X, you're likely to be Y." So while it is another term that traffics across the formal law and ordinary speech, it is not itself a logic of personhood. It is a conclusory label applied to a way of reasoning that one finds unfair. It still depends upon these logics of personhood I have described for justification. As I explain, sex stereotyping is understood to be a bad thing for lots of reasons, giving judges a tool for legal analysis that means several quite different things. Looking at the logics of personhood that help it along will clear up the confusion over its different meanings.

Sometimes embedded personhood explains the outcomes of gender discrimination cases very clearly. In cases about workplace grooming requirements, for example, judges do not even talk about gender stereotypes. They simply insist that employers can require a certain grooming standard, accept that gender is part of appearing well-groomed, and leave it at that. Only very one-sided grooming requirements are illegal, like putting women in uniforms but allowing men to wear their own clothes. In 2000, Harrah's Casino instituted employee appearance rules called the "Personal Best" policy, which required all female employees to wear panty hose, full face makeup, and colored nail polish, and to keep their hair down and teased, curled, or styled. A Las Vegas image consultant was brought in to instruct each woman in makeup application and hair styling, and the company had each woman photographed to monitor how well she kept up her efforts afterwards. Men were not allowed to wear any makeup or nail color, and were required to keep their hair cut short. The Harrah's uniform was in other respects gender neutral. Darlene Jespersen, a bartender for over two decades, was fired for not complying with the "Personal Best" policy. Ms. Jespersen felt oppressed by the demands to doll herself up, and filed a sex discrimination lawsuit against Harrah's.

She lost her case. Harrah's was within its rights to require a certain gendered look in its employees, the court held, and there was no need to get into the messy facts of whether complying as a woman was more burdensome than complying as a man.[26] Here, Ms. Jespersen was treated just as Ms. Marks was at the marketing company: neither woman was able to separate her functional individualism from the social meaning of her appearance, even though both had won accolades for their actual performance of job tasks. Stereotypes are relevant here for their absence. Why isn't it a stereotype that women should look dolled up (and that a man should not)? One could easily put it that way in ordinary language and make a sensible objection. But in the law the stereotype simply marks a conclusion: an idea about gender that is unfairly applied to an individual. Some ideas about gender—that everyone ought to have one, that it should be recognizable and appropriate—are difficult to escape. But we must also remember that it is very difficult for any of us to imagine a world without any thickly embedded ideas about gender at all.

More often, however, sex discrimination law makes it illegal to "rely on overbroad generalizations about the different talents, capacities, or preferences of males and females."[27] These overbroad generalizations are stereotypes. Some differences between men and women, like the fact that women as a group outlive men as a group, are empirically measurable and look like valid generalizations based on the evidence we have. What should we make of the fact that stereotypes often attach to something in the world that seems real, but also unjust? As K. Anthony Appiah points out, stereotypes in antidiscrimination law come in three different varieties: what he calls the statistical stereotype, the false stereotype, and the normative stereotype.[28] Statistical stereotypes are those that are statistically correlated with being a member of a group (women are weak), but that may not be true for any particular member of the group (a strong woman). False stereotypes are those that indicate a propensity in an individual because of group membership, but wherein the generalization is false as well as malicious (Mexicans are lazy).

Normative stereotypes are not simply generalizations as the first two are, but rather are "grounded in a social consensus about how [group members] *ought* to behave to conform appropriately to the norms associated with membership in their group."[29] It is a rich description of what being a certain sort of person (a person embedded in her identity and traits) ought to mean. "Jews ought to support Israel" is an assertion of a normative stereotype that draws on a consensus based on historical experiences, cultural bonds, and a sense of a unified mission. A Jew who does not think Israel should have been founded might be relatively rare statistically, but she is more than just an outlier. She is asserting something very different about the meaning of her identity. Likewise, if a transgender person understood herself as a woman but did not pursue any surgical changes or in any way change her presentation from her male body of birth, it would be very difficult for many people to understand her as a woman. She would be asserting something about what it is to be a woman (having a deep voice, facial hair, a penis) that others would see as impossible for that identity.

It is not my argument here that different identities are governed by distinct logics of personhood. Rather, as we will see with the case of women, there are always competing logics of personhood to draw upon. Legal notions like the stereotype are actually not unitary concepts. Much is swirling about under the label stereotype because we are trying hard to account for all the ways that difference both seems to matter deeply and yet should be ignored. Logics of personhood help judges, as well as ordinary people, respond to the fact that often there is something to stereotypes: their content comes from real details of the social world, but the whole question is how to explain them away, justify their use, or condemn them.

The Logic of Actuarial Personhood

Let us return to the cases discussed earlier, particularly to an intriguing detail of Ms. McDermott's dispute with Xerox. It was not that the Xerox managers thought she could not perform the job or that the social meaning of her fatness would create problems with customers. They were concerned that over the long term she might cost too much in health benefits. Xerox's managers talked about "the obese group," not about Ms. McDermott as an individual. An individualized assessment of her health at the time came back perfectly clean, but under what I call the logic of actuarial personhood, that does not matter. For the actuarial logics of personhood, difference is simply the way to place individuals within significant groupings, like people with a Body Mass Index (BMI) over 30, smokers, people who pay cash for airplane tickets, or those with credit scores below 600.[30] Persons as data points are still individuals in some sense, but they are also curiously melted into the environment. The tone of moral approbation or condemnation turns into talk of expectations, predictions, and management of costs or danger in a large field over time. The auto insurer's classic question perfectly captures this sense: where do you park your car at night? There is a "you" who matters very much, but only in relation to "where," "your car," and "at night." In the hands of professional actuaries, any and all traits are equal before they go into the calculation, and only those that are statistically significant matter in the end. But of course notions like risk and health are not just the outcomes of calculations; in the social world they are saturated with highly contested political and moral meanings.[31]

Sometimes a person's health condition is absorbed into our disability rights regime, where the logic of actuarial personhood meets the requirement to accommodate the person and to manage her difference. Consider this classic case about risk and disease. Gene Arline taught elementary school in Nassau County, Florida for fifteen years. In 1979, after a twenty year remission, her tuberculosis flared up again and she had three relapses of the disease. The school board dismissed her, "not because she had done anything wrong," but because they feared she would infect the children.[32] She sued, claiming disability rights protection as a person with a contagious disease. When her case came before the Supreme Court several years later, AIDS was a full-blown health crisis, as well as a source of panic and discrimination. The Solicitor General argued for the Reagan administration that contagiousness was not a disability and should not be given legal protection. The Supreme Court disagreed. "The fact that *some* persons who have contagious diseases may pose a serious health threat to others under certain circumstances," reasoned Justice Brennan, however, "does not justify excluding from the coverage of [the Rehabilitation Act, later to become the Americans with Disabilities Act] *all* persons with actual or perceived contagious diseases."[33] Contagious diseases as well as addictions are now considered legally protected disabilities, even though they may also be highly stigmatized. In my earlier example, the court in Ms. McDermott's case held that Xerox had considered her disabled even though she was not, and thus not hiring her just because of their concerns about the future effects of her weight was unjustified. Similarly, the school district could not just assume Ms. Arline was too much of a risk; they were required to try to accommodate her first.

One of the most fascinating and often frustrating features of actuarial personhood is that it captures empirical realities about groups of people, some of which are harmful generalizations. These are what we just termed statistical stereotypes above. But as we saw, the argument against them cannot be that they are false. Consider the 1978 Supreme Court case of *Los Angeles Department of Water and Power v. Manhart.* The city of Los Angeles had taken into account the fact that women live longer than men in setting rates for employee contributions to its pension plan. It required all women to pay 14.84 percent more each month into the plan than similarly situated men paid. The greater share that women contributed offset the greater payments that would be made to women over their longer life spans. Women therefore took home less pay than men working the same jobs. For example, the records in the case showed that one woman paid $18,171.40 into the fund, whereas a similarly situated man would have contributed only $12,843.53, taking home the balance as part of his wages. Women working for the city filed a class action lawsuit under Title VII of the 1964 Civil Rights Act, seeking an injunction against the practice and restitution of contributions that had been greater than men's.

Justice Steven's majority opinion begins with the observation that "[a]s a class, women live longer than men."[34] "This case does not, however, involve a fictional difference between men and women," he continued, noting that "[t]he Department treated its women employees differently from its men employees because the two classes are in fact different."[35] Just as in Ms. McDermott's dispute with Xerox, the solution was to focus upon the individual traits of the employee. The Court concluded that the fact that a gender-based generalization is true does not excuse its use against individual women who do not fit the generalization. Of course the city cannot know when any of its employees will die, so it simply cannot assume anything about any particular individual's life span. Risk is therefore the same kind of property of a person as her ability to perform the job, as the Court explicitly notes, and it must be determined on the same individualized basis: "Individual risks, like individual performance, may not be predicted by resort to classifications proscribed by Title VII."[36] Los Angeles had to quit funding its pension plan based on actuarial logics of personhood (though the Court did not make them offer the women a refund). Will other logics of personhood intervene to block actuarial judgments, and for whom?

The Logic of Managerial Individualism

Functional individualism is most popular for handling differences based on traits that are understood to be merely skin deep and to which we ought to be blind. The logic dictates that the truly significant trait is capacity to perform, which is somehow there to be measured and stands apart from the stigmatized trait. But what if someone really is blind? Should a manager be allowed to say that if she can't read the labels on items that need to be sorted then she just can't work there? Or, if someone uses a wheelchair and there is no elevator, do we just say "too bad"?

Justifications for accommodating difference depart from simple assertions of equal functional capacity. They query functioning itself. They acknowledge that persons function in different ways, some of which will appear as dysfunctional in certain environments or according to certain norms. Without an elevator, the wheelchair user is stuck at the base of the stairs, but with an elevator and sufficiently wide door openings she can move about the office as well as anyone else. This accommodationist impulse animates our disability rights laws, most notably the Americans with Disabilities Act of 1990 (ADA).[37] As a matter of law, anyone who files an ADA claim must meet the legal definition of a disabled person and must work out her accommodation in an organizational setting. All antidiscrimination laws define who is covered, of course, and all of them apply within organizations, usually businesses. But in disability law in particular, what I call managerial individualism has come to dominate. Managerial individualism is a process-focused, context-specific approach to differences that requires an organization to do something to accommodate the person with a disability. Managerial logics of personhood dominate disability law more than in other antidiscrimination areas like race or sex discrimination (although it is certainly present) because disability as a legal concept is uniquely individualized and highly contingent. Race and sex are understood to be self-evident attributes, but whether something is a disability is not so clear.

The difference that is disability is therefore managed as a process in the law, not as a status.

Consider the following ADA job discrimination case. Romell Carter worked for Northwest Airlines at O'Hare airport in Chicago loading and unloading baggage. His foot was crushed between two forklifts in 1999. Soon after his return in 2000, Northwest sent Margaret Sommers, a professional accommodations assessment advisor, to assess what kind of work Carter could still do. Ms. Sommers first tried to set up an evaluation at the job site with Mr. Carter, but he could not attend on the date she had set and could not notify her of his absence because he did not have a phone. She conducted the evaluation with his supervisor present instead, and found that he was not able to do his old job anymore. She began Northwest's "Alternative Duty Exploration" process with him to look for a position that would not require standing on his foot, which put him in severe pain after only a few minutes. This process went on for three months, during which time she would send him abbreviated descriptions of open jobs and then answer his questions about what each job involved. More senior employees already filled the sedentary jobs, and one job in Florida that was open to him required passing a typing test. He would have also have had to move from Chicago to Florida. Mr. Carter did not know how to type and failed the test. Northwest's insurance paid for Mr. Carter to take a keyboarding class at a local community college. He took the class, but never retook the test despite being invited to do so by Northwest on two occasions. He sued, claiming that Northwest should have provided him with an accommodation.[38]

Like Ms. Arline, the teacher with tuberculosis, Mr. Carter is legally entitled to an accommodation if he is an otherwise qualified individual with a disability under the ADA. But while stigmatized diseases cannot be presumptively excluded from coverage, a smashed foot is not presumptively included. Mr. Carter lost his case because, without making himself suitable for accommodation, he failed to qualify as a legally protected worker with a disability. The managerial process just did not work out. He would have had to have cooperated more with Ms. Sommers and to have moved to Florida. He was a person with a smashed foot, but he was also an attitude, a set of choices and behaviors, part of a relationship with a corporate professional, a skill set, an inhabitant of a certain city, and someone without a phone. Even though the ADA is also our first antidiscrimination law aimed squarely at accommodating difference rather than ignoring it, I argue that the accommodationist underpinnings of disability law quickly become diluted and contingent, vitiating the hopes that many activists and scholars had for it.

Most antidiscrimination laws grant employment rights, and so naturally the way they work in practice depends upon how they are absorbed and interpreted within the organizations they regulate.[39] Disability law and its managerial individualist logic reveal how much extra-legal organizational practices matter for deciding how to handle differences. Actuarial logics enter law's deliberations about difference because they are so important for drawing conclusions about persons in other areas of life like business (as in consumer research and marketing) and criminal justice (as in profiling and preventive detention).[40] Likewise, managerial logics supply ways of approaching persons and their difference that work to the advantage of organizations. Law's borders are highly permeable, and logics from other professional areas of expertise frequently cross over into it. Recall that Ms. Manuel, Ms. McDermott, and Mr. Carter all relied on medical professionals to examine them and to characterize their abilities and disabilities. Throughout this book I draw out the blended logics of law, management, actuarialism, and medicalization to show how they all share in determining how and why differences matter. The primary function of managerial logics, actuarial logics, and processes of medicalization is to depoliticize identity traits and to take them away from the legal and political realms. While these moves may initially attract defenders of particularly unpopular groups, I argue that they ultimately cannot supply grounds for robust political membership.

Identity

At this point one might ask, aren't the questions of justice or injustice here primarily about identities? There are not any persons, after all. There are only men and women, raced bodies, able bodies and disabled bodies. Normative stereotypes dictate how to inhabit an identity. Functional capacities, true inner strength of character, risk and dangerousness: wouldn't it be naïve to presume that these ideas stand on their own and attach to people out in the world without depending on the meaning of identity traits? And what if these ideas are primarily and invisibly produced through opposition to unmarked categories such as whiteness, maleness, able-bodiedness, and heterosexuality? Wouldn't it be folly to try to elevate ideas about personhood, whatever that is, as an explanatory concept over these other much more deeply theorized categories? Some scholars use the idea of personhood as a foil for the inhumanity or inveterately patriarchal nature of the law.[41] Martha Nussbaum points out that the concept of personhood "has in history been applied and withheld extremely capriciously."[42] Appealing to women's personhood has historically failed to compel men to acknowledge that women should be included in statutes permitting "persons" to practice law or to vote, as she points out. The idea of the person in the law only cruelly marks its actual exclusions and effacements.

I will continually insist that the best way to understand identity in the law is not as a free-floating conclusion pasted onto some kinds of designated selves (the groups who deserve affirmative action because of a history of deprivation, for example), but as a contingent outcome of constructions of personhood. Identity can always be undone, unraveled, and dispersed by accounts of personhood that preexist it and last after any particular legal account of it is gone. My use of "person" and "personhood" throughout this book is, as I noted earlier, not a normative endorsement of the term as a neutral designator (nor an aspiration), but rather an attempt to be more thickly descriptive of the ways in which our legal regime represents those whom it governs and judges. In my view, law is not *simply* a tool of the powerful that accomplishes the exclusion or effacement of persons; rather, it is a set of social practices and forms of justification that contain multiple and conflicting accounts of personhood and identity that can come to mean many things. There do not have to actually *be* persons qua persons to make studying the ways judges talk about them extremely important. My approach is agnostic about essential traits or moral demands of personhood; what I care about is the way law talks about persons. In that sense this project departs from normative political theorizing that uses the technique of abstracting from identity traits down to the level of bare personhood in order to reason about what justice requires.[43]

Strategies for Talking about What Persons Deserve: A Thought Experiment

Imagine that you are an advocate for a group that currently receives little or no legal recognition or protection but faces stigmatization, exclusion, and discrimination. That is, the group members are different from the norm in a way that is considered unhealthy, contemptible, immoral, or unfortunate. You want to use both law and political rhetoric to gain the best kind of legal identity for this group. How would you talk about the persons in the group? How would you describe their difference to convince skeptics that they deserve rights? What among all the legal strategies available would be worth wanting? One of my aims in this book is to parse out the ways that logics of personhood in the law open up or foreclose pathways to legal protection. I will argue that we can use logics of personhood and their allied strategies to foretell what it is like to try to talk about the extension of new rights in contemporary American culture, and to see more clearly why advocates have so much trouble finding a robust and liberating way to talk about why a new form of difference deserves legal protection. The rest of this book takes up weight-based discrimination in the law and imagines that the group to be defended is fat men and women. This focus will require us to explore other important groups, too, because of the ways that their claims have established options for talking about fat rights.

The current menu for establishing or increasing legal rights in anti-discrimination law includes the following options: (1) to argue that the group members can function just as well as everyone else and that their defining trait should be ignored (because it is a false stereotype); (2) to acknowledge that statistical stereotypes about the group are often empirically true, but that they should not burden a particular individual plaintiff; (3) to concede that the group members function differently or appear differently from the norm but to insist that the standards being used are not neutral, but rather constructed in favor of the dominant group to naturalize and maintain its power; (4) to analogize them to African Americans and to stress historical patterns of exclusion, segregation, and subordination (similar to the previous blame-shifting argument but including the explicit analogy); and (5) to name their difference "diversity" and describe it as an enriching and unique feature of some individuals that can be usefully integrated into the goal-oriented activities of groups.

These strategies are part of various legal doctrines, of course, but they are both more and less than that. They are more than translations of doctrine because they are accessible to us in arguments with each other in our everyday lives as citizens; and they are less than doctrine because none of these alone would be enough to win a lawsuit. Each of these strategies is made sensible through one or more of the logics of personhood I have introduced here. They depend upon a description of personhood and a justification of how a person's difference matters (or should not matter). They employ tools such as the "like race" analogy, the stereotype and the accommodation (in disability law). I highlight them to develop an account of how some logics of personhood assist some strategies for protecting difference through law and inhibit others. Logics of personhood, as I have described, are the ways we talk to each other, in ordinary conversation and in the formal law of antidiscrimination, about whether a person's difference should matter for what she deserves, and why. They can be used affirmatively to change the moral judgment attached to a trait, or defensively to ward off the application of a competing logic of personhood. The listed strategies are legally proven ways of doing so. Commitment to one or more logics of personhood explains each piece of these strategies; none on its own can explain all our impulses and justifications for treating difference. Probably several of the options outlined above seem to make sense to use on behalf of your imaginary group. You recognize them already. Indeed, judges, jurors, legislators, and ordinary people muddle through problems of difference using a hackneyed combination of logics—logics that, despite their inconsistency, nonetheless survive because of their deep roots in our ordinary lives, as well as our most powerful social institutions (notably law, business, medicine, and politics).

The Plan of the Book

This book is organized by the logics of personhood I've introduced here, but I have resisted simply marching through each logic one by one. Instead, each chapter moves our consideration of fat rights along by following the progression of alternatives for defending fat rights as the reader herself might think of them: first, making sense of the idea in the first place, then looking back to the most prominent analogies of recent history in the treatment of race and sex under the law, next on to contemporary contexts for talking about fat as a health risk or a disability, and finally reflecting on what plans can be taken from this journey. Chapter 1 sets up an analytical lens for the rest of the book using fatness. Attention to the so-called obesity epidemic in recent years has put fatness in the spotlight, and we as a society have yet to make sense of what kind of difference fatness makes. This book will, as I've indicated, use the debate over fatness in the contemporary United States to pull out and scrutinize all the choices we have to make about it. Is fat something we should ignore? Is it something that drives up health care costs and thus need regulating as a risky status or behavior? Does it give away something about a person's character? Does it make some people just unsuitable for certain roles and jobs? Could it be a disability? Is it something a person can change, or is it so hard to lose weight that it is basically an immutable trait? As I argued above, the history of our antidiscrimination laws shows an abiding attention to racial discrimination, with the result that other protected traits have succeeded insofar as they seem analogical to race. Fatness does not define a political identity group, despite the work of fat rights groups like the National Association for the Advancement of Fat Acceptance (NAAFA). We have the chance here to study a liminal trait about which no pretense of agreement exists. I show in chapter 1 all the ways we can currently conceive of fatness in the law, and suggest how the boundaries around our thinking about it also reveal the limits of our thinking about difference more broadly.

The next two chapters back up to trace out the implications of the primary tools and logics we have inherited in our antidiscrimination tradition, forged in disputes about race and gender. Chapter 2 explores the history of antidiscrimination law, showing the classic logics of personhood that drove the minority rights revolution of the 1960s and early 1970s and their transformations in the present, most notably the idea of difference as diversity. Chapter 3 draws out the logics of personhood at stake in sex stereotyping, concluding that the stereotype as a legal response to discrimination is politically unstable and individualizing, and operates to ratify the status quo even as it purports to defend difference. Difference as diversity is the pre-eminent new way to conceptualize difference in contemporary liberal law and culture, and stereotyping remains the preeminent bête noir in antidiscrimination jurisprudence. These chapters establish antidiscrimination law's classic approaches and new answers to challenges of difference, leaving us to continue on to ask how we can imagine a conception of personhood that can make sense of fatness.

The second half of the book returns to the question of the difference that fatness makes. Chapter 4 is a study of the interplay of risk, health, and medicalization in determining the meaning of a person's difference.

Actuarial personhood is an ever more compelling logic in the age of data mining, health screening, and criminal profiling. Antidiscrimination law has a few tools for responding to actuarial logics of personhood, and they are ill-suited to these challenges. Chapter 5 assesses the possibilities of our most recently enacted antidiscrimination law, the Americans with Disabilities Act, wondering what it might look like to consider fatness a disability. Disability rights seem particularly capacious in their conceptions of the person, and so we might think that the ADA offers a way out of some of the limitations I identify in the rest of our antidiscrimination canon. The conclusion takes up the challenge of normatively evaluating antidiscrimination law in light of its logics of personhood. We cannot get away from any of them, but some logics of personhood have come to dominate our law and culture more than others in recent years. Must we dwell in their contradictions, or can we find a way to shift them so that antidiscrimination law becomes something really worth wanting?

1

Imagining Legal Protections for Fatness

Introduction: How Shall We Place Fat People as Legal Subjects?

Supposedly we are a nation of ever-fatter adults and kids, and one can barely glance at the news without hearing about the so-called obesity epidemic, the diet fad of the moment, or some potentially revolutionary scientific discovery about what causes weight gain and how to control it. At the beginning of the recent wave of media attention to obesity (first taking off in the mid-1990s and reaching current levels of intense coverage within just a few years), most of the conversation about it was limited to scientific researchers and public health advocates. Fatness became an everyday topic with the release of the film *Supersize Me* in 2002, clustered with some widely publicized anti-fat books marketed to a mainstream audience.[1] Scholars from other disciplines have begun studying the social and political context of our national fat panic, asking how we are debating obesity, on what terms, with what conceptual categories, and with what political consequences. Law professor Paul Campos wrote one of the first and most widely discussed critical responses to this fat panic, arguing that it was more about elites finding an acceptable target group for their disgust and moralizing than about the nation's health.[2] Critical research by thin authors like Campos and Eric Oliver has gotten a lot of attention, but fat activists had already published their own fat-positive responses to weight stigmatization.[3] Fat academic authors wrote defenses of the fat body for a more theoretical audience, as well, situating fatness as a form of cultural transgression rather than as a fixed identity category.[4]

Recall our menu of strategies for arguing for expanded legal protections for difference: (1) to argue that the group members can function just as well as everyone else and that their defining trait should be ignored (because it is a false stereotype); (2) to acknowledge that statistical stereotypes about the group are often empirically true (statistical stereotypes), but that they should not burden a particular individual plaintiff; (3) to concede that the group members function differently or appear differently from the norm, and also to insist that the standards being used are not neutral, but rather constructed in favor of the dominant group to naturalize and maintain its power; (4) to analogize them to African Americans and to stress historical patterns of exclusion, segregation, and subordination (similar to the previous blame-shifting argument, but including the explicit analogy); and (5) to name their difference "diversity" and describe it as an enriching, unique, and morally neutral feature of some individuals that can be usefully integrated into the goal-oriented activities of groups.

Continuing our thought experiment from the last chapter for a moment, let us imagine that the group we wish to defend as deserving of legal protection is fat people. We will encounter a set of logics of personhood in the law, as well as an array of strategies based on those logics. Fatness is a fascinating trait to examine for the application of logics of personhood. It can potentially find support in all of the strategies I listed previously or be rejected within any of them. Fatness is a liminal category in the law, and therefore it enjoys openness as an analytic category that more solidified categories like race and gender do not. As a feature of identity, it both shares in and departs from the usual features of a legally protected trait. Is being fat something that a person cannot help? Is it an immutable trait? Is being fat unhealthy and therefore something we should reduce in the population, like smoking? Is it individually variable in its effects on the body, and mostly a problem for fulfilling norms of attractiveness? Is being fat the result of bad personal choices, indulgent parenting, or an impoverished life? Is easy weight gain followed by fruitless attempts at weight loss a widely shared experience? Are we in the midst of a moral panic over the so-called obesity epidemic that actually has very little to do with either science or with our actual well-being? Should a business be allowed to fire or fail to hire someone because she is fat? Could fat bodies be part of body diversity—just part of all the variation in size, shape, and abilities in the human population? Are fat people a political constituency capable of agitating for civil rights? In the public arena beyond the law, debates over fat are dominated by presentations of obesity (the more common term) as a national health crisis, and supplemented by a much smaller fat rights movement that disputes the evidence that fat is always unhealthy and lobbies for doctors who are more understanding, an end to dieting, more accessible public spaces, and less discrimination.[5]

"I watch them get up out of their chair": Common Sense, Stereotypes, and Individual Abilities

Recall the case of Arazella Manuel, the applicant to the Texas airport bus company. She passed the first step in evaluating her functional capacities with flying colors. The company conducted an in-person interview, checked her references, and administered a road test, all of which found Ms. Manuel to be, as the manager who interviewed her later swore under oath, "very impressive" and "very personable." But then she had to undergo a federally mandated physical examination. Department of Transportation (DOT) regulations specify that a prospective driver should not have such conditions as an amputation of an arm or a leg, blindness, alcohol or narcotic addiction, or a history of heart attack, and must keep a Medical Examiner's Certificate in possession at all times.[6] Obesity is not an automatic disqualification under the federal rules. Ms. Manuel's functional individualism quickly went from consideration of her driving abilities to assessment of her health. Her examination involved much more than a determination that she did not have any of the prohibited conditions: the company doctor assessed her as a person embedded in fatness and relied on what he called his own "common sense" rather than upon professional expertise.

When she went to Dr. James Frierson's office for her examination, Ms. Manuel stood five feet seven inches tall and weighed 345 pounds. In his deposition in the eventual lawsuit, Dr. Frierson explained his method of conducting DOT exams, beginning with an observation of the way people walk from the reception area:

> When I call their name up front, I watch them get up out of their chair. That tells me a good deal; and I watch how they walk back to the office, how they sit down, how they undress—well, women, we don't undress them—and then we take their blood pressure and listen to their heart.

He observed that Ms. Manuel was "literally waddling down the hall; and I would say it took her, oh, roughly five times as long as it would somebody else." He was surprised, however, to find that her blood pressure was normal and that she did not have any health problems. None-theless, Dr. Frierson declined to issue a Medical Examiner's Certificate for Ms. Manuel to drive for Texas Bus Lines because of her obesity. He felt that he "owe[d] the public and other people the right to have a driver that [could] give them some protection in case of an accident or fire or something like that." Under questioning, Dr. Frierson admitted that he lacked any special training in what it takes to be a bus driver and that he had not followed up his observations with agility testing. He responded that, well, he knew about driving a bus because he had ridden in buses plenty of times, and that he knew Ms. Manuel was not agile from watching her get out of her chair and "waddle" to the exam room. "Common sense" and "experience," he claimed, made it clear to him that very fat people like her should not be hired as bus drivers. Because Dr. Frierson would not supply the medical certificate, Texas Bus Lines withdrew its conditional offer to hire her.[7]

Ms. Manuel sued Texas Bus Lines in federal court for discriminating against her under the federal Americans with Disabilities Act (ADA) under a "perceived disability" theory (also called a "regarded as" claim) and won. The ADA offers a way for those who are not actually disabled by obesity to file lawsuits, which is to claim that the firing, failure to hire, or exclusion was based on a perception in others that the claimant was disabled.[8] The judge interprets Ms. Manuel's case as a classic case of discrimination by what K. Anthony Appiah calls a false stereotype: a malicious generalization about an individual based on her group membership that is not empirically true (for example, Mexicans are lazy, or here, fatness means disability).[9] The judge uses strategy (1), insisting on her functional individualism and requiring that her fatness be ignored. The concept remains tethered to the definition of disability under the ADA: a person must either have a physical impairment that causes her to be substantially limited in a major life activity, or be regarded as having an impairment that is substantially limiting in a major life activity, all while being qualified to perform the essential functions of the job. A physical impairment is defined as a physiological disorder or condition that affects a body system.[10] Even though being overweight is generally not considered a disability under federal law, the bus company was not permitted to assume that Ms. Manuel couldn't perform the job just as well as anyone else. Presumptions based on "common sense" and "experience" were not allowed to override her right to be hired based on her qualifications.

With this understanding of antidiscrimination law, then, the wrongness of the employer's act stems from the use of a certain kind of knowledge: an irrational misjudgment based upon a false stereotype. The law exists to protect people like Ms. Manuel from negative "common sense" perceptions about them—that they are unhealthy, slow, and risky to have on the job. Dr. Frierson drew on common sense, what we each use every day to move about in the world and by which we treat other people as socially embedded persons. But what I've been calling common sense can sometimes be simple prejudice. Banning the use of common sense in an antidiscrimination case means it is illegal to judge the plaintiff in a richly detailed context of norms and impressions, as the doctor did using observations of Ms. Manuel's walking style and his past experience riding buses. Ms. Manuel's case exemplifies use of the first strategy I defined: arguing that group members can function just as well as anyone else and that their defining trait should be ignored. Ignoring the trait is the solution because our reasoning about it is thought to be so corrupted by this natural-seeming "common sense."

Could we say that in promoting this view of Ms. Manuel, we are promoting her inherent dignity as a human being? Wouldn't talking about that be a strategy, too? A logic of personhood that rests on inherent dignity would also ban reasoning based on surface-level characteristics. This transcendental logic of personhood best fits with a quasi-religious concept of the person in which there is absolute equality, because, of course, this dignified core of personhood does not vary based on our outwardly appearing talents and traits. We rarely find such a logic beyond the hortatory surface of American antidiscrimination law, however, because law must choose between persons and justify unequal allocations of scarce resources like jobs (some lofty rhetoric in preambles notwithstanding).[11] If fatness per se is banned as a legal proxy for selecting employees, telling an employer that she must instead choose candidates based on the inherent dignity of every person does not give her much with which to work. The law must fall back on fact-gathering about other permissible factors that can be measured and which have meaning and value in the sphere that law regulates, namely organizations. Can this person pass the driving test? Can she type a certain number of words per minute? This logic promotes fitness into smoothly running organizations, efficient performance of tasks, and predictability of behavior. It condemns disgust, stigma, and false stereotyping, and in their place promotes measurements of functioning as the tools of justice for persons. These measurements are understood to be morally neutral replacements for biased social judgments based on appearance. Looking to functional individualism makes a lot of sense in employment law. Firms are trying to get workers to perform certain jobs so that the firm can make money.

Indeed, its use for free market efficiency combined with its resolute opposition to identity politics has made functional individualism very appealing to conservatives,[12] though there is no denying that the language of functional individualism reaches far beyond any one ideology to veritable saturation in our culture. Recall the invocations by fat rights supporters discussed in the Introduction: "Appearance is widely accepted as a legitimate consideration in employment matters. However, for most jobs appearance has no bearing on an individual's ability to perform."[13] "I guess all I can say is that people shouldn't judge others because of how they look. What's important is whether or not they can do the job."[14] Use of such language is popular among many other groups, too. Said one African American woman who suspected she had been a victim of racial and gender discrimination: "Why should I be judged just by how I look instead of what do I have to offer as far as merit and ability? That's the bottom line."[15] The logic of functional individualism is a discourse of first resort across the political spectrum because for liberals, it deflects invidious prejudice and affirms the abilities and worth of marginalized persons, and for conservatives, it promotes can-do individualism and economic efficiency.

Measures of functioning are practically useful and politically clean. That is, the framework of functional personhood presents us with a moral epistemology that offers a means of knowing who deserves what in our society that is neither a power grab by identity groups (which seems to be difficult to justify with a principle that could apply to everyone), nor a gesture toward the transcendental dignity of every person (which is hard to use to account for differential outcomes precisely because it applies to everyone equally). Functional individualism nonetheless retains some basic moral appeal by connection to other prominent values of our culture; it honors can-do individualism and promises that no one will be held back by tattered stereotypes attached to her outward traits. Its rootedness in the priorities of the economy—efficient, instrumentally rational workers striving to be selected for their "merit alone"— also helps it persist as an alternative discourse to social movement discourses that could compel uncomfortable redistributions. It is ahistorical: what really matters is what this person has to offer in the present, not the history of her people and their struggles. It offers both a liberation story—freedom from burdensome stereotypes and the opportunity to prove one's worth—and an eminently presentable account of failure that keeps failure individualized: "It's not because she's a ———, it's because she just couldn't meet our standards."

Role Modeling and Appearance

What about a job that is explicitly about role modeling, though? Doesn't appearance sometimes send a message about the kind of person I am in ways that employers shouldn't have to ignore? What if the job is to be a role model for health and fitness? The notion of role modeling depends on the logic of embedded personhood. An embedded person is one who cannot be fully understood without taking seriously the meaning of her appearing traits. Sometimes the way we look really *does* say something about who we are, the group memberships we share, and the ways we want to be interpreted by others. Either a court must reject the basic idea that role modeling is important for a particular job, or, since fat discrimination itself is not illegal in most areas, a court could simply allow the employer to impose whatever kind of role modeling (or customer satisfaction) obligations it wants, including being slim.

Role modeling implicates what Appiah considers the "most interesting" kind of stereotyping in American antidiscrimination law: normative stereotyping.[16] Normative stereotypes are thick descriptions of roles. They understand the person as the embedded person, richly described in her community and its norms. They tell us what it is to occupy a certain identity. Antidiscrimination law is very much in tension with the logic of embedded personhood and is most often engaged in trying to suppress it, ignore it, or domesticate it. That is why calling upon normative stereotypes is not one of the strategies for gaining legal protections that I listed earlier. (For the same reason, calling upon the embedded personhood recognized in some tort law claims is not a strategy for antidiscrimination law either, though below I discuss the possibilities for sympathy that could be generated there.) But, to echo the communitarian critique of liberalism, it seems that antidiscrimination logics deny embedded personhood but also depend on it, work around it, and sometimes accede to it.

I want to stress that embedded personhood is not necessarily oppressive or liberating. Even though it appears in the fat discrimination cases as pure anti-fat bias, I will discuss it again in chapter 3 as a deep source of meaning for gendered lives that is more than gender bias. Gendered appearance norms can be unjust and constraining, but they can also "serve as potential instruments in the construction of a dignified individuality," as Appiah puts it.[17] Describing embedded personhood may sound very much like reference to Appiah's normative stereotypes, in other words, but these are not always bad. Examples of normative stereotypes would include religious rules that certain groups observe, like abstaining from pork or alcohol, or wearing certain clothes, or the speech inflections and hand movements among youth in urban hip hop culture. I argue that these normative stereotypes are important not only for our dignified individuality, but also for their community-generating powers. They are the ways we recognize and understand each other. A dignified individuality is not just pure uniqueness; it is embeddedness within an identity recognized communally as worthwhile. It has quickly gotten complicated to simply opt for strategy (2), then: banning any kind of generalization about a group as a stereotype even when it is grounded in some real features of the group's life. What kind of stereotype? Is it a true one in some way we should care about? Is it a meaningful one?

The connection between Appiah's normative stereotypes and what I have called embedded personhood in the law is communal recognition. Role modeling is sending signals within a community in order to bring up the youth of the community into identities considered valuable. Antidiscrimination laws give a range of answers about how and whether to accede to normative stereotypes, and these conflicts produce not only incoherent doctrine but also stagnant politics. Appiah suggests that we should accept the existence of normative stereotypes and refrain from making it illegal to judge persons based on them. Much of antidiscrimination law recasts these normative stereotypes as invidious, however, and demands that employers treat employees as if they did not display any race, gender, or religious affiliation. Communal recognition is, after all, only as enlightened as the community itself. Persons can be embedded down in racism, orientalism, sexism, pity, or contempt. But laws reflect the values of society as much as they reform them, and I will argue in chapter 3 that sex discrimination law is committed to maintaining at least some normative stereotypes for gender.

So what does law make of fat role models? What is fatness allowed to mean for an employee's identity, character, or ability to bring up the youth in the values of the community? Consider the following cases. Mary Nedder taught in the Religious Studies Department at Rivier College, a small Catholic religious institution in Nashua, New Hampshire, for about six years, during which time she weighed around 375 pounds and stood five feet six inches tall. In 1994, the school did not renew her contract. She sued under the Americans with Disabilities Act. Ms. Nedder assembled evidence in her lawsuit that Sister Jeanne Perreault, the college president, had previously stated that losing weight is part of promoting the health of the whole person (an explicit part of the school's mission).[18] The college's mission statement also includes a commitment to "an environment in which integrated learning is the shared responsibility of students, faculty, staff, and administrators, and is pursued in all the curricular and co-curricular programs of the College" and urges those who participate in the life of the college to "take responsibility for ourselves and for others, and to engage in dialogue about basic human issues facing society, especially the plight of the poor and powerless."[19] Sister Perreault also said that faculty members should serve as good examples of the college's mission, and that she believed that fat teachers did not get much respect from students.[20] Sister Perreault's opinion that students would react negatively to fat professors (finding them "less disciplined and less intelligent") came from a report on the subject that she had circulated among some other faculty members.[21]

Ms. Nedder, however, prevailed upon a perceived disability theory under the ADA and received back pay and reinstatement at Rivier. The court found that the college's belief that her weight kept her from being a good role model and a respected teacher amounted to an erroneous conclusion that Ms. Nedder was substantially limited in her ability to teach (even though she was not so limited). The *Nedder* case is a fascinating example of a court enforcing functional individualism in the face of evidence that the trait may indeed have some bearing on job performance. Being a teacher and role model at a small private religious college may indeed call for looking beyond brute functional capacities toward things like collegiality, friendliness, and so on. (What would the bare-bones functional capacities of a professor be, anyway?) Mary Nedder's weight was an externally appearing trait that signaled a character defect to her employer, and since possessing and displaying a certain character within the college community was a requirement of the job, her weight made her seem dysfunctional to Sister Perreault. But even Sister Perreault's proffered empirical evidence that fat teachers did not get as much respect as role models was not enough to override the college's obligation to ignore Mary Nedder's weight when it judged her fitness as a teacher. The court insists that even though her job is to represent the college's close communal values when she stands up in front of students to teach, it does not permit the social meaning of fatness to count in her job performance.

Teaching then becomes the kind of job that is imagined to be measurable in terms that are separable from the appearance of the self. But in the close-knit, values-laden community of Rivier College, can lecturing, evaluating students, and mentoring students be separated from the appearance of the self? What if it were true that the students did not respect Ms. Nedder as much because of her weight? The court's decision in *Nedder* is an effort to transform the social meaning of fatness by rendering it illegitimate as a part of Ms. Nedder's teaching and role modeling, even in a community in which embedded personhood undergirds the relationships between faculty and students.

Jennifer Portnick earned credentials to be an aerobics instructor through the Aerobics and Fitness Association of America and applied to Jazzercise, Inc. for a job in San Francisco. The company refused to hire her, however, because at five feet eight inches tall and 240 pounds, Portnick did not meet the company's requirement that instructors look fit (read: slender, athletic). She filed suit under San Francisco's "height and weight" civil rights ordinance, and after mediation by the San Francisco Human Rights Commission and much publicity, the company agreed to change its policy. Portnick triumphantly reported that "[f]rom now on, the evaluations of applicants will be based on their skill."[22] Acknowledging studies showing that people of varying weights can still be fit, Jazzercise, Inc. conceded that "the value of 'fit appearance' as a standard is debatable."[23]

Ms. Portnick's case is the successful version of what happened to Deborah Marks, the saleswoman I discussed in the Introduction. She had been named "Telemarketer of the Year," but when she pressed her company to promote her to salesperson (a face-to-face selling job rather than a telephone-focused job) they promoted another "thinner and cuter" woman with fewer job accolades as a telemarketer ahead of her.[24] When she complained, her supervisor told her that for "outside sales, presentation is extremely important" and "Lose the weight and you will get promoted."[25] Ms. Marks sued under Title VII of the 1964 Civil Rights Act using a "sex plus" discrimination theory, alleging that the personal appearance rules held women to a standard of physical appearance—particularly, being slender—that did not apply to men. But because she was not able to point out any overweight men in the sales department either, the court found no sex discrimination. The company simply did not hire any fat salespeople at all.[26] Without the hook of gender discrimination, her case fell apart because discrimination based on weight alone is not covered under Title VII.[27] Congress would need to be convinced to add weight to the list of protected categories in Title VII for this outcome to differ. Without that, fatness is just like any other undesirable trait that employers are free to keep out of their workplaces, like drunkenness, smoking, dirty uniforms, or foul language.

The concession that it might not be such a bad thing to have a variety in body sizes among Jazzercise instructors is a result of San Francisco's attempt to shift social norms through municipal laws, precisely because the appearance of the teacher to the students can be a fundamental part of what takes place in the class. The law helps change the content of that message from "thin is in" to "being fat isn't incompatible with a healthy, fit image." Perhaps Jazzercise wanted its message to be "do this program and you'll look like your thin instructor." ("Exercise and stay basically the same size" isn't a very compelling message, after all, if clients came for weight loss.) The question here is whether San Francisco succeeded in transforming social norms or just tweaking functional individualism to include a fatter instructor as long as she could do the job just as well and in the same way as a thinner one. Presumably Ms. Portnick could lead the same class in the same exercises for the same amount of time at the same pace that other instructors did. Presumably the company also wants to maintain its brand consistency, avoiding mixed messages or radical shifts in what its employees present as Jazzercise. Mechanical motions of the body, easily tested and compared to others, constitute one reading of the job description. When the job in question has easily testable components, functional individualism simply requires that fat employees perform just as well as any other employee, and in exchange, the employer dismisses misgivings about the effects of their appearances.

Notice that this strategy and its enabling logic of functional individualism close off use of other protective strategies. There is no reason to change the standard of measurement of a good employee in any of these successful cases because the argument is based on the fundamental equality and sameness of the fat women in comparison to their thinner counterparts. One cannot easily argue that Ms. Manuel's fatness should be ignored *and* that it contributes to diversity within the company, that it should be accommodated though modifications to the bus or that the bus company should take fat culture into account in its workplace policies. If we are supposed to ignore fatness, why should we change our thinking about it? If there is anything that matters about fatness—positively, like its contributions to diversity or cultural enrichment, or negatively, like increased risks or costs—then functional individualism and the strategy of ignoring it will not provide a way to approach that meaningful difference.

Costs and Risks: Adjudicating Statistical Generalizations about Difference

What if an employer's standards include an interest in keeping health care costs low, and the employer believes that fat workers will cost more? Should the outcomes of such cases turn on whether the employer can prove that they actually do cost more? What is antidiscrimination law supposed to do with generalizations about people that may be empirically true but are still harmful? Strategy (2) aims to dissolve the power of stereotypes even when generalizations about the stigmatized group are empirically true (by defending the individual as exceptional). Antidiscrimination law deals with false stereotypes, for sure, but it also must address statistical stereotypes. Those are a bit trickier, as we found normative stereotypes to be as well. That most women are physically weaker than most men is true as a generalization, though of course there are some women who are stronger than some men. A feminist cannot simply dispute the fact of the generalization; she must both come up with a way of talking about why presumptions of strength organize opportunities the way they do and work to dismantle those presumptions at the same time that she defends the right of any strong woman to do the work of a strong man.

Antidiscrimination law expresses skepticism on behalf of protected traits and does not just accept an employer's account of a statistical truth. The legal device is the disparate impact lawsuit under Title VII. Title VII does not permit use of rules or practices that disproportionately impact employees based on race, color, region, sex, or national origin unless they are justified by business necessity. If the rule is that any employee must be able to lift 100 pounds, the employer must prove that it is really necessary to hire people who can lift that amount. If an employer thinks that rule means all women are excluded, the law says he is being narrow-minded. In that sense disparate impact law is directed against false stereotypes: they are simply prohibited. It is directed against statistical stereotypes in a more complex way: the exceptional individual must be able to fight her way past them and prove that she can lift 100 pounds, for example. Employers are not allowed to use a protected trait as a proxy, say, by avoiding physical weakness among employees by hiring only men. Courts have found that employers really do not rely on their standards for strength, height, and other traits nearly as much as they claim to, and so requiring proof can operate to banish the norm of masculinity from a category of jobs like policing and firefighting, while also keeping standards high enough to get the jobs done.[28]

So what kind of stereotype is the idea that fat workers cost more: false or statistical? Does our law allow employers to assume whatever they want, or does it compel proof? Would proof end the inquiry? Since weight is not a protected trait under Title VII, there is no way to use disparate impact theory to combat workplace rules that disadvantage fat workers. Where fat discrimination is not illegal, employers can fire or refuse to hire fat people based on any assumptions they have, empirically defensible or not. Where courts manage to find fat discrimination illegal (again, mostly using disability law), they display an ambivalent attitude toward the question of statistical truth. In one case in which a nursing home refused to hire Ms. Cook, a fat nurse, and was held liable under disability antidiscrimination laws, the employer's use of actuarial reasoning about the nurse's future claims on the worker's compensation system and the assumption that she was too fat to help evacuate patients in the event of a fire functioned as "a graphic illustration of an employment decision based on stereotyping—exactly the sort of employment decision that [disability rights law] seeks to banish."[29] The assumption that she was too fat to assist in an emergency is the same assumption Dr. Frierson made about Ms. Manuel, and the court in the latter case wanted proof, not presumptions. But no one did agility testing on Ms. Manuel as part of the fact-finding, so the court fell back on all the other successful measurements of her abilities (individual data instead of statistical generalizations). The judge for the fat nurse condemns the lack of real evidence, but also inveighs against norms of thinness. The employer failed to look into what exactly the applicant's physical limitations were, if any, "and instead relied on generalizations regarding an obese person's capabilities."[30] The harm was to the true, individualized self: the failure to make a " 'fact-specific and individualized' inquiry" into actual job performance.[31] "In a society that all too often confuses 'slim' with 'beautiful' or 'good,' " the judge wrote, "morbid obesity can present formidable barriers to employment [and] . . . those who erect and seek to preserve them must suffer the consequences."[32]

So would this judge accept a "fact-specific and individualized inquiry" concluding that Ms. Cook was indeed likely to cost a lot in worker's compensation? We would still have our culture of confusing slim with beautiful and good. Individualized inquiries do not necessarily promote anyone's dignity or transform social norms. If these inquiries are conducted as medical examinations, then Ms. Cook would simply have been put into Ms. Manuel's place. The judge in Ms. Cook's case is using a logic of personhood (functional individualism) that cannot address his real concerns. He wants a strategy that can condemn the cultural hegemony of thinness, and he uses the notion of stereotyping to describe the type of reasoning he wants to prohibit. He has to presume the employer was using false stereotyping, not statistical stereotyping, but he has no language to talk about the difference. That is because functional individualism has no answer to statistical stereotyping except to hope for the individual plaintiff's exceptionalism. In other words, it can only supply a justification for hiring strong women and agile fat people.

Yet Another Reality: Not Fitting into Spaces Designed for Smaller Persons

What if the problem is not stereotyping or stigmatizing, but just that a fat job applicant does not fit in a place she needs to fit to do a job? It is not a false stereotype that fat people are bigger than non-fat people; it is understood to be a fact, like the fact that someone who uses a wheelchair cannot use stairs. But as we have seen in the previous cases, just announcing something as a fact about difference does not resolve the issue. Consider the case of Stacey Webb. Ms. Webb applied to the Swartz Creek Community School District in Swartz Creek, Michigan for a job as a substitute school bus driver in August 1996. On the first day of training, Ms. Webb found that the steering wheel pressed into her abdomen. At the time, she was about five feet eight inches tall and weighed between 320 and 330 pounds. The next day, the test drive supervisor dismissed her from the training program because she could not fit behind the wheel, at least not without the wheel pressing into her body. Even though this case arose in Michigan, the only state in which employment discrimination based on weight is expressly prohibited, the court found that the supervisor lacked "discriminatory animus" because "[she] only found Webb's weight to be a problem because it prevented Webb from driving the bus safely."[33] Ms. Webb was not disabled, either, according to the court. Nor was she perceived as disabled; she was just perceived to not fit behind the wheel. The supervisor never made derogatory remarks about Ms. Webb, and even suggested applying for other jobs in the school district. The district had decided not to adjust the seat on the bus any further because it would require structural modification, possibly in violation of other safety standards (something the district had also been unwilling to do for other applicants).

Ms. Webb lost her case even though she was covered by Michigan's state law extending protection in hiring based on weight. The Michigan law came about, writes one state judge, because "the Legislature was concerned that overweight people would be cast aside on the basis of inaccurate stereotypes about their abilities."[34] The law is rarely used, however.[35] When it went into effect in 1975, according to Art Stine of the Michigan Department of Civil Rights, it was used by women who would have been kept out of traditionally male jobs by *minimum* weight requirements, such as the 120-pound minimum for being a police officer.[36] The school district did not base its refusal to hire Ms. Webb on stereotypes (despite the legislature's anticipation that stereotyping was the problem they were fixing—false stereotypes, presumably). Rather, the decision was based on the fact that she could not physically fit behind the wheel. Her lack of fit is understood to be just a fact, not evidence of any injustice. The judge in her case pointed out that everyone seems to have been quite nice to her. Ms. Manuel, Ms. Portnick, and Ms. Nedder could perform the jobs for which they had been hired according to the same specifications that applied to everyone else, and their employers' negative views were based upon deference to others' social norms and conjectures about future hypothetical situations. Ms. Webb (or anyone else her size), on the other hand, would have needed some kind of accommodation in order to take the job, presumably moving the seat back or the steering wheel forward and adjusting the controls.[37]

When justice means protecting the capabilities of the self, then there can be no reason to modify the bus to allow Ms. Webb to take the job. The difference that matters about her is a difference in her capacity to function in the same setting as everyone else. There is nothing unjust about the fact that the norms of school bus construction probably always assumed that drivers would have a certain body size; the conditions of the work site are simply given, and thus legally understood as the neutral terrain upon which discrimination may or may not occur. Such an understanding fits well with strategies (1), defending fat people's functional individualism generally against false stereotypes, and (2), arguing that even if fat people generally have diminished functional capacities, *this* individual does not. The idea that justice requires modifying the bus would stand upon different justifications altogether. It would use a strategy capable of securing redistributions of resources backed by a political commitment to transform the lives and opportunities of fat people. It would redescribe their difference as something that emerges through the unjust construction of the social world (and school buses in particular), not something rooted in Ms. Webb's incapacities. That strategy is the third one I outlined: conceding that fat people have bodies that depart from the norm, but insisting that the norm itself is unjust and serves to naturalize the privileges that thinner bodies in our culture enjoy. This third strategy grounds disability accommodations, as well as redistributive practices like affirmative action and disparate impact discrimination suits.

Accommodations hone in on past injustice done to the group through the operation of hegemonic norms that displaced or marginalized bearers of that identity trait. They acknowledge that the physical world has been assembled in the interests of some people's functional capacities and against others' interests. It is not simply neutral terrain upon which proper or improper functioning happens, but rather it helps to create and maintain the dysfunction of some people and promote the abilities of others. Buildings only accessible by stairs are fundamentally unfair because not everyone's mobility comes from walking, for example. The problem is the lack of ramps, not that people using wheelchairs have something wrong with them.

For functional individualism, as we saw, difference in capacity is just a politically unproblematic way in which persons vary. Problematizing those differences requires problematizing the ways that differences in capacities emerge, gain recognition, are reproduced within institutions and social practices, and come to be seen as deserving of goods or advancement (or alternatively, of criminalization, medicalization, or contempt). To do so, one would concede that the group members function differently or appear different from the norm but nonetheless insist that the standards being used are not neutral, but rather constructed in favor of the dominant group to naturalize and maintain its power. These strategies defy functional individualism by shifting the blame from the person's capacities to the social structures that produced the standards for or the site of functioning.

Some means of litigating an antidiscrimination case begin with this kind of political commitment to the advancement of a named identity group and an acknowledgment that that group has been unjustly held back. I've just referred to disability rights law, which is an obvious example. We do not treat wheelchair users as Ms. Webb was treated. Disparate impact theory is available to combat rules that disadvantage women, as I noted earlier. Rose Mary Boyd applied to be the first and only woman pilot at Ozark Air Lines but did not fit properly in the cockpit because she was too small (too short to see out at the right level, specifically). She successfully sued Ozark under Title VII on a disparate impact theory, and the airline had to lower its height requirement from five feet seven inches to five feet five inches so as to allow more women to qualify as pilots.[38] There is no logic of personhood politically available to shift the blame from Ms. Webb to school bus designers, however; therefore, there is no way to argue for modifying the bus to accommodate her.

Creating Protected Communities for Embedded Persons

We've already seen in Ms. Mark's case (about the failed promotion of the telemarketer to a face-to-face sales job) how embedded personhood can mire an employee down in others' distaste for her appearance.

However American law sometimes entices us to try to understand each other as embedded in other contexts besides antidiscrimination law, most notably in deliberations about whether a person behaved reasonably as is required by tort law or the law of personal injury. Tort law does not use categories in the same manner that antidiscrimination law does; rather it proceeds by standards like reasonable behavior, avoidance of negligence, and mitigation of damages. I bring up tort law in a study of antidiscrimination law because the question of judging difference is big enough to engage more than the most obvious area of law. Tort law is about our duties not to harm each other, and those duties sometimes vary based on our differences: children have lesser duties than adults, for example, and homeowners have greater duties than guests. Stereotyping is not a key concept in personal injury law, so we do not find judges talking that way. But they are trying to figure out the same thing about a person: does this difference about him matter? The lawyers for the fat teenagers in the infamous McDonald's lawsuits were hoping that the public could easily understand the temptations of fast food and sympathize with the teens, particularly if they were misled by advertising stating that frequent consumption was compatible with a healthy lifestyle.[39] However, personal responsibility has dominated the response, with the House of Representatives' passage in 2005 of the Personal Responsibility in Food Consumption Act (shielding fast food companies from such lawsuits) and the adoption by many state legislatures of similar measures. It is supposed to be common sense not to eat too much fast food, and so there has not been much sympathy for lawsuits that are based on consumer ignorance that eating McDonald's can make one fat.[40]

What would make understanding and sympathy about weight gain possible in the law? Does embedded personhood have potential for something more benign than distaste or contempt? Consider the following personal injury case, in which a fat person's reasonableness in attempting to lose weight is the key issue. While trying to get out of a whirlpool tub in a Best Western Starlight Village Motel in Ames, Iowa, Bruce Tanberg fell and injured his back. He brought a personal injury lawsuit against the hotel corporation, claiming negligence in its operation of the tub. Best Western argued in its defense that Mr. Tanberg's failure to lose weight (from over 300 pounds at the time of the fall) constituted comparative fault and a breach of the duty to mitigate damages.[41] Plaintiffs must do what is reasonable to treat injuries rather than letting them get worse and then blaming the defendant for that, too. Often that means following doctors' orders. Several doctors testified that his weight could have contributed to the back injury, or at least kept it from healing properly, and that he "had not been as faithful in following his diets as he should have been."[42]

Should he have been more faithful to his diet, or was it reasonable that he did not manage to lose the weight? Is the proper fat person always trying to lose weight? Considering that the vast majorities of diets fail to keep weight off and that dieting can cause weight gain over the long term (so-called yo-yo dieting), it would seem that dieting failure is something many people can understand.[43] Interestingly, the law does not require that the plaintiff actually lose weight, just that he make a reasonable effort to do so. This required display of reasonable effort is the dominant normative stereotype for fat people: regretful, wishing to be thin, always dieting. The jury did not have to ignore any feature of Mr. Tanberg's personhood; rather, the legal standard embedded him fully in both the medical and moral presentations of his fatness. In the end, he did not get any money because the jury found that he was more responsible for his injury than the motel was. Other juries have felt differently about plaintiffs in Mr. Tanberg's position, finding that it was understandable when the plaintiff could not lose the weight.[44] Are some fat people worthier of sympathy and others less so? Does our sympathy come from our own understandings of how difficult it is to look just the right way, or does it come from the gratification we get when someone has humbled himself, declared his weakness, and begged to be excused?

American law is filled with different rules for persons whose difference makes a difference, though these have often been controversial. As I noted earlier, antidiscrimination doctrine is a particularly difficult place to squeeze in accommodations for embedded persons because of the predominance of functional individualism. Other areas of law show somewhat greater evidence of compromise. Native American tribes are entitled to self-governance on Indian lands and to operate casinos, tort law provides different standards of negligence for children, the Amish do not have to send their children to public schools until they are sixteen as other parents must, and some federal judges have employed a gender-specific standard of "the reasonable woman" for judging the severity or pervasiveness of a sexual harassment claim. Fat people would have to be understood to have a coherent identity as fat people, and to be able to make claims on the dominant culture to preserve and enhance that community. Given the backlash against the McDonald's lawsuits and the animosity directed toward fatness in our culture, strategic reliance on a positive version of embedded personhood for fat people seems exceedingly far off.

The "Like Race" Argument for Fat Rights

And what of the last two strategies: (4) analogizing fatness to being a member of a racial minority group (quintessentially, African American) and (5) invoking diversity? What logics of personhood would make these strategies tenable, and what are their strengths and limits? As a practical matter, there is no chance that either of these arguments will see the interior of a courtroom. That is not our primary concern here, though. It's still worthwhile to sift through how these arguments would be made. Let's take (4), the "like race" analogy, first. It is a strategy designed to shift the blame from individualized deficiency to social inequality. The blame shifting logic of personhood would remove the stigma of medicalized deficiency and moral turpitude from fatness and redescribe it as a feature of a person that admittedly makes it harder for her to succeed, but only because systemic oppression surrounds her and has burdened her group over past decades. Blame-shifting, as I indicated in the Introduction and explore in detail in the next chapter, has been most thoroughly implemented as a response to racial oppression.

Fat discrimination would have to be regarded as a more serious threat to equal citizenship than any of these other forms of discrimination except for that based on race. To claim that one's group is like African Americans is to reach for the brass ring in the context of constitutional rights under the 14th Amendment's equal protection clause. Dismantling slavery and its effects (like school segregation and Jim Crow laws) was the primary purpose of the Civil War Amendments (the 13th, 14th, and 15th). Fourteenth Amendment jurisprudence has always held out racial discrimination as the paradigmatic evil that a government must be prevented from perpetrating upon its citizens. Policy development in civil rights traces the power of the "like race" analogy, with groups who were most able to make the analogy convincingly also more easily able to achieve the same policy benefits (principally affirmative action measures) that had been designed with black Americans in mind.[45] The argument would have to be that fatness has been subject to invidious discrimination, that it is an immutable trait (or at least practically immutable), perhaps genetically based (as race is imagined to be), that it causes isolation and exclusion of a group of people from public life and opportunity (as segregationist practices did), and that fat people as a group are marked by their fatness in a way that is tempting for government to use to subordinate them (as skin color can be used).[46] There is plenty of social science evidence that fat people, particularly fat women, suffer reduced life opportunities because of their body size, receiving lower incomes, reduced job opportunities, greater isolation from health care, and high levels of stigmatization.[47]

The benefits would mean that the government could not classify citizens with regard to their body size (no report cards with a child's BMI sent home to parents, no exclusions from state-sponsored programs on the basis of weight) except for the most compelling reasons. But since the Supreme Court interprets the benign use of a trait in the same strict way as an invidious one, any program targeting fat people for some special benefit would also be very strictly evaluated (as in the University of Michigan's use of race in its admissions programs). This is all very far-fetched, of course, because now the medicalization of fatness as obesity means that it can be separated from moral turpitude while remaining an imminently reasonable way to classify people in the interests of health. After all, the first thing that happens on any visit to the doctor is stepping on the scale. Health of the population could even be a compelling justification that would allow government use of weight even if the trait received the highest judicial scrutiny. As long as being fat is like being a smoker, it will never be like being black. Likewise, public opinion seems to favor a view of fatness as behavioral rather than immutable, and fat people themselves often dislike being fat and try to lose weight (rather than seeing themselves as part of a distinct social group of oppressed people, on the model of a tribe or racial minority group).

Pushing a "like race" argument in such an inhospitable environment may be futile, but it may also neglect the ways that fatness as a category can help deconstruct ideas about what constitutes a deserving category of people in the law. Kathleen LeBesco argues that fatness is like queerness in its open challenge to conventional norms and in its fluid boundaries.[48] When what is considered fat varies widely between different subcultures and situations, when persons drift in and out of the category, and when its meaning has undergone significant historical shifts, doesn't that suggest that it would be preferable not to shoehorn it into an awkward analogy and risk losing grip on its unique implications for identity politics? As Janet Halley points out, making the "like race" analogy solidifies an account of the identity being defended, creating a community that has discrete interests and, in Appiah's terms, a corresponding normative stereotype for what it is to share that difference.[49] Such a construction in the law would also open up fatness to all the criticisms leveled against identity politics: its false unity over dissenting members, its inability to account for intersectional identities, its essentialist tendencies, and so on.

Invoking fat persons as part of the fabric of diversity might seem like another way of making a "like race" argument, since diversity as a legal concept is a defense to using racial classifications. Supporters of affirmative action have switched to talking about diversity instead of racial balancing or proportional representation. But I argue that diversity means much more than this narrow "like race" interpretation suggests, and this wider meaning also makes some room for traits that are considered unconnected to systemic oppression to be part of diversity. In one study of the expansion of diversity rhetoric within corporations, the authors found that Hallmark defined diversity as including the legally protected traits, but also "lifestyle" and "thinking style," and Westinghouse announced that it sought to mix "quiet [people] with talky people."[50] Diversity is a multifaceted term that crosses between and blends legal obligations to prevent discrimination based on certain traits but also seeks to maximize corporate "synergies" by bringing people together who are thought to vary in their different approaches to problem solving.[51] Difference as difference in problem solving approaches thus leads to the inclusion of cultural background, attitude, and other features of the interactive person. The difference that matters is the difference in the mind, as expressed through ideas, suggestions, and new perspectives. The traits are desired insofar as they are proxies for the likelihood of expressing a helpful idea in a group setting.

The redefined managerial conceptions of diversity in the above-mentioned Edelman study did not include any mention of appearance or any feature of employees that is primarily appearance-based (besides the legally mandated ones like race and sex).[52] In fact, appearance and experience are in tension in diversity management because diversity is often understood to be an alternative to traditional concern with specific groups demarcated by appearance: racial and ethnic minorities and

women. The basic impulse of diversity management is to substitute experience and perspective for appearance. Appearance on its own would
not suggest this likelihood of insightful provision of ideas; appearance
would have to be connected to an experience or community upon which
the organization wants to draw. The person is then a conduit for these
things into the working group. Fatness as a useful life experience could
be attractive to a company looking to market to fat customers. Disability is a similar experience, however, and managerial diversity has not
shown the same enthusiasm for employees with disabilities as they have
for "talky people," suggesting that this marketing interest may be fairly
limited. But marketing products to fat people could be big business,
probably greater than marketing to people with a wide range of different disabilities, and perhaps it will turn out to be a compelling reason
to include fatness within diversity management. Fatness as diversity
would, in this view, be the ultimate expression of what diversity's critics
claim it really is: the absorption and deflection of the political claims of
minority groups into a meaningless array of commodity-driven plati-
tudes.[53] But talking in terms of "body diversity" could find a wider way
into institutions like schools and universities that are not so tied to business interests and which could serve as incubators for a more cosmopolitan view of body forms. There is already a familiar critique of the ideal
feminine form in feminist circles (and a very popular topic with undergraduate women). Perhaps it would not be too much of a stretch to include not only the oppression of being a size 10 in a size 4 world, but
also of being a size 22. University diversity programs are also uniquely
poised to present body diversity in a context that emphasizes the cultural and historical contingency of our ideas about the ideal or normal
body (its whiteness and heteronormativity, for example).

Conclusion: Using Fatness to Press Logics of Personhood

Logics of personhood tell us how to talk about a person to make her
seem deserving of some kind of protection from stigmatization directed
against her difference. These logics of personhood link up with a limited
set of strategies to increase rights protections. The full menu of strategies included (1) arguing that the group members can function just as
well as everyone else and that their defining trait should be ignored (because it is a false stereotype); (2) acknowledging that statistical stereo-

types about the group are often empirically true, but that they should not burden a particular individual plaintiff; (3) conceding that the group members function differently or appear differently from the norm but insisting that the standards being used are not neutral, but rather constructed in favor of the dominant group to naturalize and maintain its power; (4) analogizing the group to African Americans and stressing historical patterns of exclusion, segregation, and subordination (similar to the previous blame-shifting argument but including the explicit analogy); and (5) naming their difference "diversity" and describing it as an enriching and unique feature of some individuals that can be usefully integrated into the goal-oriented activities of groups.

The first pair of strategies (1 and 2) both redound to functional individualism, the first totally and the second after a quick concession about the group generally. They deflect "common sense" judgments, even from a doctor against a fat patient. They can even deflect actuarial personhood, as when Xerox predicted Ms. McDermott would be a drain on the health benefit system. The next options (3 and 4, critiquing the normal standard or summoning the "like race" analogy) give up on functional individualism and turn to a blame-shifting approach to recast inferiority as systemic injustice. They can summon redistributions and accommodations for acknowledged difference such as disability rights, disparate impact litigation, or affirmative action. Fat plaintiffs have not been able to make much use of either of these strategies in American antidiscrimination law, though there have been a few wins in court under disability rights (not perceived disability, which is really about functional individualism, but the claim of an actual impairment, which depends on a medicalized view of fatness). The last option, (5), responds to the culture of corporate diversity management. It attempts to create a group identity that gives its members special knowledge and marketable perspectives.

Studying fatness does not give us any entry to understanding how logics of personhood make justifications for affirmative action possible. It does not give us much purchase on practices like diversity management or disability accommodations management, since it is not well recognized in them. What would it mean to reconstruct fatness as diversity or fatness as disability? To understand that, we have to see how these concepts help logics of personhood justify and protect differences. I turn to these analyses in later chapters, assisted by studying other salient identity traits that have much more purchase on questions of diversity and accommodations. But let us reflect for a moment on the pressing issues that studying fatness does illuminate.

First, fatness brings into stark relief the interplay of appearance and functional capacities in both our moral intuitions and the formal law. It is not possible to pretend that all stereotyping is just false stereotyping covering over persons' true abilities. The truth of the statistics behind stereotypes lurks and cannot be wished away. And then there was the pull of normative stereotyping, forcing acknowledgment of the role of appearance in role modeling and the many meaningful cultural practices of our lives. These dilemmas only get more difficult when we consider the ways that legal thinking about gender may presage approaches to fatness—a subject I take up in chapter 3. Second, fatness directs our attention to medicalization, particularly to the ways that the professional expertise of physicians interacts with the formal law as well as the life of organizations. Pre-employment exams were the paradigmatic example here. Is talking about health the new way to sanitize stratifications among persons and to justify distributions of jobs and opportunities? Medicalization sits easily with functional personhood, actuarial personhood, and managerial personhood, and it is only with a trait like fatness that we see its full reach into law's deliberations about difference.

No single logic of personhood can supply an adequate justification for why a person's difference should not make her undeserving. If these strategies I have laid out here seem to be full of gaps and contradictions, that is because they rest upon logics of personhood that are themselves partial and conflicted. This partiality prevents their reification by keeping them susceptible to innovation and critique. Nor does the field of the formal law control or capture all the ways to define persons. The ways doctors understand fat patients and the ways that corporate managers regard fat employees are at least as important if not more important than judges' ideas about what difference fatness makes. Being partial, conflicted, and colonized by professionals from other fields does not make American antidiscrimination law necessarily unjust or weak. It just means that we have to understand how the law works from a perspective that acknowledges and anticipates this partiality, conflict, and colonization.

2

Shifting the Blame

Introduction: Reasoning about Persons and Racial Disparities

In the previous chapter, we saw how functional individualism cannot interrogate the norm of proper functioning for an identity like fatness. Capacities were the main features of persons that differentiated them; differences in appearance were not supposed to matter. Norms of proper functioning are simply given by the demands of the job. They are not understood to be politically formed, biased, or designed by a dominant group to maintain its privileged position. Functional individualism provided one answer to the question, why do inequalities exist and how can they be justified? What other methods do American lawyers, judges, and ordinary citizens have for answering that question, though? We leave fatness and turn to race, the most important aspect of difference in American antidiscrimination law.[1] We suspend our discussion of fatness because it cannot tell us anything about how the logics of personhood we possess have developed. Struggles over racial inequalities (and secondarily, as I shall explain, sex inequalities) have been the critical sites for forming the ways we reason about persons and their differences in the contemporary United States. The following two chapters on race and gender critically and fully examine the law and politics that any new rights campaign will inherit.

When one looks around and sees racial disparities everywhere, how might one talk about differences between people without verifying a functional individualist picture in which some racial groups look like they deserve their lower place? That is, if it is true that functional individualism is the dominant logic of personhood within which discussions of racial injustice must take place, what is the defensive logic to which one would naturally turn? The primacy of functional individualism leads to the following debate: is the reason located within the person (physical capacities or character, the core of the functional individualist logic), or is it external to her (discrimination or deprivation)? If the reason is something external, then her position is not entirely her fault. Functional individualism seems unfair because the person's merit and ability are not entirely her own. We then find ourselves struggling to come up with policy solutions that are helpful without being paternalistic, redistributive while still attracting majority support, targeted without being stigmatizing. This balance is notoriously difficult because it arises only when a logic of personhood we otherwise celebrate breaks down and requires amendment in a deeply antagonistic fashion.

While this polarity between the internal and the external is admittedly reductive, I nonetheless insist that backing up to this first move illuminates much of the later debates. As I shall show, it has been very difficult to find terms in American antidiscrimination law that one might use to talk about why racial inequalities are unjustified, because the logic of personhood necessary to do so contains a radical critique of the dominant logic—functional individualism. After a period of batting around the idea of what I call shifting the blame, a much more comfortable account has arisen: difference as diversity. Thus, when a campaign for fat rights turns to the history of black civil rights for inspiration, it will find that the most radical tools have been dismantled and that a new logic has supplanted them. Indeed, prominent fat advocates already talk in terms of "body diversity" and "weight diversity."

In this chapter I argue that the historical moment of the adoption and implementation of the 1964 Civil Rights Act provided the conditions necessary for transforming the logic of functional individualism, but in fairly limited terms. The challenge of combating racial discrimination in the 1960s and 1970s prompted legislators and judges to turn to the logic of blame-shifting, in which personhood is no longer the site of natural capacities but instead is a site of social construction under conditions of inequality. Capacities are not simply given, but made. Crucially, they are understood to have been enhanced for some and stunted for others, and on the basis of group characteristics like race. The blame-shifting logic relies on techniques for detecting differential treatment among persons as group members sharing a trait that is protected under the 1964 Act: race, color, sex (including pregnancy by later amendment), religion, and national origin. Making businesses report how many minorities and women they have hired, for example, is a sensible strategy when injustice is conceptualized as social and group-linked. (Functional individualism presumes that if fewer members of a group were hired, that was simply because they did not measure up.)

Vestiges of this political movement to shift the blame from individual dysfunction to social debt remain, but they have been largely eclipsed by an account of difference as diversity. Difference as diversity deflects concern for socially created group-level dysfunction in favor of celebrating persons as unique, useful contributors to group enterprises like college learning. If differences in achievement across groups still persist, however, a diversity approach cannot say why those differentials are unjust.

When Is Functional Individualism Unjust?

Despite the fact that American antidiscrimination law is highly individualistic, pockets of it still regard the person as fundamentally socially situated and group-bound.[2] As noted earlier, there are two basic ways to claim employment discrimination under Title VII of the 1964 Civil Rights Act: (1) disparate treatment on the basis of a protected trait or (2) disparate impact of a rule or practice on a protected group. Disparate treatment is an individualized wrong, such as when one worker receives negative job treatment because of her race. Disparate impact, however, is a wrong done to a group of women or a group of employees of one race, for example.[3] If a seemingly race-, gender-, nationality-, or religion-neutral employment practice turns out to have a disparate impact on the hiring prospects or working conditions of a protected group, it is illegal under Title VII of the 1964 Civil Rights Act unless it can be justified as a business necessity. Restrictions on height and weight, strength and endurance tests, or verbal skills tests are examples of policies that have been frequently targeted for their disproportionate impact on women or minority groups. The test for the legal wrong is the aggregate outcome (what proportion of women failed the strength test versus men?), not intent of the employer to discriminate. The notion of the harm is entirely removed from individual subjectivity, bad motives, and unjust stereotypes. So unlike the individual woman who gets to prove herself in the face of a statistical stereotype that women are weaker than men, this protected group would include all the women who failed the test. They would not be arguing for their exceptionalism in the face of an otherwise valid generalization; they would ask for the rule to be changed so that more of them could pass. Legal action would force the employer to justify the test. The Supreme Court's 1971 decision in *Griggs v. Duke Power Company* established the disparate impact theory of discrimination under Title VII, and Congress later wrote (and re-enforced) the disparate impact theory into statutory law in the Civil Rights Act of 1991 after the Supreme Court had narrowed its application in an earlier case.[4]

Recall that the dispute in *Griggs* began over the fact that Duke Power Company required either a high school diploma or a passing grade on a general intelligence test for new hires and internal transfers within the company. As I mentioned earlier, jobs at the Dan River Steam Station in Draper, North Carolina were organized into five categories: Labor, Coal Handling, Operations, Maintenance, and Laboratory and Test. Prior to 1965, African Americans could only get jobs in Labor, which paid less than the other four categories, and the remaining departments were filled with white employees. When, in 1965, Duke Power instituted a high school graduation requirement for transfer from Labor to any other department, it was only white employees working in other areas who did not have high school diplomas who kept their jobs and continued to achieve promotion within the other four departments. On July 2, 1965, the day the Civil Rights Act of 1964 went into effect, the company instituted an additional requirement—the successful completion of two aptitude tests—for a job in any department except for Labor. The tests screened out vastly greater numbers of black employees than white, though there was no proof that Duke Power had instituted the test hoping for such an outcome. Black employees at the Dan River Station filed a class action lawsuit under Title VII.

The Supreme Court concluded that "practices, procedures, or tests neutral on their face, and *even neutral in terms of intent,* cannot be maintained if they operate to 'freeze' the status quo of prior discriminatory employment practices."[5] The timing of the policy change—on the day the highly contentious Civil Rights Act went into effect—seems to indicate discriminatory intent, but the Court expressly avoids making that accusation. Instead, the Justices dwell upon the group level inequalities perpetuated by racist policies they were then in the thick of unraveling: school desegregation.[6] Justice Burger, writing for a unanimous eight-member court (Justice Brennan did not participate) pointed out that "[b]ecause they are Negroes, petitioners have long received inferior education in segregated schools and this Court [has] expressly recognized these differences."[7] Apartheid laws created and perpetuated black educational inferiority, in other words. Functional individualism requires widespread acceptance that the basic starting conditions have been equal for everyone. At certain historical moments that notion is cruelly laughable (and understood to be so by enough elites for policy change to occur). In those moments, antidiscrimination law cannot rely upon functional individualism to justify unequal distributions. School segregation spurred Supreme Court judges to engage in blame-shifting rather than draw upon functional individualism.

Functional individualism and the questions of how much blame to shift and where to shift it were interestingly intertwined in those years, emerging most clearly in discussions about how to bring black men into better-paying jobs. Black men's unemployment had been a primary concern for legislators at the time the Civil Rights Act was enacted. One senator had argued for the passage of the Civil Rights Act of 1964 to increase black employment in broad terms, not in terms of black functional individualism: "The rate of Negro unemployment has gone up consistently as compared with white unemployment for the past 15 years. This is a social malaise and a social situation which we should not tolerate. That is one of the principal reasons why the [Civil Rights Act] should pass."[8] Additional justifications circulating at the time of passage had also focused on the irrationality of allowing one group's skills to go untapped. "Through toleration of discriminatory practices, American industry is not obtaining the quantity of skilled workers it needs," argued one Congressional news source in 1964. "A nation need not and should not be converted into a welfare state to reduce poverty, lessen crime, cut down on unemployment, or overcome shortages in skilled occupational categories," the argument continued. "All that is needed is the institution of proper training programs and the elimination of discrimination in employment practices." The "economic straitjacket in which the Negro has been confined" amounted to simple "economic waste."[9]

There are two ways to understand this suppressed personhood. One sees the functional individual forced into a straitjacket by racism. If released from his "economic straitjacket" he will get a job and have an equal chance at prosperity.[10] In this view the straitjacketing does not constitute the person it restrains; it just takes an otherwise functional person and makes it so he cannot use his (metaphorical) arms. This view suggests a one-time fix of racist practices followed by a return to functional individualism. The alternate view would be to understand the metaphorical straitjacket as constituting the person it restrains in a more complex manner, such as the way that an inferior education influences the range of abilities a person is able to develop in the first place. This view implies that fixing impairments caused by racism must continue over time and across generations. Persons are not just restrained by external forces, but can also be constituted through "feeling[s] of inferiority as to their status in the community that may affect their hearts and minds in a way unlikely ever to be undone," as the Supreme Court worried black schoolchildren may be in *Brown v. Board of Education*.[11] The attention in *Griggs* to the effects of a segregated educational system suggests this second interpretation, but the idea that Title VII would fix racial inequalities by taking off straitjackets implies that a functional individual was imagined to spring forth more easily ("All that is needed . . .").

This tension is never really resolved in race discrimination law nor in the terms of debate in our wider culture; it is built in from the beginning and remains with us. Disagreements across the political spectrum about the exact nature of the racist deprivations of the past and how long their treatments should remain reflect this basic tension. Conservatives tend to find the first interpretation more agreeable; liberals gravitate toward versions of the second. Both sides grapple with the reality of continued inequality—conservatives blame black culture and want to stop shifting any blame to whites, and liberals point to the lingering effects of discrimination and conclude that redistributions must continue. Conservatives veer toward implying innate inferiority; liberals risk characterizing minorities as lacking in agency and dignity. My aim here is not to resolve these debates, presented here in sheared-down form, but to show how they are anchored within and intelligible through competing logics of personhood. Any attempt to place blame and suggest solutions, no matter where it is rooted ideologically, must use these logics to explain the relationship between race, functional capacities, and desert. The account of that relationship determines the range of political perspectives with which we are so familiar, and explains their persistent insolubility.

Managing and Counting: Ethno-racial Identity Categories under Blame-Shifting

Congress created the Equal Employment Opportunity Commission (EEOC) when it enacted the Civil Rights Act of 1964. Initially the

EEOC had weak enforcement powers and was soon overrun with complaints of discrimination. In response, the EEOC switched from a strategy of relying on individual complaints (which would each have to be investigated and validated, and there were thousands and thousands of them) to a more bureaucratically rational approach of surveying employers and measuring representation of racial groups. There was already a system in place for counting members of minority groups. As John Skrentny explains, the President's Committee on Government Contracts initially drafted the EEO-1 form in 1956 to require counts of "Negro," "other minority," and "total."[12] The form evolved over the next few years, in part because of lobbying from groups who wanted greater specificity than "other minority." Mexican Americans got "Spanish-Americans" and Chinese and Japanese Americans got "Orientals." Jews were not included on the grounds that they were not an economically disadvantaged group, and "American Indians" were added by David Mann, President Eisenhower's director of surveys, on account of their economic deprivation as a group.[13] Sex was also included though it never seemed fully analogous to race. By the time implementation of Title VII moved into high gear, a sense of "taken-for-grantedness" pervaded the choices of which groups to measure and why. The metric was "similarity to the economic deprivation of African Americans," in other words, and the analogies proceeded within civil rights bureaucracies without a great deal of debate. Affirmative action plans cohered around these agreed-upon groups and were enthusiastically implemented as conditions for receiving government contracts. The Supreme Court validated private affirmative action plans for the same reasons that disparate impact discrimination cases were allowed: "abolish[ing] traditional patterns of racial segregation and hierarchy."[14]

Not surprisingly, the courts worked with bureaucratic formulations and adopted a similarly aggregate-level measurement of disadvantage, allowing EEOC-gathered statistics to stand as evidence of racial discrimination in employment. Civil rights bureaucracies created rules for interpreting data as they had created definitions for who counted as a minority. The EEOC established the "four-fifths rule" for detecting discrimination in disparate impact cases:

A selection rate for any race, sex, or ethnic group which is less than four-fifths (⅘) (or eighty percent) of the rate for the group with the highest rate will generally be regarded by the Federal enforcement agencies as evidence of adverse impact, while a greater than four-fifths rate will generally not be regarded by Federal enforcement agencies as evidence of adverse impact.[15]

The idea was that "it is ordinarily to be expected that nondiscriminatory hiring practices will in time result in a workforce more or less representative of the racial and ethnic composition of the population in the community from which employees are hired," as the Supreme Court observed, and evidence of a disparity would therefore be probative (but not dispositive).[16]

Notice that the blame-shifting logic as implemented in civil rights law requires bureaucratic tools for measuring and counting. (The blame-shifting logic would also be compatible with an individualized assessment, such as when a jury finds a criminal defendant less culpable because of mitigating circumstances like a deprived childhood or past abuse.[17]) The counting of persons is not exactly actuarial because it does not involve risk projections about the future, instead only counting up the rejections of the past. These past failures are evidentiary proxies, perhaps for intentional discrimination, perhaps for the accreted effects of a thoughtless and biased policy. Nor are the bureaucratic practices the same as what I call managerial individualism in chapter 5, meaning an individualized accommodations process overseen by management professionals. Bureaucratic practices necessary for implementing policies grounded in blame-shifting are group-focused rather than individualized. This aggregate focus is exactly what makes the blame-shifting account sit uneasily within a tradition focused on persons as individuals.

Critics of disparate impact discrimination seize on this number-crunching feature to argue that businesses will simply install hiring quotas to evade triggering the four-fifths rule, for instance.[18] "Quota" is an epithet because it signals straightforward redistributions, denying that functional capacity is the critical feature of persons that matters. Businesses, worried about being able to defend the necessity of job tests, may just abandon them and, the argument goes, hire less qualified people. These conservative critics support retaining functional individualism as the way to justify the distribution of jobs. The threat of antidiscrimination lawsuits to business owners has been greatly exaggerated, however.[19] The number of actual cases litigated under a disparate impact theory is extremely low (around 2–3% of the total).[20] The legal claim has to be tied to a discrete practice that results in the disparate impact, and pinpointing such a practice or rule in the contemporary workplace is extremely difficult. Most employment discrimination cases are disparate treatment cases, in which the plaintiff alleges that she was discriminated against as an individual, not as the result of a neutral policy impact on her group. Plaintiffs lose more than they win, and evidence suggests that relatively few employees who have experienced discrimination will ever file a claim, much less proceed all the way through the system.[21]

African American poverty and displacement from skilled work has a history. There was no problem acknowledging the dysfunction of African American workers in 1964, because there existed sufficient political consensus to sever its link to personal failure, laziness, or lack of innate ability. Rather, the problem was "toleration of discriminatory practices," as the Congressional news service put it. That is, tolerance by whites of discriminatory practices by whites. That is as simple as the blame-shifting logic of personhood can possibly get: the problem is white racism and its legacy, not black functional individualism and its failures. The hope was that once better jobs and education became available, dysfunction would be transformed into proper functioning. The standards for proper functioning would remain the same but minority races would be assimilated across all levels of employment and educational achievement.

These expectations now seem optimistic and naïve. We now know that generations of discrimination and poverty have not been corrected by Title VII, though there is evidence that it did improve wages among black workers.[22] Problems like incarceration rates, credit and lending discrimination, housing discrimination, and lack of adequate health care were never meant to be addressed in Title VII and their reach into minority communities has been crushing. But it is critical to see that when, for a brief period, a national consensus formed, it made a discourse of personal failure impossible and installed group-targeted remedies. From a perspective supportive of blame-shifting, the problem was that justifications and accounts of personhood able to account for the constitutive effects of unequal treatment in a group over time never appeared, at least not in a way that was translatable to judges and legislators. Blame-shifting was really only embraced in the straitjacket removal sense, and once antidiscrimination laws were in place it was difficult to account for why racial disparities persisted. From a functional individualist perspective, this history of blame-shifting is a shameful liberal legacy of coddling and excuses that has in fact helped to perpetuate the underclass. The conservative perspective now dominates, and one never hears a defense of affirmative action, for example, that does not also insist that every selected person is also a fully meritorious functional individual. It is then easy to see why an account of difference as diversity has enjoyed wide acceptance from the Supreme Court to the boardrooms of major corporations.

Difference as Diversity: A New Account of Personal Merit and Functionality

The Supreme Court held that an interest in maintaining a diverse student body could be a compelling justification for considering applicants' race as one part of the admissions decision in the 2003 companion cases from the University of Michigan, *Grutter v. Bollinger* (the law school case) and *Gratz v. Bollinger* (the undergraduate case).[23] These are constitutional equal protection cases, whereas I've been discussing Title VII statutory employment law up to now. The jurisprudence between the two is quite different: Title VII permits claims based on aggregate-level disparities without proof of discriminatory intent, while the constitutional standard for when the government has wrongly considered race is individualized and intent-based.[24] The Supreme Court has not been willing to read a *Griggs*-type disparate impact theory into the equal protection clause, insisting that "the Fifth and Fourteenth Amendments to the Constitution protect *persons,* not *groups.*"[25] The kind of discriminatory purpose that is actionable under the equal protection clause is not merely knowledge of the consequences of a law or a willingness to put up with regrettable results, but rather an affirmative desire on the part of the decision maker to bring about the harmful consequences to the affected group.[26] Critical race theorists have rained down criticism upon the Court for its adoption of such a strict standard for proving discrimination, claiming that it misses much of what discrimination really is.[27] Another significant feature of the Court's race jurisprudence is its refusal to evaluate so-called benign uses of racial classifications more leniently than invidious ones; that is, affirmative action meant to assist minorities is scrutinized in the same way as a segregationist law would be. Using race in admissions practices is clearly both intentional and, for supporters, benign. The question was, in the Michigan cases, would the Court be able to justify the use of race? Diversity turned out to be wildly successful in repackaging functional personhood into what I call diverse personhood. Diverse personhood is closely related to functional personhood: it is a new way of talking about how individuals can perform unique functions in group situations by bringing their unique style to bear on a problem-solving or learning situation. I isolate it as a logic on its own to show its differences from functional personhood, particularly its emphasis on uniqueness and individuality rather than the movement of a body at a task or possession of a certain skill set. I have also described the invocation of diversity as part of a strategy to argue on behalf of one's group that one's traits contribute to diversity.[28]

Under the 14th Amendment's equal protection clause, governmental use of a racial classification can only be justified by a compelling state interest, and then must also be narrowly tailored to achieve the interest. In *Grutter* and *Gratz,* white applicants who had not been admitted to the undergraduate program and the law school challenged the University of Michigan's admissions policies, claiming that the university used race impermissibly to guarantee certain percentages of minority students at their expense. The previous statement on affirmative action in university admissions had been the 1978 *Regents of the University of California v. Bakke* medical school admissions case, in which the Court struck down the Davis campus medical school admissions policy of setting aside a certain number of spots for non-white medical students. The *Bakke* case banned racial balancing, remedying societal discrimination, and increasing the number of doctors who might serve minority communities as possible compelling governmental interests.[29] It did not make all affirmative action in higher education illegal, however. Justice Powell's opinion for the plurality announced that because of the weight of the First Amendment tradition of academic freedom, the attainment of a diverse student body could be a compelling state interest that could justify the use of race as one factor among many in an assessment of an applicant's merit. The University of California system was unconstitutional because it carved off a set number of places in each class for non-whites and was thus considered too rigid. Justice Powell extolled the Harvard system, described as a flexible system of individualized assessment of each applicant in which violin players, applicants from rural areas, and racial minorities would all be considered for their unique traits. But because the Court was split in *Bakke,* Powell's single-authored opinion stood alone in using diversity as a possible justification for affirmative action until his idea was finally validated in the 2003 cases.

In *Grutter*, the case challenging the use of race in the University of Michigan Law School's admissions program, Justice O'Connor's majority opinion affirmed the diversity interest from *Bakke* and found also that the law school's procedures were sufficiently narrowly tailored. The interesting question was, how would this relatively conservative Court differentiate between the University's expressed interest in getting a "critical mass" of minority students and the supposedly improper interest in racial balancing per se? A pure functional individualist perspective would have excluded race from consideration in the usual color-blind sense. But in refusing that track, the Court did not embrace anything like the idea that minority applicants bear a history of discrimination that has produced lower test scores (i.e., blame-shifting). Differentials in standardized test scores by racial groups do not matter at all in the Court's reasoning.

Instead, O'Connor defends the "critical mass" concept through its capacity to produce educational benefits. When there are enough members of a minority group present, their variation from each other defeats group-based stereotypes as well as solves the problem of minority group members having to serve as spokespeople to whites for their entire race. Yet O'Connor's discussion ranges much wider. She goes on to say that "legitimacy in the eyes of the citizenry" for our prestigious institutions requires that they be "visibly open" to members of all races. [30] The opinion also explicitly acknowledges the weight given to *amicus curiae* briefs from the U.S. military and from major corporations in support of the University, explaining how a diverse officer corps and diverse corporate leadership are necessary for success.

Imagining an individualized selection process is the Court's antidote to the group-based redistributions envisioned under blame-shifting. Not only is the idea of group-based redistributions based on race repugnant under this line of jurisprudence, but a bureaucratic process that effaces individuality is the touchstone of illegality. The University of Michigan used several different administrative review systems for the thousands of undergraduate applications it received, but a common thread was the imposition of a bureaucratic framework upon each application. The sheer volume of applications received made it desirable to overlay the process with bureaucratic management based on numerical data. Its point system was the most hotly debated in the subsequent litigation, particularly the award of 20 points in a 150 point scale (where 100 points meant admission) for being a member of a minority race. Chief Justice Rehnquist's majority opinion in *Gratz* held that the program was not narrowly tailored because it did not provide individualized consideration but awarded 20 points based on race where the only question involved was the applicant's actual membership in that racial group. (O'Connor concurred that this is a "mechanical" system.) The mechanical nature of the admissions system was the division of the applicant into a collection of traits, each with a point value. A press release from the University of Michigan announcing a new undergraduate admissions policy promised "highly individualized review" in a "flexible" process, however, including new essay requirements to gain the "richest possible picture of the student's intellect, character and personal values."[31] As a direct result of the Court's decision, the University hired fifty-one new personnel to assist with admissions, and spent an additional 1.8 million dollars in fiscal year 2004 (projected to decline to about 1 million above 2003 levels thereafter).[32]

The attainment of racial diversity is understood as a communal product, not solely a matter of individual capacity. One cannot be diverse alone; the racial contribution to diversity is to stand not only as a signal of one's race in a learning group but also simultaneously to communicate an individuality that is uninflected by race-specific content. A person's ability matters insofar as she is imagined to contribute to a learning community, in which she is projected to debate, discuss, and express her individuality as a member of her outwardly-appearing identity group. In Appiah's terms, the hope was that all three kinds of stereotypes—false, statistical, and normative—would be challenged by an array of minority students who defy them by appearing in sufficiently large numbers that they cannot constitute their own homogeneous subculture. Diversity assigns a deep indeterminacy to racial difference. Individualism is a conflicted notion: there can be no normative stereotypes for racial identity, leaving it wholly self-guided, yet it is undesirable to have an all-white environment. Pictorial racial variety is required for the visible openness of institutions O'Connor wants, but must be assumed not to mean anything in particular for any individual. This is a deeply perplexing account of what difference racial identities ought to make— none and all at the same time?

Conservatives protest that an individualistic account of racially de-fined functional merit (let's call it "diversity") is a faddish cover for sim-ple proportional representation of certain minority groups that would not otherwise be so well represented.[33] That is one explanation for the contradictions here: admissions officers really just want to increase mi-nority representation and do care about race itself and assume that it has social meaning, and so it is only pragmatic to find a way to recast that concern in individualistic terms to keep critical mass from sounding too much like a quota. While exchanges between racially different stu-dents will be beneficial, in this view it would primarily be desirable for white majority students to learn about the experiences of minority class-mates and a fairly limited range of racially inflected moments of class-room discussion would do just fine. In other words, progressive admis-sions officials hope for a sharing of normative stereotypes in a positive and enriching context, not for utter individuality or wholly contingent racial identities among students. Remember that all the other blame-shifting rationales for affirmative action practices are now unconstitu-tional, so there is no way to use that logic.

While diversity certainly has its critics among critical race theorists, it has actually been widely embraced on its own terms in a way that sug-gests it is not simply a Trojan horse for race progressives.[34] Evidence from psychological, educational, and complex systems research suggests that people really do come up with better ideas and come to see each other's differences more positively in well-constructed, diverse groups than in more isolated or stratified settings.[35] For our purposes it is most interesting to assume that it has grown into a complex meaning that is shared across contexts—legal, political, business, military—and that its tensions indicate its usefulness in our culture. To take interest in what diversity means requires unpacking what it does for the range of arguments we can make about persons and their differences. Diversity avoids focusing on who or what is to blame for lower minority test scores (the test of functional capacity for the dominant culture), and in-stead recreates a new story of functioning (one that dodges the blame question entirely). It remains true to the functionalist paradigm, sticking to the ways that diversity assists in management and in learning, but it preserves attention to race only insofar as it insists that this identity marker cannot be presumed to mean anything in particular. It is not strictly color blind, though. It doesn't have to be, because the new con-tingency of race means that it won't be so distracting. The Court's requirement that the review be "flexible" and "non-mechanical" is the route to honoring the true self, who must be appraised as a unit, not as a collection of traits that are distributed optimally within a population of admitted students.

Process rather than identity is the route to avoiding shifting blame for unequal access to higher education (encapsulated in test score differentials). Process is contingent and content-free; identities carry historical and social meanings. *Griggs* blamed school segregation and other structural inequalities for test score differentials between black and white applicants. Here, however, all applicants are imagined as unique contributors to the educational process, equally capable of doing their part to enrich diversity. It is as if high-stakes standardized tests did not exist, nor massive inequalities by race at the secondary school level. A *Griggs*-type shift in blame would have relied upon some version of the prohibited justifications for affirmative action: making up for group-level deprivations by redistributing opportunities to group members *qua* group members. Substituting process ("flexible individual evaluation") for stable identity ("underrepresented minority group member"), by contrast, secures a new form of homage to the uniqueness of the individual person. The constitutional concept of diversity takes flexibility and individualization as the defining features of just process. The process is of course the admissions process, but I mean to make more of the idea of process than that.

Just process is at the heart of the rule of law. Ordinary people obey the law because they feel like the process treated them fairly even if the outcome was less than favorable for them.[36] Process is often counterposed to substance. In law and policy this means that there is often a choice between creating a process (a right to sue, for example) and creating an entitlement (a right to a substantive good). Shep Melnick's work on education rights for children with disabilities shows how it is often easier to create right through a process (in this case, the right to an appropriate public education, enforced by giving the parents certain procedural rights) than to define who exactly is a child with a disability and what exactly such a child is entitled to receive.[37] So in one view, process is foundational to justice and preserves respect for the individual and her particular circumstances. In another view, process is a part of the sham of rights, in which the needy child gets a right to litigate for an education rather than an education. The key here is to see how setting up a process is a way to avoid specifying the meanings of identity traits for personhood. The admissions process and the learning community the student later joins will generate the context for the individual to show and share her identity, but there is nothing predetermined about it.

Most defenders of affirmative action would prefer a wider rhetorical field upon which to defend affirmative action, such as drawing upon constitutionally prohibited justifications (representation as just in itself, or as a route to better provision of legal and medical services throughout society). Progressive legal scholars, when they are inclined to be honest, have to admit that they support race- or gender-sensitive redistributions for constitutionally proscribed reasons, such as preventing the accretion of all the best jobs in the hands of whites or men only. Those defenders do not need to lean so much on process because they embrace the substance of racial meanings in some way: there must be at least a meaningful cluster of students from disadvantaged minority groups, and the main challenge is finding them, recruiting them, and assuring their success. They have been forced to adopt the language of diversity as the only jurisprudentially viable justification for race- or gender-consciousness in governmental practices. It was clear that diversity was the last rationale for defending the use of race in admissions, and by the time of the inevitable lawsuit, educational researchers had assembled a portfolio of studies about the benefits of a multi-racial learning environment.[38] But entirely aside from its uniqueness as a legal idea, diversity had become a prominent topic among management professionals in the business world by the mid-to-late 1980s.[39]

Diversity is thus a cross-over concept with wide-ranging usefulness across professional arenas and within the law. Military leaders and heads of major corporations filed amicus briefs with the Supreme Court in the Michigan cases arguing that they relied on the service academies and the elite public institutions to provide them with a diverse leadership group. The military generals' amicus brief specifically pointed to the imbalances between the all-white officer corps and the multi-racial enlisted men as the source of much Vietnam-era disorder.[40] As a result, the military adopted quite explicitly race-conscious policies from promotion decisions to monitoring disciplinary actions. For their part, General Motors argued in its brief that

> only a well educated, diverse work force, comprising people who have learned to work productively and creatively with individuals from a multitude of races and ethnic, religious, and cultural backgrounds, can

maintain America's competitiveness in the increasingly diverse and interconnected world economy.[41]

There is a tension in this shared air between the idea of diversity management and the legal or constitutional notion of diversity as a justification for the governmental use of race. It boils down to this: does diversity have a special place for race, disadvantage, and racialized disadvantage in particular? Or is it more about using individuals' different perspectives and modes of problem solving to come to better decisions, where politically salient identity traits have no necessary relationship to those perspectives? The military's perspective is the most straightforward: they need black and Latino officers because there are proportionately many black and Latino enlisted men and women, and only some rough balance will prevent racial tensions from arising. This sounds a lot like the unconstitutional reason, racial proportionality. The corporate perspective, however, includes within diversity such traits as "lifestyle," "position within the organization," and "culture," and imagines "mix[ing] quiet with talky people, electrical engineers with software and quality-assurance engineers."[42] General Motor's plea for a diverse workforce to work in a globalized world suggests they need people who speak Mandarin or Hindi more than they need American-born black employees from disadvantaged backgrounds or mothers returning to work after taking a few years to raise children. When difference is celebrated as contributing to organizational functioning or group decision making, there is no reason to conceive of difference as inequality or socially produced dysfunction. Difference then begins to look like an aesthetic matter, a problem to be solved through private markets, or simply as the array of unique traits individual people bring to work. Diverse personhood cannot be a way to talk about some racial differences as particularly pressing or more meaningful than others. It cannot be a way to talk about dysfunction, lifestyles, and subcultures that are held in disdain, and the often ugly realities of racialized inequality in the contemporary United States.

Conclusion: Sharing, Not Blaming

There is a very fundamental choice to be made when we see that difference maps very closely to patterns of social inequality. Inequality along racial and ethnic lines has been the most important site for wrangling over difference in the law, historically and today. What shall we make of the fact that whites do better than African Americans, Latinos, and Native Americans on nearly every measure of social and economic well-being? Are these outcomes explained by features of the people themselves, or should some blame be directed not at them but at some other structure or set of persons, such as discriminators or patterns of historical exclusion? One major issue is whether the level of analysis should be at the level of the individual—her choices, life circumstances, opportunities, and constraints—or whether the frame should be opened up to include historical events that occurred before she was born, like slavery, or structural factors, like educational funding that depends on the local tax base. In other words, is racial difference explicable by an accretion of past injustices that continue to matter in ways we should consider in law and policy? Or is racial difference just one part of human variety that does not necessarily mean anything for who a person is? The fact that so much of our cultural and legal debating over racial inequalities takes this dyadic form can be traced back through logics of personhood and their shifts in response to tensions over time.

This chapter has been a reflection on the different ways we have made that choice as a society over the last several decades as well as a consideration of why we talk that way in the first place. Law's stories about why people are different and what justifies their differential treatment are explained through logics of personhood. The original conception of what I call the blame-shifting logic considered black Americans to be held in straitjackets by racism, which if released by antidiscrimination laws, would free them to fulfill their true functional individualism. In the meantime the blame-shifting logic upended the normal science of functional individualism, requiring redistributions and aggregate measures of disadvantages between groups. The transformation of a norm of personal failure into a concept of state-owned social debt is the defining feature of the most successful modification to the functionalist account that has recently taken root in American law. Conditions for that transformative moment included the black civil rights movement (the peaceful marches and the more violent occasions of urban unrest that were contemporaneous with it), presidential and legislative struggle and compromise over the 1964 Civil Rights bill, bureaucratic implementation and logical extension of the "like-black" paradigm of legal protection, and the Supreme Court's embrace and redescription of sustained government-fomented inequality in *Griggs*.

Certainly the power of the blame-shifting account has almost entirely melted away. It crystallized in an historical moment that in retrospect—as I watch grainy footage of Birmingham protestors thrown against walls by water hoses or pretty girls in bobby socks being loaded into paddy wagons—is so singularly easy to condemn in the most basic moral terms. The fact that we collectively remember the black civil rights struggle in that way renders the blame-shifting logic strangely calcified and inapplicable to contemporary problems of inequality, which seem much more complicated. It is no longer a dominant discourse for explaining why racial minorities and white women seem to fail to perform as well as the dominant group. There is no longer any sense that powerful people may have defined proper functioning to describe themselves and then taken steps to maintain their privilege. Instead, conservatives have harnessed the language of race-blindness to defeat affirmative action with ballot initiatives (as in California), and the Supreme Court has similarly outlawed racial redistributions in government contracting (where the masculine concept of entitlement to skilled trade jobs perhaps had its greatest chance of acceptance within an equal protection analysis, if the same blame-shifting impulse had been present). The rhetoric of diversity in higher education remains to justify a new kind of affirmative action, though it has fully replaced any consciousness of the social production of unequally performing citizens with attention to the conditions for a racially individualized process of democratic-managerial enculturation of the student body. This managerial gloss on individualism is in ascendance across multiple spheres of social life.

I have argued here that diverse personhood instructs us in one way to understand difference. It has significant costs because it dislodges us from other ways of understanding difference that are better able to account for power differentials and sustained forms of inequality. But it is fair to ask, what else can we do in the pluralistic, globalized contemporary world? Could we hope that diverse personhood could become more richly contextualized, moving toward a combination of embedded personhood and democratic politics in a way that assists us in understanding more about those who are different from ourselves? I happily concede that the dominant legal-corporatist account of diversity that I describe here is contingent, and that its meaning could change. Diversity does not have to be a servant to glossy aesthetics of corporate responsibility. It could genuinely help us to be less ethnocentric and more imaginative. To do so, it would have to be separated from its process-focused understanding of individualism and reconnected to the ways in which we are embedded within what we express as our diversity.

If a rights-seeking movement like the fat rights movement were to try to reintroduce the logic of blame-shifting, advocates would have to ask many questions about it. How are the causes of inequality determined, and how are the agents responsible identified and described? What is it to think of shifting the blame to some agent or to some structure or institution? We cannot imagine that these processes would be any less politically constituted than the alternatives. It is likely that the vague critical sensibility of the blame-shifting critique would easily become fixated on some bugbear of the day. The leftist critique of Big Food, high fructose corn syrup, suburbanization, and television is an example of blame-shifting in the fat discrimination context that, although it shifts attention away from the bodies of fat people, redirects attention to other causes that fit well within a particular version of neo-liberal anxious healthism.[43] These critiques reconfigure fat people as hapless victims and still cannot explain why, if all of these forces are so vast and omnipresent, we are not all fat. If the panicky tone of the national discussion about fat can be reduced a bit, perhaps we can think through an explanation of fatness that finds its origins in genetic predispositions and in structural changes in the ways we live rather than in the fault of the individual. Perhaps diversity could be politicized rather than individualized if we learn to talk about its context as a contest for benefits and burdens distributed across stratified groups rather than as an already-set task to which fat people may bring their own unique perspective.

3

Balancing Functional Individuals and Embedded Selves

Introduction: Stereotyping and Personhood

An employer deducts more pension contributions from its female employees' paychecks than from male employees' paychecks because women as a group live longer and cost more as pensioners. A woman loses her bartending job because she refuses to wear the full face makeup that her employer requires. A Texas father sees his son, born out of wedlock in Vietnam, deported back to Vietnam after many years in the United States because he did not take extra steps to establish citizenship for his son as a boy. If the young man's mother had been a citizen it would have been automatically conferred. A brash, foul-mouthed woman at a major accounting firm fails to make partner because the all-male partners find her behavior unbefitting a woman. How do we talk through what happened to these men and women and come to see it as just or unjust? We differ from each other in all kinds of ways: actuarial projections about our life spans, what we do to look well-groomed, whether we are the partner who gives birth, and how congenial and appropriate we are in the workplace. Gender is always implicated in these differences. Gender, like racial difference, has been a critically important site for building up the ways we use antidiscrimination law to decide when difference matters and why. The tools constructed in sex discrimination law—the idea of the stereotype, in particular—will be applied to new debates about fat discrimination. In the last chapter, we saw how the legacy of racial discrimination has given us a few important ways to talk about persons and what they deserve. In this chapter, we turn to the ways we talk about gender in the law. The stereotype is probably the single most important concept in sex discrimination law, and so here I focus in on its use in debates about what persons deserve.

Talking about stereotyping is one way to talk about how a person has been unjustly misapprehended because of some trait that she bears. In common parlance, people use it to designate an irrational misjudgment of someone. Use of the stereotype is a crucial tool in the first two strategies for defending someone who is different in an unpopular way: (1) arguing that she can function just as well as everyone else and that her stigmatized trait should be ignored or (2) naming the norms and assumptions of the dominant group stereotypes and argue that they are false or, even if empirically true, that they should not burden her. As I explained in the Introduction, K. Anthony Appiah has parsed out three different conceptions of a stereotype floating about in American antidiscrimination law: false, statistical, and normative. Recall that the first strategy invokes functional individualism and presumes a false stereotype about capacities (women are weak and irrational, Mexicans are lazy). The second strategy also calls upon functional individualism but combats statistical stereotypes that are accurate as generalizations and not necessarily malicious (women live longer than men). Judges sometimes still insist that an individual should not be burdened even by a true generalization about a group to which she belongs—that is, when that kind of person is understood to deserve robust protection from generalizations of a particular sort.

The third variety of stereotyping is tricky because it is deeply incompatible with the common impulse of antidiscrimination law, which is to dismiss false and statistical stereotypes. Normative stereotypes are generalizations about traits that tell a rich story about what it is to be that kind of person. Gender conventions, patterns of sexual attraction, religious and cultural practices—these are not inaccurate generalizations nor are they bare empirical conjectures about what a particular person is like based on her group membership. They are deeply rooted feelings, practices, and communal connections, and without them one would no longer be that kind of person. There is something deeply silly about utterances like: "It's just a stereotype that Christians accept Jesus as the son of God" or "It's just a stereotype that heterosexuals are attracted to people of the opposite sex." Normative stereotypes may certainly oppress non-conformists, but they are simultaneously so constitutive of our identities that it is hard to imagine our personhood without them.[1]

Normative stereotypes describe embedded personhood, under which we are understood to be inseparable from our salient traits (as opposed to being functional individuals whose capacities can be measured while ignoring those traits). The inseparability (or sense of inseparability) in normative stereotyping is a kind of non-biological essentialism, in the sense that one considers something to no longer be the same entity without that trait. "Me, but a different race" just does not make any sense, that is. Stereotypes thus capture conflicting logics of personhood and involve several different kinds of generalizations: mean false ones, accurate ones, and ones that richly describe our life patterns. This ability to refer to different things at different moments in antidiscrimination law leads to incoherence and to stark limitations on the power of the stereotype to describe injustice against persons. As I will explain, courts have come up with a wide range of answers for the plaintiffs whose cases I briefly described above. In each case, antidiscrimination law refers to stereotypes to generate an account of when and how differences matter. But what is really driving the decisions is personhood: namely, decisions about whether to elevate a functional individualist conception of gendered personhood or to honor gendered persons as embedded persons.

Gender organizes all kinds of silly false stereotypes about women and men's functional capacities. But there are also many empirically valid generalizations about gender (statistical stereotypes) to contend with, from biological differences like pregnancy to actuarial projections about life span, disease, and criminal activity. And finally, appearances in the world as visibly gendered persons are so foundational to identity (normative stereotypes) that it is difficult to imagine ourselves without gender, even as demands for gendered appearance can also be cruel, limiting, capricious, and unimaginative.[2] This is not to say that one might want gender to be very different from what it is now, but to say that whatever it is, it is hard not to place it centrally in one's self-concept. Law acknowledges this in a way that it does not for race, even though race plays an equally central role in the self-concept of many people (especially those marked as non-white). So while I do not take a stand here between which aspect of identity is more foundational—gender or race—or even frame that as a necessary choice, I insist that law's ambivalence about gender means that it is much less willing to unseat it. That is also what makes it a fascinating site of study here.

A Critical Genealogy of the Sex Stereotype

No one really gave much thought to sex discrimination when Congress enacted the Civil Rights Act of 1964, which included "sex" as a prohibited basis for discrimination. It was at best a distraction and at worst a cynical ploy. As David O'Brien notes, "in historical perspective there is no gainsaying that the primary purpose of the Civil Rights Act [of 1964] was to combat the persistence of racial discrimination."[3] President Johnson's speeches in support of the Act, committee reports, and debate in both the House and the Senate focused overwhelmingly on race discrimination, particularly the very controversial Title II, which barred race discrimination in all places of public accommodation that had any relation to interstate commerce.[4] The prohibition against discrimination based on sex, in contrast, was introduced by an eighty-year-old segregationist Democratic Representative, Howard Smith of Virginia, who was chair of the Rules Committee and known for manipulating procedural rules to block civil rights legislation.[5] He was also a supporter of the Equal Rights Amendment (ERA), though, and thus adding "sex" to Title VII would promote both his segregationist interests (if it caused the defeat of the civil rights bill) as well as his pro-ERA stance (if it passed).[6] The amendment caused "pandemonium" in Congress, because many liberals feared that Smith's amendment would defeat the entire bill (an outcome he intended, or was at least indifferent to).[7] The amendment was approved 168 to 133, and after a five-hundred-hour-long filibuster in the Senate (in which the focus remained almost entirely on race), the Act passed with the prohibition on sex discrimination written in. It had gotten only brief discussion as Smith introduced his amendment with sarcasm and to hooting and laughing.[8] In defending women's employment rights, for instance, Smith read a constituent's letter about a lack of husbands for women and asked who would protect "our spinster friends and their right to a nice husband and family?"[9] According to O'Brien, the media reported the amendment "for what it was—a tactical move to derail the strongest civil rights legislation since the Reconstruction Amendments."[10] John Skrentny observes that while rights for blacks in 1964 were "simple but threatening," women's employment rights were "complex but funny."[11]

In any case, it is clear that Congress never considered sex discrimination as a problem of structural inequality or historical accretion of wrongdoing, nor did the body seem to self-consciously address itself to remedying gender-based injustices when it passed the 1964 Act. Consideration of women was limited to legislative strategizing about whether to include "sex" as an amendment (which many white women's groups did not support, fearing it would derail the civil rights bill entirely, though some women in Congress defended its inclusion), derisive laughter, and worries that white women would be left out if black women gained legal protection on account of their race. Southern representatives in the House explicitly warned that employers would hire black women over white women if the sex amendment were not included. Interestingly, this part of the debate is the only part in which black women are considered explicitly, and then only as a potential foil to white women's interests. Accounts of why "the Negro" needed access to better jobs were otherwise consistently framed as men's need to enter skilled manual labor markets—to compete with white men, not women of any race—and to raise the economic status of "the Negro." Black men were understood as workers and as heads of households: the people who would need well-paid employment in order to stabilize their communities. The person being described as deserving was one who had suffered under the yoke of American racial apartheid, with the attendant markers of physical exclusion, alienation from acts of citizenship, and historical roots in slavery, *and* who needed access to better wages and eventually to middle class society as a head of a household.

What is also significant about this legislative history, such as it is, is its lack of presentable justifications for why "women" require antidiscrimination protections. There is simply nothing for courts to refer back to when explaining why Title VII applies to sex. Because court decisions cannot refer back to legislative history (as they often do in Title VII race discrimination cases), gender cases often lack the invocation of historical wrongs (such as the reference to institutionalized school segregation in *Griggs*), and, when put up against Congressional intentions to address race discrimination, seem less single-minded. The only substantive discussion of why women should be included only reinforced the whiteness of the category "women."[12] Despite the rather odd legislative history surrounding the addition of "sex" to the list of protected traits, courts have nonetheless worked with the prohibition, often with a nod to its strange birth but without any deference to the idea that its inclusion might have been disingenuous or racist.

The result has been to take one idea—the sex-based stereotype—and to define it as the essential wrong that Congress was aiming at with the sex prohibition. The banned sex stereotype is most commonly a stereotype about preferences or abilities (women don't want to do or are unfit for manual labor, they are especially suited for jobs requiring nurturance, and so on). The goal of Title VII, courts often repeat, is "to strike at the entire spectrum of disparate treatment of men and women resulting from sex stereotypes."[13] Because there was never any story about the systematic devaluation and suppression of women's abilities, there is no *Griggs*-type justification for policies meant to benefit women. The notion of the sex stereotype fills in instead, bearing the entire weight of law's story about what's wrong with gender relations in our society.

Courts were beginning to wrangle with sex discrimination under the 14th Amendment's equal protection clause at about the same time as they had to come up with a way to talk about the ban on sex discrimination in Title VII. The idea of the stereotype was shared across both areas of law and anchors both in similar ways today. In the classic cases that established 14th Amendment equal protection against sex-based classifications, states were not allowed to presume that men as a class would be preferable to women as a class in the role of executor of a deceased person's estate (stereotype: men are more likely to have the training and capacities to handle being an executor);[14] that husbands as a class are not dependent on their wives for support while wives as a class are dependent (stereotype: men as wage earners and women as housewives);[15] and that women would not thrive in a harsh military school environment (stereotype: women as cooperative learners who thrive under nurturance and men as future citizen-soldiers who thrive under adversity).[16] Each of these cases enthusiastically condemns old-fashioned stereotypes about women.

In all these instances, however, it was generally true (as a statistical stereotype) that most women lagged behind most men in attaining the kind of education and public role experience associated with being an executor of an estate, that wifely economic dependence was much more common than the reverse, and that very few women expressed interest in or succeeded in the military school environment. A stereotype does not have to be statistically false to be illegal. Instead, in these cases the stereotype is declared off-limits for reasoning about what any particular woman deserves in spite of its truth as a generalization about most women's lives at the time. Stereotypes function as a way to relentlessly individualize women in spite of widespread patterns of gendered living and working.

One well-known Title VII discrimination case, *Los Angeles Department of Water and Power v. Manhart* (1978), confronted the fact that female employees entitled to pensions live longer and cost more as retirees than males. The city of Los Angeles had taken this fact into account in setting rates for employee contributions to its pension plan, requiring all women workers to pay 14.84 percent more each month into the plan than similarly situated men paid. Records in the case showed that one woman paid $18,171.40 into the fund, whereas a similarly situated male would have contributed only $12,843.53, taking home the balance as part of his wages.[17] Women working for the city filed a class action lawsuit under Title VII of the 1964 Civil Rights Act and won.

The problem was not sexist assumptions about functional capacities or preferences; women really do live longer than men. As previously noted, Justice Stevens, writing for the majority, conceded that "[t]he Department treated its women employees differently from its men employees because the two classes are in fact different."[18] As discussed in the Introduction, just as in Ms. McDermott's dispute with Xerox, the solution was to focus upon the individual traits of the employees. Actuarial risk (for women, anyway) is the same kind of property of a person as her ability to perform the job, as the Court explicitly notes, and it must be determined on the same individualized basis: "Individual risks, like individual performance, may not be predicted by resort to classifications proscribed by Title VII."[19] "Practices that classify employees in terms of religion, race, or sex," wrote Justice Stevens for the majority, "tend to preserve traditional assumptions about groups rather than thoughtful scrutiny of individuals."[20] The Court is in effect ordering a subsidy by men of women's wages because the city was perfectly correct about its costs over the longer term and on average. But because the idea of paying women the same as men for the same work enjoys such strong consensus and because of the easily available fix of individualism, even a valid statistical stereotype cannot count as a difference that matters.

The individualistic bent of the judicial parry against the statistical stereotype assumes structural inequalities away by separating an imagined litigant from everyone else in her group. There is no end to that reasoning—as applied hypothetically to each individual in the group *seriatim,* one could go on and on until no woman lived longer than the male average. Thus it loses its power for condemnation—"What you, employer, think of women is deplorable, and you ought not use your powers to advance that view"—in its turn to individualized, inaccurate reasoning—"But you, employer, cannot assume that what may be true of women generally is true of this one in particular."[21] Consider another well-known case in which an employer refused to hire women with school-age children because of the belief that their duties as caregivers would interfere with their abilities to devote their full attention to their careers.[22] The employer in *Phillips v. Martin Marietta* did not mind hiring men with young children. Though the hiring practice was held to be illegal, the employer was correct in his reading of gendered labor in the home. There was then and still is to some degree an unequal sharing of child care in heterosexual couples that amounts to a second shift for working women.[23] So even if women generally still occupy subordinate roles at home, an employer cannot presume that this particular working mother will be any more busy, distracted, or overburdened than a working father. The point is that there is nothing built into our thinking about the illegal statistical stereotype that can detect widespread conditions of gender inequality.

This strategy of conceding the generality while defending the particular is a classic lawyerly move and a favorite of liberal judges who want to establish a helpful ruling in a particular case without having to refute the empirical basis for the stereotype or, critically, having to reframe it. Justice Ruth Bader Ginsburg's majority opinion in *United States v. Virginia* (1996), an equal protection case ruling that if any young women could succeed under the adversative method of the Virginia Military Institute then the school had to open its doors to them, has this flavor. Cadets live in spartan conditions and during their first year, exist as "rats" subject to humiliation and bonding rituals on the "rat line." Physically and psychologically exceptional female applicants were ordered admitted into the hyper-masculine and militaristic environment, even as the Court acknowledged that most women would not be suited to such a college learning environment. *Virginia* is considered the strongest equal protection sex discrimination case yet because its doctrinal interpretation of the relevant standard defends exceptional women against generalizations that would be valid as applied to most women.

There is no leverage for redescribing gender roles, or concepts like weakness, adversity, and citizen-soldier, however. And yet, where differences between men and women have to do with pregnancy, childbirth, or the capacity to become pregnant, the Supreme Court's equal protection jurisprudence permits differential treatment and fails to interrogate whether these differences also owe their meaning to cultural constructions. In its most recent ruling on the distinction between a real sex difference (which laws may permissibly take into account) and a stereotype (which laws may not rely upon), the Court held that regulations requiring extra steps for unwed fathers to legitimate biological children born overseas were constitutional because birth mothers (who were not required to take these extra steps) always have a point of contact with a child at the time of birth that fathers may lack.[24] Connection to the citizen parent establishes the right to citizenship, and thus the regulations can treat fathers and mothers differently based on the different potential for that parent-child relationship. No matter that in the particular facts of the case the boy's father had actually raised him in the United States after turmoil in Vietnam separated him from his mother, who was never located. The father had not completed the steps to certify his parenthood, however, and so could not pass on citizenship to his teenaged son. After the teen was convicted of a sex crime, he was ordered deported to Vietnam, a country he had not grown up in and whose language he did not even speak.

The son's fate turned on different rules applied to mothers than to fathers. In his opinion for the majority, Justice Anthony Kennedy argues that the greater burdens on fathers to claim paternity address "an undeniable difference in the circumstance of the parents at the time a child is born . . . [that] does not result from some stereotype, defined as a frame of mind resulting from irrational or uncritical analysis."[25] He continues,

> There is nothing irrational or improper in the recognition that at the moment of birth—a critical event in the statutory scheme and in the whole tradition of citizenship law—the mother's knowledge of the child and the fact of parenthood have been established in a way not guaranteed in the case of the unwed father. This is not a stereotype.[26]

Of course mothers are present at the birth of their children, and fathers may or may not be present. But the legal rules about acquiring citizenship are there to make sure that a certain relationship to the United States is possible in the child's life (to prevent fraudulent claims to citizenship). The simple event of birth cannot carry the full weight of the relationship unless one reads much more into the mother-child relationship versus the father-child relationship, something that is only accomplished by assuming that mothers are naturally very different parents than fathers.[27]

What counts as a sex stereotype in the first place is determined by preconceived ideas about what is socially or biologically determined. Moreover, we can see how normative stereotyping (here, mothering and what it is and what it should be) is particularly susceptible to being used politically by judges to evade the criticism that they are complicit in sex stereotyping at all (by reframing a normative stereotype as an observation of biological fact). In the Title VII context it is illegal (normative and probably also statistical) stereotyping to assume that a working mother will be a less reliable employee than a working father because of the meanings and gendered practices of motherhood in our culture. But the event of birth was enough in *Nguyen* to constitute a real difference between mothers' and fathers' different abilities to convey U.S. citizenship readiness to their children born overseas, a transmission that would presumably take place through later parenting, not through the umbilical cord. Both the citizenship case and the working mother case are about parenting and what it means for women and men, but they both also illustrate how slippery and full of unstated content the concept of a stereotype can be, especially when what are at stake are deeply gendered practices and positions like mothering, not simple assertions of sex-based capacities or incapacities. (Straightforwardly malicious false stereotypes are usually cloaked in litigation.) Rather than interrogating distinctions between the biological and the social, stereotypes evade them (as in *Nguyen*) or ratify them superficially (as in *Phillips*).

Sometimes the Supreme Court speaks as if it wishes to undo even fairly deeply rooted normative stereotypes about gendered appearance and behavior. In a famous 1989 Title VII case about a woman who failed to make partner at Price Waterhouse, the Court issued a seemingly broad denunciation of sex stereotypes. Ann Hopkins "was generally viewed as a highly competent project leader who worked long hours, pushed vigorously to meet deadlines and demanded much from the multidisciplinary staffs with which she worked."[28] She used foul language at work and was considered a taskmaster, even as she successfully managed multi-million-dollar accounts. When she was not promoted to partner in the accounting firm, a senior male colleague advised her that her chances might improve if she would "walk more femininely, talk more femininely, dress more femininely, wear make-up, have her hair styled, and wear jewelry."[29] The Supreme Court recognized that gendered expectations (here, a double bind of requirements, femininity plus masculine, high-powered competence) amounted to sex discrimination for Hopkins. In a man her behavior would be evidence of toughness while in a woman it was unseemly. In ruling for Hopkins, the Supreme Court declared that "we are beyond the day when an employer could evaluate employees by assuming or insisting that they matched the stereotype associated with their group."[30] *Price Waterhouse* suggests that Title VII means that being a woman should not require anything more than doing the job successfully: functional individualism free of normative stereotyping, in other words.

How far does the celebration of freedom from gendered norms of appearance and behavior really go in Title VII, though? Two recent federal circuit court decisions point in opposite directions. In the first case, Jimmie Smith, a male-to-female (MTF) transsexual firefighter in Salem, Ohio, won a sex discrimination case against the city for its treatment of him during his transition.[31] Coworkers had begun to inquire about his appearance, noting that he had begun to look insufficiently masculine as he began the process of becoming a woman. The city suspended him and tried to figure out a way to fire him, but he sued. Neither transsexualism, gender identity, nor gender expression is listed as a protected category in the statute, but the federal Sixth Circuit Court of Appeals held that sex encompasses "gender non-conforming behavior and appearance" and therefore transsexualism or transgenderism.[32] "After *Price Waterhouse*," the appeals court explained, "an employer who discriminates against women because, for instance, they do not wear dresses or makeup, is engaging in sex discrimination because the discrimination would not occur *but for the victim's sex*."[33] Under what has been called the sex-flipping test, judges imagine the person as the opposite sex and ask, would the discrimination have occurred (a "but for" causation test)?[34] Applying a sex-flipping analysis to Smith's situation, "it follows that employers who discriminate against *men because they do wear dresses and makeup, or otherwise act femininely,* are also engaging in sex discrimination, because the discrimination would not occur but for the victim's sex."[35] "Discrimination against a plaintiff who is a transsexual—and therefore fails to act and/or identify with his or her gender—is no different," the reasoning continues, "from the discrimination directed at Ann Hopkins . . . who, in sex-stereotypical terms, did not act like a woman."[36]

The *Smith* case reduces the story of gender oppression to a story about stereotypes and makes MTFs into men who wear dresses and makeup. Smith's sex was fixed as male, and gendered signals such as clothing are simply objects of personal choice. Most men do not usually wear dresses and makeup, but if one happens to want to then he should be allowed to do so. Most women do not want to go through the "rat line" as cadets at the Virginia Military Institute, but if one happens to want to then she should be allowed to do so. Transsexuals or transgender people per se do not really exist in the *Smith* opinion; there just happen to be some men out there who want to wear dresses. Sure, men in dresses are rare (like the woman who is stronger than many men), and we can allow them to keep and get jobs without much upheaval for everyone else because the law can treat them as exceptional. The reasoning empties out the content of normative stereotypes about gender— what we look like and act like as recognizable men or women—and makes them into contingent personal choices that do not have anything to do with the constitution of our gendered identities (and that only a few people will make in dissenting ways). The court fits a normative stereotype into the usual framing of statistical stereotypes: most men are stronger than most women, and most women wear clothes that most men do not wear. But there are some unusually strong women, and there are some men who wear women's clothes. Smith is a man who just happens to wants to put on some signs of femininity (a mirror opposite of Hopkins, a woman who did not want to put them on and put on masculinity instead).

Notice that the reasoning has to work this way because of the sex-flipping test, which assumes rigidity in the polar male/female categories. Would Smith have been fired if, as a woman, he had begun to look more feminine? Of course not, and hence the story of causation: because of sex. Leaving aside the double bind of anyone trying to be simultaneously a feminine woman and a firefighter, a court can easily imagine that a similarly situated woman would not have been fired and thus Smith was fired because of his sex. The sex-flipping test plus the vagaries of sex-stereotyping theory yields the *Smith* decision. The image of gender is still rigidly polar (men/women), and the normative content of gender is held at bay and transformed into a matter of accessorizing, of simply adding a little femininity or masculinity to the actual sex we already are.

Followed to its completion, the *Smith* application of *Price Water-house* would say that employers cannot require any gendered look or behavior of any kind from employees no matter what their biological sex is understood to be. Those men who are statistically unusual in wanting to wear dresses must be allowed to do so (because remember, that's what we are supposed to think trans identity is). But there are many other cases affirming enforcement of normative gender stereotypes under Title VII. Courts have consistently upheld gender-specific grooming requirements, such as makeup for women and short haircuts and neckties for men.[37] As long as the requirements do not burden one sex more than the other, employers can require everyone to appear as the professional version of maleness or femaleness, matched respectively with current biological sex. Across the country and for several decades, courts have rejected the idea that these requirements amount to illegal sex discrimination. It is as if *Price Waterhouse* has no implication whatsoever for employee appearance. In the grooming requirements line of cases, gendered appearance is reduced to something like cleanliness: it has nothing to do with sex equality in the workplace, and is just such a basic and natural requirement that it is beyond much question.

Consider this example, handed down in a different jurisdiction from the *Smith* case and strongly inconsistent with it. Darlene Jespersen, a bartender for over two decades at Harrah's Casino in Reno, was fired for not wanting to comply with Harrah's "Personal Best" policy, which demanded that she wear pantyhose, full face makeup, and colored nail polish and that she wear her hair down and "teased, curled, or styled."[38] Harrah's brought in a Las Vegas image consultant who did makeovers on the women and photographed them afterwards. Managers would then compare the women to the photographs to see how they were keeping up their "after" looks. Jespersen felt oppressed by all the makeup, which she normally did not wear. She sued Harrah's for sex discrimination. According to the Ninth Circuit in its ruling for Harrah's, "Grooming standards that appropriately differentiate between the genders are not facially discriminatory."[39] She did not even have the basis for a sex discrimination claim. The court refused to speculate about the added costs for women in the purchase and application of makeup or in the time spent teasing, curling, and styling their hair (as compared to men, who only had to keep their hair trimmed above the collar and were prohibited from applying any makeup or nail color).

The grooming requirements cases, because they affirm employers' rights to dress their employees in a gendered way that maps biological sex, are in direct conflict with the reasoning of *Smith*. Why can't Jespersen say she should have the right to look less classically feminine and still keep her job, when Smith was able to look less masculine and keep his? Can't most any gender-tailored grooming rule be redescribed as a stereotype about what men and women are supposed to look like? If we use the sex-flipping test, we could say that if Jespersen had been a man and refused to wear makeup, she would not have been fired (indeed, men were prohibited from wearing any makeup). The *Jespersen* court was perfectly aware that it hovered on this precipice. "If we were [to hold that an objection to a makeup rule for women only could give rise to a claim of sex stereotyping under Title VII]," the majority opinion observes, "we would come perilously close to holding that every grooming, apparel, or appearance requirement that an individual finds personally offensive, or in conflict with his or her own self-image, can create a triable issue of sex discrimination."[40] In *Smith,* the court specifically said that Smith was not being considered under the special category of transsexual (because Title VII does not cover discrimination because of transsexualism). So, he was allowed to bring a case because looking masculine was in conflict with his self-image (to borrow the *Jespersen* court's formulation), but not because he was a transsexual. Either the *Smith* court was evading the fact that Title VII does not cover transsexualism or it would have struck down the makeup requirements. To get around the fact that supposedly sex discrimination law makes gender stereotyping illegal, the *Jespersen* court recasts gendered appearance requirements as rules one would react against in a highly idiosyncratic ("find[ing] personally offensive") way having nothing to do with resisting a dolled up femininity.

The Ninth Circuit did not even cite to the *Smith* case (though it did not have to, since it was from another jurisdiction) or any other transgender cases from any jurisdiction. The opinion suggests that gender non-conformists may still press cases for sexual harassment, that employees may not be forced to wear uniforms that are too sexually provocative (and are not related to the job), and that conforming to the gendered image should not impede the worker from doing her job. The *Jespersen* makeup and hairstyle requirements for women, however, are understood to be just ordinary, reasonable requirements without any implications for sex discrimination law. Thus it looks like it is illegal sex stereotyping to fire a trans employee who is transitioning (with all the violations of traditional gender appearances that may come up along the way, especially before passing is possible), but it is not generally illegal to require women (presumably overwhelmingly non-trans women) to wear some makeup at work and to seem feminine in a non-extreme way, whatever that means. The point of drawing out this puzzle is to illustrate how gender stereotyping as a legal idea lives quite comfortably with inconsistency. Judges, supposedly in the business of squelching sex stereotyping, switch registers very quickly from considering broadly social ideas about women's roles to isolating a woman's preference down to mere individual preferences. Once again the stereotype produces the line between the idiosyncratic and the deeply gendered (just as it produced the line between the biological and the social in the equal protection cases), pretending to discover it.

It would be easy to condemn the *Jespersen* case as a sell-out decision that forces women into made-up roles not because they are not based in sex stereotyping but just because they are so pervasive. The Ninth Circuit did not want to be so activist as to throw out all gendered grooming requirements. Makeup is, after all, easy to isolate as a petty and superficial part of gendered appearance. Yet if we understand it as one of a collection of signals that we all use in ordinary ways every day to display our gender, it is not so clear that a world in which those signals were illegal would be such a desirable world. Looking more feminine was deeply important to Jimmie Smith, after all, so much that he was willing to go through all that is required to make an MTF transition. Those of us who are relatively comfortable in our sex assigned at birth can make light of the sexism of makeup requirements, but we should recognize that we are assisted by that very comfort into imagining that those things are petty.

The *Smith* jurisprudence takes a wide swath of what gender is for most people—most notably, being in one gender over a lifetime that is visible and meaningful in community with others—and makes it illegal to enforce as a pernicious false stereotype, manages it as if it were a statistical stereotype that simply defends the exceptional needs of men who happen to start looking feminine one day, and pretends that it has no normative stereotyping content that matters at all. Starkly different ways of talking about gendered personhood—as functional individualism and as embedded personhood—flourish alongside each other because stereotyping can simply be redefined or ignored depending on which logic best fits the court's program of gender transformation or gender preservation.[41]

Exceptions for Explicit Sex Discrimination in Employment

I have so far described the vagaries of sex discrimination law as derived from the use of stereotyping to cover over what is really judicial management of difficult problems of gendered personhood and justice. The law is clear at one level that sex stereotyping is illegal in employment, but I have conceded that there are both statistically real differences between men and women, as well as deeply normative but nonetheless compelling stereotypes, that are well worth preserving in some ways. Judges are then working with a tool that could be too blunt if it were actually used with full force, and so they must adapt it in incoherent ways. The problem is that the legal system remains politically unaccountable for these adaptations, and the ways we all talk about it obscure the way sex discrimination law really works.

There are moments of greater transparency, however, and they mimic the tensions and resolutions we have already seen. Title VII sex discrimination law sometimes permits employers to choose their employees based on sex, using a loophole called the bona fide occupational qualification, or BFOQ. If it is absolutely necessary to have women as employees, say as strippers at a strip club, then the business may legally refuse to hire men in those jobs. A BFOQ permits a business to differentiate among employees based upon gender, religion, and national origin because of the implausibility of wiping away all the socially meaningful content ascribed to these traits in job performance.[42] A BFOQ is an excuse for otherwise illegal overt discrimination. To qualify as a BFOQ, a job qualification that keeps an otherwise protected class of people out of the job must "affect an employee's ability to do the job" and "must relate to the 'essence' or to the 'central mission' of the employer's business."[43] It is legal deference to normative stereotypes, which I have argued are so meaningful to our lives that often we don't want to banish them. It is embedded personhood sneaking in disguised as functional individualism. This aspect of Title VII also shows that our antidiscrimination regime is not interested in totally transforming gender but rather prefers to interact with gender in a selective way, altering some of its meanings in some contexts.[44] We happily ban stereotyping that is understood to be old-fashioned, such as dictating professional or family roles, but we balk at undoing gender in ways that would completely transform sexuality, gendered appearance, and privacy, even when those rules are clearly based on cultural preferences about gender roles.

At the time of the Senate debate on the Civil Rights Act of 1964, floor leaders made it clear that they wanted the BFOQ exception to protect religious enterprises from having to hire non-believers, even where the purpose of the business was something other than direct proselytization. (Title VII otherwise prohibits discrimination on the basis of religion.) The example on the Senate floor of how it would work was to safeguard "the preference of a business which seeks the patronage of members of particular religious groups for a salesman of that religion."[45] Door-to-door Bible salesmen could obviously be required to be Christians. Courts have held in subsequent cases that a Jewish Community Center could refuse to hire a non-Jew as their youth director (despite his training in the Torah and Hebrew language ability);[46] that a Jesuit university could refuse to hire a Jewish professor because the spot was reserved for a Jesuit candidate;[47] and that a U.S. helicopter company hired to fly over Mecca, Saudi Arabia, a holy site closed to non-Muslims, could refuse to hire non-Muslim pilots even though the mission was only to prevent fires in pilgrimage camping grounds and to monitor the crowds.[48] Protecting communities of religious belief is quite attractive as a use of the BFOQ exception because there is no social program elsewhere in law to transform the content of religious beliefs, as there is to transform the content of beliefs about gender.

Courts have always insisted that the BFOQ for sex be construed very narrowly, because it has the power to subvert the goals of Title VII as a whole. To be excused from the ban on sex discrimination, then, the employer must prove that there is a "factual basis" for the belief that "all or substantially all women [or men] would be unable to perform safely and efficiently the duties of the job involved."[49] Most of the time courts refuse to permit normative stereotypes about what it is to work as a man or to work as a woman to have much pull. In one dispute over sex as a BFOQ, for example, a fine dining establishment argued that it should be able to hire only men as servers since customers at such a restaurant would expect male servers, and they presented a better image in their tuxedos than women would present. The court rejected the argument on the grounds that the basic purpose of Title VII was to frustrate such norms, not to accommodate them.[50] In another BFOQ case, an oil corporation argued that it ought to be permitted to discriminate against women in hiring for its director of international operations because the cultural expectations of the exclusively male South American working environment would make it much harder for a woman to occupy a powerful position successfully. The court denied the BFOQ even if a female director would have to deal with men who would find her unsuitable for the job.[51] The Supreme Court also struck down the attempted use of the BFOQ by a battery manufacturing company that did not want to hire any fertile women to work in the manufacturing process because of the danger of lead exposure to any developing fetuses.[52]

The employers say they are simply honoring a reality about gender that is just a part of life: men look better than women in tuxedos, a woman forced to work with old-fashioned men could have a harder time directing a company than a man would, and only women can get pregnant and expose fetuses to a known teratogen. The courts do not dispute that they are probably right about normative stereotypes for elite waiters' and oil executives' appearances and correct about the statistical stereotype that only women gestate fetuses. Normative stereotypes about elite job performance in restaurants are understood to be gendered, but not very socially important. Rich people should just put up with having a female server in a tuxedo, and likewise for the sexist South American businessmen and their dealing with female executives. The lead exposure case is a bit closer, but it is easy to see how keeping nearly all women out of an entire job category would be hard to square with a statute intended to open up more jobs to them.

In cases involving bodily privacy, however, courts have granted BFOQs to preserve the dignity of clients whose bodies would be seen by the employee. In an early case of this type, a lower federal court allowed a nursing home to hire only women as nursing aides performing intimate bodily care for elderly patients, almost exclusively women, because "female guests would not consent to having their personal needs attended to by a male."[53] Since then, judges have granted the BFOQ exception in other contexts that relate to the display of the body such as labor and delivery rooms,[54] mental hospitals,[55] and a shower and bathhouse, permitting sex-specific hiring matched to the sex of the people being cared for.[56] In cases involving staffing in labor and delivery rooms, hospitals submitted anecdotal evidence that women in labor would not want a male nurse, and that an even larger percentage of their husbands would not want them to have a male nurse. The judges accepted the hospitals' reasoning that modifications to shifts or hiring extra female nurses in case a woman requested a change would be too burdensome.

Interestingly, Congress considered and rejected an amendment to

Title VII that would have included race as a BFOQ in some cases. During the 1964 debate over the Civil Rights Act, Rep. John Williams, a Mississippi Democrat, introduced an amendment in the House to permit race-based hiring under the BFOQ exception, arguing that "Negro businesses" ought to be able to continue hiring only blacks at the risk of losing the primary character of their businesses.[57] Supporters also argued that face-to-face salesmanship jobs ought to be race-based since "a Negro salesman would be best in dealing with selling to Negroes."[58] Here, race is not an external trait of a core self, nor a marker of historic and systemic deprivation for which lawmakers have responsibility, but rather it is an aspect of the embedded person in a community ("dealing with selling to Negroes"). The amendment failed due to objections that permitting such an exception would vitiate the basic principle of the law, that hiring should be done "based on [employees'] individual qualifications, not on the color of their skin."[59] Even as the predominant justification for the Act was to undo the effects of systemic deprivation of opportunity (for would-be skilled black male workers, in particular), functional individualism defeated the BFOQ for race.

Conclusion: The Incoherence of Gender Difference

Talking about stereotypes is the most common way for Americans to defend someone's difference in ordinary language. It is quite plausible that invoking the language of stereotypes will become an important part of defending fat citizens from stigmatizing associations (they eat all the time, they don't care about their health). Gender stereotypes are already supposedly a primary target of Title VII employment discrimination law. I have tried to take the vaunted place of the stereotype in anti-discrimination theory down a notch or two. Once we see that what is really going on is deciding between whether to isolate an individual from her gendered social reality or to endorse keeping her embedded within it, then it is clear that stereotyping as a legal concept simply covers over a set of tense and complicated decisions about the meaning of gender difference. First, under *Price Waterhouse* (the accounting firm partnership case), gender difference was understood to include patterns of speech, appearance, word choice, and demeanor. Even these deeply constitutive features of gender performance were banned from consideration in employment decisions. The *Smith* case involved a biological male taking on physical and social femininity through sex reassignment as protected gender-based activity in the workplace. These cases suggested the widest possible field for gender difference as self-determined, unregulated, and unburdened. In this vision of sex difference under law, no one can be required to look or act in any certain way because of others' interpellation of them as a man or a woman. This is functional individualism showing off its potential to protect radically different forms of gender expression as long as these manifestations of gender are understood to be unconnected to ability to perform the job. I argued that these cases cannot really be as strongly disruptive to normative stereotypes as they seem to be since elsewhere sex discrimination law is determined to preserve gender differences, even ones that entrench certain appearances and behaviors.

Second, gender difference can be understood as statistical reality but nonetheless inapplicable to any particular individual. So in *Manhart,* it was generally true that the women would cost the city more in pension outlays, but the city could not ask any particular woman to pay more because of that possibility. In *Phillips,* the employer had to ignore the fact that his employees who were mothers of small children probably would have a second shift waiting for them at home. Disparate impact under Title VII works in a similar fashion: if a strength requirement is necessary for a business it can keep it even if the rule disproportionately screens out women, but an individual strong woman must be given the chance to prove that she is exceptional. If requirements disproportionately keep women out but are not necessary, they must be changed to accommodate more women in those job categories. It is not that gender difference does not matter or cannot be acknowledged, but rather it must be carefully managed so that it does not harm any women who can overcome it. I argued that this approach to difference often ratifies the status quo by raising up an individual woman above the stereotype while also conceding its general truth.

And third, gender difference sometimes matters utterly. Sometimes gender difference matters because of the strength of normative stereotypes. The BFOQ exception most clearly captures those moments when it is impossible to pretend that gender expression is unconnected to job performance. Certainly a man can change an elderly lady's diaper just as well as a woman can, but courts have recognized that functional individualism is not what anyone cares about there. In the case of Darlene Jespersen, the Harrah's bartender, the court refuses to even consider a sex stereotyping analysis because it seems so minimally burdensome and appropriate to require women to wear makeup and fix up their hair. Of course both sexes can make drinks and serve them, but the point is also to project gender in a certain way while doing so. Sometimes gender difference matters because biological realities hold overwhelming social significance, as in the *Nguyen* citizenship transmission case. Gender difference was not just a statistical reality there because the Court did not want to simply raise up the individual mother and ignore general social patterns (as in the *Phillips* case about the working mothers). In *Nguyen,* the individual mother actually had not done much mothering; the father had raised his son in the United States. The court had to insist that giving birth is one of those events that cannot logically be the subject of a stereotype at all, therefore evading the need to consider functional individualism (here, of the father). Birthing is just a bare sex difference, and thus it could be the basis for governmental classifications.

Gender conservatives would certainly say that the preservation of some differences that might be labeled stereotypes is a good idea. (They would have a very short list of true stereotypes, embracing instead a view of biological difference as properly determining social roles.) Gender liberationists would likely concede that a world in which we are all gender-less functional individuals is undesirable. No matter what one's view of gender justice, then, it would be very difficult to come up with a principle to delineate what should be preserved and what should be transformed, especially if one grants a bit of pluralism and employer autonomy. Courts have tried to fashion one—a ban on sex stereotyping—and it has fractured into incoherence. It is incoherent because it embraces functional individualism but cannot completely let go of embedded personhood. Functional individualism pushes *Price Waterhouse*-type reasoning along, and embedded personhood pushes *Jespersen*-type reasoning along. One logic tells us that wearing or not wearing makeup has nothing to do with job performance, and the other tells us that makeup can be required for job performance.

One might think that law works by declaring something an injustice (a certain kind of reasoning about women, for instance) and then ruling case-by-case on allegations that such an injustice has taken place. That would be a coherent jurisprudence that would inform everyone ahead of time what kind of conduct is illegal. Many fat rights activists hope that legal coverage for height and weight discrimination will help drive stereotyping about fat people underground (or eradicate it) in exactly this way. My point here has been that we should look ahead to developments in sex discrimination law by asking not, "Is this a case involving a stereotype?" but "Does this case push the limits of gender transformation just a little too far or just far enough?" Overturning all grooming requirements was unlikely because it would have pushed gender transformation a little too far, not because grooming rules are not about stereotypes. The reality of sex discrimination law is that it does not follow clear rules to banish agreed-upon injustice. I did not expect it to, of course, but it was nonetheless crucial to trace out exactly what it does do.

Sex discrimination law is actually fairly predictable in the political sense once we understand the balance being struck between functional individualism and embedded personhood, and we see stereotyping as nothing more than a convenient judicial tool to maintain that balance. Any legal question of identity in which outwardly appearing traits (like modes of religious dress, for example) have deep meanings for the embedded person and yet attract the prejudice of others will face this same type of adjudication. The application to fat rights may not be direct, since gender currently does more to organize our individual and social worlds than fat does and thus the range of meanings gender holds for us is wider. But at the very least we should anticipate that to invoke antistereotyping from the law is to invite judicial use of a tool, not to make a clear moral argument. It would be a useful tool against some of the worst false stereotypes, but would not have much to say against statistical stereotypes (currently put in actuarial terms), and without a full-throated defense of fat identity, this tool might just further promote the normative desirability of thinness.

4

Governing Risk
Medicalization and Normalization

Introduction: Health and Functioning in the Workplace

Joyce English, an African American woman and a college graduate, stood five feet eight inches tall and weighed 341 pounds when she applied for a job as a Customer Service Representative at the Philadelphia Electric Company (PECO).[1] She passed all pre-employment tests and then had to submit to a physician's examination. The medical department at PECO refused to certify Ms. English for employment because they believed that her obesity would create risk of medical problems that might result in excessive absenteeism, low productivity, and other costs to the company. The Human Relations Commission, from which this case was appealed, had concluded that Ms. English was a handicapped person protected by antidiscrimination laws because she belonged to a class of morbidly obese people who were susceptible to potentially severe restrictions on mobility and breathing.[2] But the doctor who examined her found that she was not in fact limited in her functioning by any of the usual health problems that fat people are assumed to have. She reported being perfectly able to do a normal day's work. Moreover, regulations adding perceived disability claims to the Pennsylvania law were not promulgated until after Ms. English filed her case, and the court chose not to draw on them. Therefore, the Pennsylvania court concluded that Ms. English was not legally disabled. Ms. English's weight put her well outside the company's weight charts (which pegged her proper weight at 140 plus a 40 pound allowance) and the court defended the employer's "inherent right to discriminate among applicants for employment [based on risk of loss to the company] and to eliminate those who have a high potential for absenteeism and low productivity."[3]

Ms. English was understood as an actuarial person, not as a functional individual. The logic of actuarial personhood represents persons as members of a population who exhibit characteristics that can be used to calculate risks, costs, and behaviors like crime commission or likelihood of defaulting on a loan. Its tools are data gathering, actuarial science, and generalizations about demographic groups. Under the logic of functional individualism, by contrast, Ms. English would have been exempt from even a valid generalization about fat people after the doctor's exam showed that she personally did not have any obesity-related health problems. That logic protected Arazella Manuel, the Houston bus driver, after Dr. Frierson failed her in the physical exam. In Ms. Manuel's case, the legal mechanism was perceived disability under the ADA, which holds employers liable for discrimination when they think a person is disabled even if she actually is not.

In Ms. English's case (in which that rule did not apply), she was healthy and therefore could not be disabled, so then the company was free to decide under its own weight charts that she was too fat to be hired. Those weight charts are neither functional nor individualistic in the way we have been considering: they claim to predict health care costs and morbidity, but for an imaginary person in the population rather than for a particular individual. An individual's height and weight can be plotted on the chart, of course, but that is not the same examination as taking Ms. English's pulse, blood pressure, or glucose levels (all of which were normal). The weight charts do not measure anything in particular about Ms. English's body, such how it functions in the workplace at PECO or how she would handle customer service inquiries. She is simply measured against a norm of the productive worker's body size, and then her abnormal size is given medical significance as part of an insurance calculation. Ms. English's case perfectly illustrates the entry of actuarial personhood into antidiscrimination litigation.

Actuarial personhood is an ever-growing account of the person that is only going to become more influential as concerns about health care costs, disease, obesity (as it's termed in these discussions), and longevity become more and more salient for employers and in public policy generally. Insurance is a private market, and actuarialism is its profit-making technique. But the problems it solves for us are not simply private consumer preferences. Protection against deprivation and suffering is the first reason to enter into society and to pool resources, after all, and so insurance techniques must be at the forefront of wrangling over distributions of those protections. The American situation is particularly unique. Health care law and employment law are deeply intertwined in

American law because we have no national health care system. Health care costs are paid by employers with employee co-pays and contributions (if they offer health plans, that is), by the government for people who are either over sixty-five or sufficiently poor (Medicare and Medicaid), or by individuals purchasing their own coverage. People without jobs (or with jobs that do not provide insurance) and who do not qualify for a government program either go without or pay out of pocket. A fat person who tries to buy private health insurance because her job does not offer it can simply be refused on the basis of her weight alone.[4] There is no law to prevent this. Even when a state guarantees that everyone will be able to purchase health insurance, the price may be too exorbitant. Actuarialism also governs the lending industry in home insurance and mortgages, for example, and home ownership is the primary source of wealth and savings for many Americans. Finally, purchasing life insurance is an important way to guard against financial devastation for dependents or to pass on an inheritance.

The Fractured Politics of Risk and Identity

Should we think of insurance as pooling risk with as large a community as possible or should we hope to be placed in an actuarial group that excludes as many high-risk individuals as possible so that we pay only what we as individuals are likely to cost?[5] The first choice would push public policy toward nationalized health care or at least ban insurance companies from pushing out certain groups of people, while the second choice would embrace techniques that gather as much information as possible about actuarially relevant characteristics and then narrow the groups who get favorable coverage. We have evaded this fundamental choice in American law and policy, and instead have a hackneyed combination of state and national laws that borrow from the anti-stereotyping language we have been discussing to protect some groups who are politically sympathetic. Along with the classically protected groups, some rent-seeking professional or sports groups have managed to convince state legislatures to offer them favorable regulations in the insurance market.

Nearly every state (but not all) restricts the use of race in selling and pricing insurance, and the majority of states include other categories central to antidiscrimination law: color, creed, religion, and national origin. Alaska, for example, prohibits use of "an insurance score that is calculated using the income, age, sex, address, zip code, census block, ethnic group, religion, marital status, or nationality of the consumer as a factor" in selling personal insurance. Sex differentials in insurance are much more likely to be allowed than racial or ethnic traits. Reflecting a recent national trend, Alaska, along with seventeen other states, also bans discrimination in insurance based on a history of having been domestically abused.[6] Bans on the use of genetic information are also popular, enacted in fifteen states and the District of Columbia. Other protected groups, conditions or activities in various state codes include sickle-cell disease, sexual orientation (particularly as a proxy for HIV/AIDS), participation in snowmobiling, being an optometrist or a cosmetologist, past military service, declination by another insurer, age of residence or economic condition of the area (for property insurance), physical disability, diethylstilbestrol (DES) exposure, history of foreign travel, or being in a civil union. The level of protection varies in these laws: some protect only against being rejected or canceled but not against pricing differentials, and most list different categories protected in different kinds of insurance (rejecting blind people for motor vehicle insurance is acceptable, for instance, but rejecting them for life insurance is illegal in many states). A few states like Mississippi have no protected categories in their insurance code at all and do no more than ban "unfair trade practices" in insurance as compelled by the Unfair Trade Practices Act (UTPA), a model law developed by insurance commissioners and adopted nationwide by 1960. These laws prevent "unfair discrimination between individuals of the same class," but do not regulate any of the methods used to create the classes.[7] Other state laws name a group that cannot be burdened in underwriting but contain a loophole stating that differential treatment is acceptable if it is "based upon an unequal expectation of life or an expected risk of loss different than that of other individuals," as Colorado's law covering blindness and physical disability does.[8] Weight is not listed as a banned criterion for insurance underwriting in any state law.

These regulations are most important for individual buyers of insurance (such as property or life insurance) who are not covered by laws governing employment benefits. Most people with health insurance have it as an employment benefit, however, where it is subject to Title VII antidiscrimination rules that offer much greater protections than these state laws. Title VII requires equal treatment of men and women in employee health insurance under its ban on sex discrimination, for instance, while a woman purchasing on her own would be charged more because of likely childbirth-related expenses.[9] The Health Insurance Portability and Accountability Act (HIPAA) of 1996 makes it illegal to single out, exclude, or charge higher payments to unhealthy members of group plans, thereby helping those who already have health insurance through employment to hang on to it.[10] Because once a company hires someone, it must offer her the same health benefits at the same price that it offers everyone else, companies have an incentive either not to hire obese workers (or other putatively unhealthy groups) in the first place, or to try to improve these workers' health on the job. About two-thirds of U.S. companies in a recent survey reported requiring medical testing of new hires, current employees, or both.[11] Worksite health promotion programs have also become quite popular. HIPAA permits companies to encourage healthy habits in employees but restricts their ability to punish employees for being unhealthy. Before HIPAA, for example, if a pregnant employee did not attend prenatal care classes and go to the doctor, one company refused to cover her birth costs and kept the new baby off the mother's health plan for one year as punishment.[12] Now companies are more likely to offer incentives like extra pay for attending exams or classes or to tone down such punishments.

This is the larger world in which actuarialism matters. But this is a book about difference and personhood and how antidiscrimination law grapples with what differences matter for justice and why. Whose personhood is subject to actuarialism in the law and whose gets protected from it? Antidiscrimination law could declare every group-based generalization, including empirically accurate statistical stereotypes, illegal as an insult to the unique life of the individual. Making unhealthy people pay more or not insuring fat people could be the height of injustice. Or law could step back entirely and let the market rule, in which each person is measured on every relevant axis and then made to pay according to her tailored risk profile. Being left out or charged a lot more would not be the basis of a claim of injustice.

But there is no such single vision. Instead, antidiscrimination laws do several different things in response to actuarial logics of the person: (1) turn to functional individualism, in which the aim is to describe the individual as exceptionally healthy or able even if the statistical stereo-type about her actuarial group is accurate or even if she actually has a disease or disability that is risky; (2) call upon the tools of data analysis to fight actuarialism, in which the aim is to sniff out redlining, for ex-ample, by analyzing lending by race of the applicant populations and to force companies to underwrite more loans for targeted groups; or (3) statutory bans on consideration of some factor understood to be unfair even if it is actuarially relevant, such as race or genetic predisposition to a certain disease. None of these responses really grapple with actuarial personhood on its own terms, however. I maintain that American anti-discrimination law lacks any principled way of addressing how a per-son's departure from the norm burdens her, as well as any real vocabu-lary for talking about the new understandings of individualism and groups that actuarial personhood brings.

The Logic of Actuarial Personhood

I've just noted how state legislatures have intervened to remake actuar-ial personhood through policy interventions designed to protect certain groups and activities, but it is worth assessing actuarial personhood on its own theoretical terms, as well as considering law's adaptations to it. The salient features of actuarial personhood, considered as an ideal type, are: (1) the collapse of traits of the person as a bodily individual with other features of her environment, family health history, and so on, such that the relevant description of her includes many details beyond her character or control; (2) the use of these features to project into the future and to assign risk estimates based on a population-level norm; (3) the reconstruction of group categories as populations grouped by relevant statistical factors rather than along the lines of social groups or protected classes; and (4) the infiltration and use of actuarial techniques from other professional spheres into the law, particularly from public health medicine, demography, statistics, and actuarial science.

The politics that accompany actuarial personhood are strangely de-natured: amoral, based upon aggregates that are not interest groups and redescribed in seemingly scientific terms. It does not call fat people glut-tons, just too costly. There is no longer the ruling class, just the strata of people defining the statistical norm. These politics combine with the more recognizable moral politics against fat that have dominated mainstream American culture for the past century and the vigorous self-policing by many of us in the form of vegetarianism, organic food consumption, dieting, exercise regimens, vitamin and supplement use, and vigilance against allergies and pollutants.[13] Actuarial personhood, then, is not built into antidiscrimination law the way that the logics of functional individualism, diversity, and blame-shifting are—it does not share enough of the moral underpinnings of those logics. It comes into law from outside, but can fit very well because of its resonance with the technologies that regulate the body and its health with which we are already so familiar in modern life. We've already discussed empirical generalizations about groups of people in the law under the term statistical stereotype. Actuarial personhood describes the subject of statistical stereotypes.

Let us return to Joyce English. Defendant corporations such as PECO describe fat job applicants as risky hires because they perceive fat workers as likely to miss work more often, to become disabled, and to suffer more health problems than thinner employees.[14] Companies bluntly state that regardless of the prospective employee's present health, a fat applicant is rightly rejected on an actuarial basis. Ms. English lost her case because the court deferred to PECO's policies against risk of loss without finding her to be legally disabled. But recall Catherine McDermott, the fat woman whom Xerox did not want to hire for the same reason. She also presented no health problems and was perfectly able to do the job. In the Introduction I explained that in her case, she forced Xerox to evaluate her as a functional individual rather than as an actuarial threat. Specifically, Ms. McDermott won her case because the court turned Xerox's concerns about her health risks into a disability rights issue. The New York court reasoned that the fact that Xerox had rejected her based on her status as "a medically unacceptable risk" in the future could mean that her obesity constituted a legitimate medical impairment in the present (for which Xerox could not refuse to hire her without violating disability antidiscrimination laws).[15]

The twist is a bit disingenuous: the Xerox managers did not think Ms. McDermott was disabled in the ordinary sense of the term; for a range of reasons they simply thought she was likely to cost too much later on. Perhaps they would be wrong, but they preferred not to take the chance. Xerox's projections were not about Ms. McDermott in any individualized sense, but were simply a product of actuarial science that helped them manage financial risk. Her future risk calculation became a civil rights category in the present for the court: disability (or perception of disability). Xerox was ordered to offer Ms. McDermott an equivalent position, give her back pay, and pay damages for hurt, humiliation, and mental anguish.[16]

Disability rights laws like the ADA are supposed to challenge the idea that there is one normal way for a worker to function and to frustrate the classic cost/benefit calculus that says that doing more for people with disabilities is simply too burdensome to justify given their relative small numbers in the population. Without these two key critical concepts, workers with disabilities would just be evaluated using the logic of functional individualism and their differences would provide plenty of reasons to fire or to not hire them. The Xerox case uses disability law to frustrate normalization by equating the company's use of weight charts with perceiving Ms. McDermott as disabled. The Xerox court understands disability as that which defies normalization—the abnormal, the "off the chart" data point—not as a medical condition afflicting a person. One might think that this interpretation would be the only way to have a disability rights law with any teeth, and thus expect that most courts would use the ADA in a similar way. But actually this interpretation—challenging normalization rather than medicalizing the individual—is the exception rather than the rule. As I explain later in this chapter and more extensively in chapter 5, ADA interpretation is extremely porous and suffused with several conflicting logics of personhood, making it politically weak and susceptible to takeover by actuarial, managerial, business, and medical interests.

Governing Difference with Actuarial Personhood

What understandings of difference do we find in actuarial personhood? How does the logic of actuarial personhood reframe individualism and group membership and their significance for antidiscrimination law? When is bad health (and other risks, like bad credit) a difference that makes a difference, and when are persons protected from stigmatization, firing, and higher costs because of their categorization as a risk? Recall my example from the Introduction about the auto insurer's question: where do you park your car at night? Every word in the question will help to frame the risk of underwriting: "you" matter as an individual, but in relation to "where" you park "at night." In other words, actuarial personhood is simultaneously more expansive and more restrictive than the more familiar group categorizations of antidiscrimination law.[17] It is more expansive because the person is blended into the environment: the same person with the same car may pay very different rates to insure at a Manhattan address than at a rural upstate New York address. That is because risk is a product of many factors that depend on the behaviors of others (their likelihood of smashing one's windows, perhaps), even as it is tagged onto one individual purchaser of insurance. It is more restrictive because only a few variables really matter, and not the ones that traditionally have been a part of merit-based calculations. Moral character does not matter; number of speeding tickets within five years does.

Difference is understood as risk in the future based on membership in groups that are defined in sometimes stable, sometimes shifting, but usually politically invisible ways. Medical knowledge about persons and their bodies is a critical way of parsing difference that has particular resonance for fat rights and disability rights. Categories may include overweight or obese employees, home mortgage applicants from certain neighborhoods, and those most at risk for contracting HIV or developing diabetes. One view is that these are simply new ways of demonizing the same groups. Fear about disease has been a classic part of moral panics directed against gay men, immigrants, and other socially marginalized people, after all: might some of these be the same thing? Evidence suggests the media often discuss obesity in exaggerated terms and with hyperbolic metaphors, and when discussing blacks and Latinos, refer to poor food choices much more often as the cause.[18] People who express negative attitudes toward fat people are likely to also express negative beliefs about racial minorities and poor people and to display authoritarian personality traits.[19] Perhaps the lazy fat black or brown person is the perfect villain. She can conveniently be redescribed from Welfare Queen to Diabetes Time Bomb, with the same old contempt covered over by expressions of concern about her health.[20] This "old wine in new bottles" critique of risk profiling is indeed compelling, but I argue that we should take seriously what is new about actuarial personhood that sets it apart from these more familiar forms of demonizing difference. Specifically, there is a new role for professionals and their norms and practices in constituting persons, and there is a new concept of a group.

Actuarial personhood does not traffic in moral condemnation, at least not explicitly. It requires some consensus within some professional community—physicians, demographers, public health experts—that data exists to mark the group or lifestyle as risky or in need of intervention. These professional communities present themselves as genuinely concerned with the well-being of the people they study, and no doubt many are. This is not to say these actors should not be regarded as enforcers of knowledge and power, but simply to say that their embeddedness within research-conscious professions is significantly different in form and structure from that of politicians or judges, for instance. For an actuary looking after a company's health benefit plans, a fat person is simply a member of the "obese group," classified by a chart and tables, and marked with a certain risk of making demands on employee benefit funds. She is not an individual in any ordinary sense of the term; the actuarial framework loses all the boundaries and content of what we understand a person to possess.

Nor is the actuarial person embedded within a community or only understandable through her appearing traits. There are no normative stereotypes about actuarial persons because the aim of these professionals is to simply predict and plan for their behaviors, illnesses, or accidents, not to incite them into any particular way of inhabiting an identity. Any economic pressures or incentives—to wear a seatbelt, for instance—are not aimed at constituting the cultural life of a group but simply at reducing costs. If some fact does indeed have cultural meaning, such as pit bull ownership, then it is not supposed to effect the underwriting decision. Brian Glenn argues that underwriters do in fact rely on thick narratives about risk that are culturally embedded, including penalizing households with pit bulls as not the right sort to insure.[21] The history of insurance underwriting, he argues, shows that stigmatized groups like blacks, Jews, and Mexicans were described in the scientific terms of the day as inveterately destructive and uninsurable.[22] I do not mean to argue here that actuarial personhood is never supplemented by other logics of personhood or that it always or even regularly appears in its ideal form described here. Glenn's point is that underwriters do not rely on real data, and he implies that if they did then much discrimination would disappear (sidestepping the problem of statistical stereotypes that appear in actuarial data and are empirically valid but still unjust). In other words, even critics of cultural embeddedness in actuarial practice still assume that there is some true version of actuarialism in which those meanings should not hold sway.

Under the blame-shifting view of personhood, dysfunction or lack of capacity is not the person's fault alone, but a result of state policies that must be compensated for. The blame-shifting view of personhood locates the individual within a deprived social group. One's group membership matters because it was the source of the inferior treatment doled out on a large scale with the aim of keeping all group members in a subordinated position (such as poorly educated in segregated schools). Blame-shifting accounts of the person can explain group-level differences in achievements that functional individualism must otherwise validate. These two contrasting views of personhood illustrate the dominant approaches to the problem of the individual in relation to the group: functional individualism demands that group membership be ignored, while blame-shifting gives the group a history and a current status based on its treatment at the hands of the state (or at the hands of a dominant group). Diversity, as we saw, diffuses the heavy meaning of group membership in favor of an individually expressed background that doesn't just explicitly lack content, but rather expresses assistance in group tasks or pluralistic living. Diverse personhood represents a pendulum swing back toward more individualistic accounts of achievement because it empties the structural critique of blame-shifting out of the notion of the group. Being black means having a new perspective to share, not being marked as inferior in a systemically racist society.

The twists and turns of these three accounts of personhood undergird the various theories of discrimination and remedy in American civil rights law, as I've set out in previous chapters. Even as variable as these accounts of group membership are, they still share nothing in common with group membership under actuarial personhood. Groups of actuarial persons are assembled by experts, not by events in the world or by shared social ties. Actuarial persons do not even know they are in the same group; their group exists in data but not in ordinary life. Jonathan Simon cautions that "[t]o the extent that group differences created by historical processes of domination are demoralized by actuarial representations (as they are for insurance in insurance premium setting) it becomes more difficult for disadvantaged groups to generate political power."[23] Actuarial practices create new groups—people living in homes built more than fifty years ago, people with body mass indexes (BMI) over thirty, kids with learning disabilities (LD)—and distribute benefits and burdens in society along these lines. These new groups are not contiguous with socially salient identities, and their production has the effect of blurring or dispersing other more politically charged identities while promoting these more easily managed categories.

Groups as figured in the most heavy-handed affirmative action or the most pictoral "Colors of Benetton" approach to diversity are both real things, however, in the following sense: people who belong to them know they belong, they can describe the markers of membership and recognize others who belong, and various terms of speech and interaction work by reference to the realities of group membership.[24] The groups that appear regularly in U.S. law—in class actions, school desegregation, disparate impact discrimination, affirmative action, and laws governing corporations—are not a distribution of factors, but rather a more or less coherent entity with properties that law can treat as fixed and with interests the law can envision and protect. The justification for corporate personhood is to render the entity capable of suing and being sued, for example, in order to render its actions more easily compared to and interchangeable with those of human persons. Named plaintiffs in class action suits must accurately represent the other real and identified people (counsel must make efforts to identify them no matter how large the class) who are part of the certified class in order to speak for them. The group-level antidiscrimination measures like disparate impact and affirmative action are meant to benefit a discrete subset of people—minority applicants living in the area who may not otherwise be hired, for example, or female applicants who could have become firefighters if it were not for the strength test requirement.

The previous two chapters explained how personhood accounts for law's handling of racial difference (as either blame-shifting or diversity) or gender difference (as stereotyping). We needed to understand those critically important categories so that we could see how persons come to be seen as worthy of legal protections and on what terms. If fatness were to gain more antidiscrimination protections, we see what terrain it would enter upon. But now we return to the ground upon which debates over fatness are waged in the present. The actuarial person is not the subject of moral strictures or individual fitness tests; instead, she is subject to medicalization and normalization. These techniques describe her difference and enter into law as reasons to justify certain treatments of her. As we will see, antidiscrimination law sometimes absorbs and sometimes reflects them.

The Medicalization of Fat: From Gluttony to Obesity

Medicalization is the process by which some problem comes to be defined, diagnosed, and treated as a medical problem rather than say, a personality quirk, random misfortune, or sinful habit.[25] Alcoholism is an example of a deviant behavior (excess drinking) with a long and complex socio-legal history, now widely regarded by both experts and ordinary people as a medical condition.[26] Medicalizing fatness could remove the stigma of gluttony and replace it with the notion that fat people cannot help being fat because it results from their genes, their hormones, or some complex combination. It also supplies a huge market for anti-obesity drugs and for weight loss surgeries, billed as health interventions rather than as aesthetic treatments. Talk about fat in contemporary U.S. popular culture is dominated by a discourse of health, at least among elites and in the mainstream media: fat as unhealthy, fat as costly, fat as driving increased rates of diabetes, cancer, and heart disease.[27] The term "obesity epidemic" evokes disease and widespread death in the population. Medical researchers, physicians' organizations, and state agencies have organized for many decades around obesity as a medical problem, holding conferences, publishing standards, classifying it as a disease in official publications, and researching treatments: medicalizing fat, in other words.[28] Obesity has been listed as a disease in the International Classification of Diseases since 1948, but it was not until the mid 1990s that international groups of researchers at the World Health Organization began to formulate standards to measure obesity worldwide. The International Obesity Task Force (IOTF) was formed in 1996 with the goal of "alert[ing] the world to the growing health crisis threatened by soaring levels of obesity."[29] Its members are concerned that obesity is not being recognized as a disease quickly enough. The IOTF is not a disinterested scientific research organization, however; it was started with funds from several major pharmaceutical companies and continues to receive most of its funding from those companies.[30]

We are in the middle of a fascinating period of upheaval over the politics of fat. Professional and governmental assessments share a medicalized view of obesity, though there is no consensus on what causes it or how it might be cured. Most ordinary people do not consider fat people to be victims of a disease, however; instead, most people think that getting fat is primarily caused by bad behaviors like eating too much and failing to exercise.[31] It is considered a garden-variety character flaw, like getting into too much credit card debt. Sloth and gluttony are two of the seven classic sins, after all. As Rogan Kersh and James Morone explain, public views of something as a private vice can shift to acceptance of it as a social problem requiring public intervention. These shifts share a pattern: first social disapproval, followed by scientific backing for claims of harm, self-help movements, demonization of those unwilling to go along with self-help, criticism of the industry supplying the product, topped off by social movement or interest group action that finally spurs policy making.[32] American politicians have only just begun to embrace regulatory actions against fattening food, however, and with fairly low levels of enthusiasm (perhaps removing soda machines from schools, but stopping short of ordering restaurants to list the calorie content of all entrees).[33] Support for the fast food industry against lawsuits by fat consumers also indicates that politicians are unlikely to do much more to regulate Big Food anytime soon.[34] European countries, by contrast, have much more regulations: limiting television advertising about junk food to kids and more stringent labeling requirements, for instance.[35]

Fat acceptance groups, the Health at Every Size (HAES) movement, and other anti-dieting, anti-surgery groups are gaining more attention, particularly as professionals engage in data wars over what exactly the health effects of being fat even are. The most widely reported study that obesity causes 400,000 deaths per year and would soon overtake smoking as the leading cause of preventable death in the United States, for example, had to be revised because of an error that had inflated the numbers by about 35,000 and then was challenged by another study showing that the number of total deaths was about 26,000 per year and that those in the moderately overweight category (BMI 25–29) were least likely to die.[36] A recent issue of the *International Journal of Epidemiology* featured debate among obesity researchers and social scientists over whether the so-called public health crisis is really actually a moral panic. Researchers on the moral panic side raised questions about data establishing the most basic arguments of obesity researchers: that the more fat one has, the more dangerous it is, as well as the idea that losing weight is a feasible and effective cure.[37] Critics respond that actually, data available for the last ten years shows that mortality is highest for those with either very large or very thin body sizes, and even when one gets to a BMI of 40 or more (3.2 percent of the U.S. population in 2001, according to the U.S. Department of Health and Human Services Medical Expenditure Panel Survey), mortality differences are not yet statistically significant.[38] Critics also maintain that the amount by which we have gotten fatter has been greatly exaggerated by media, and that in fact it seems that yo-yo dieting and use of diet drugs may explain a lot of the health problems that fat people often have. Increased exercise is one clearly beneficial treatment for many conditions considered to be linked to obesity, but then, it is also beneficial whether weight loss occurs or not. The crux of the debate is whether fat per se deserves so much attention, or whether the real concern should be with the poor eating habits and sedentary lifestyles of Americans of all sizes, and of course with the larger problem of lack of access to health care at all for millions of American citizens.

The response to the moral panic critique by an international anti-obesity policy expert was to reiterate that the "field of medical and scientific research has never been more unified in expressing its concern about the medical and personal disadvantages associated with excess weight gain," maintaining that the evidence for increased health problems and early death from excess fat were clearly documented in many studies that should not be undone by one contrary study.[39] Finally, libertarian voices like the Center for Consumer Freedom (CCF) keep media attention on these missteps and disagreements in order to diffuse support for governmental restrictions. The CCF is funded by the restaurant and food lobby, and many anti-obesity researchers are funded by pharmaceutical companies who manufacture weight loss drugs. The politics of food and fat is a churned up mess with plenty for diet advocates and skeptical critics to argue about for years to come.

The medicalized view of obesity is certainly the most powerful at the level of research and policy, but does not seem to explain ordinary people's attitudes toward fatness. Moreover, the medicalized view is often expressed in terms of population-level obesity increases that can be interpreted as simply an epidemiological description of gluttony run amok. Thus far population-level data and professionals' warnings have been compatible with discourses of personal responsibility and moral blame. Even if population-level public health interventions replace moral criticism as the most prominent response to rising obesity, I would still expect Americans, especially the elite, to maintain a highly personal and closely monitored relationship with eating that affirms their moral sense and which bolsters their sense of self-control. Eating, after all, is not like a vaccine that one shows up to get every few years —it is a steady part of one's everyday interaction with one's body and its pangs and pleasures. It is simply available as a focal point of self-improvement and self-monitoring, particularly in comparison to others, in a way that many other features of the self are not (like sexual practices, for example). This combination of readiness for population-level monitoring with relentless self-interaction makes the politics of fat both intensely personal and vividly governmental at the same time.

Normalization: Weights and Measures

Along with the politics and morality of health come the actuarial techniques that track, classify, and define the norm of human functioning. Medicalization requires normalization, so we can measure and track changes in the population and define its optimal condition. As Jonathan Simon points out, the practices of test-taking, filling out forms for insurance companies, and answering polls are "familiar and banal" to most of us, yet these activities are also "central components of a new regime of social ordering linked to myriad exercises of social control and power, e.g., hiring, admitting, campaigning, selling, sentencing, and educating."[40] Talk about fat has not abandoned the moralistic tone that came with the sudden anti-fat shift in American culture around the turn of the last century, but more and more concerns about fat are expressed with demographics, Body Mass Index (BMI) ranges, and cost projections.[41] Any generalization about the population requires standardization: setting the normal and abnormal weight ranges. The BMI measurement, which is a single number based on height and weight, classifies people into four categories: underweight (below 18.5), normal (between 18.5 and 24.9), overweight (25 to 29.9), and obese (30 and over). According to the BMI measurement, 64.5% of Americans are overweight or obese and 30.5% are obese. A five foot eight inch man or woman would be overweight at 165 pounds, for example, and obese at 197 pounds. (The average American woman is thirteen pounds heavier now than in 1970s, and the average American male is seven pounds heavier.)[42]

The BMI was developed in the 1830s by Adolphe Quetelet, a Belgian astronomer and social statistician. "By gathering together a number of individuals of the same age and sex and taking the average of a set of their constant measurements, one obtains a series of constant figures that I would attribute to a fictional entity I call the average man for this group," Quetelet wrote.[43] He is famous for pressing the idea that statistics could help explain social phenomena like crime or suicide rates and for developing the normal bell curve distribution for wide use.[44] François Ewald observes that Quetelet came up with a "new way of judging individuals. . . with reference to their position in a group, rather than by paying close attention to their essence, their nature, or their ideal state of being."[45] The average man displays the norm for body size, and the development of a normal curve can then account for variation as departures from the norm both at the right and left sides of the curve. Ewald points out that normalization and standardization have been necessary for all the momentous developments in Western culture—measurement, production, industry, consumption, even grammar and vocabulary.[46]

In recent years, the standardization of the BMI measurement has been in flux. From 1980 to 2000 governmental guidelines used a cutoff of 27.1 for overweight, and in 1985 the National Institutes of Health (NIH) recommended a gender-specific cutoff for overweight of 27.8 for men and 27.3 for women.[47] After the World Health Organization (WHO) promulgated a cutoff for overweight of 25, there was pressure to bring U.S. standards into line. In 1998, the NIH subsequently revised its standard down to 25–29 to define "overweight" for both men and women, which is where it stands now. As Eric Oliver points out, when the NIH report lowered the BMI standard for overweight, "overnight, 37 million Americans suddenly became 'overweight' even though they had not gained an ounce."[48] A person with a BMI of 25 (a five foot five inch woman weighing 150 pounds, for example) would look very out of place among fashion models, but would look perfectly acceptable to the vast majority of ordinary Americans. Media coverage suggests that Americans have become very fat in large numbers, though it is more plausible that millions of us are carrying a few more pounds than in the past at the same time that the standards were revised downward.

Fat people are often explained through actuarial personhood as the first alternative to a straightforwardly bigoted approach that explains them as disgusting or gluttonous. There are no legally imposed limits on the actuarialization of fat. But of course antidiscrimination law grapples with the "abnormal" bodies and potential risks of members of other protected groups quite frequently, notably in disability law and fair housing and credit policy. In the next sections, I examine how antidiscrimination laws explain and combat actuarial risk as features of persons in these areas of law where the response is more developed.

Law's Reactions to the Logic of Actuarial Personhood

Individualizing Risk in Disability Rights Law

Gene Arline taught elementary school in Nassau County, Florida for fifteen years. In 1979, after a twenty year remission, her tuberculosis flared up again and she had three relapses of the disease. The school board dismissed her, "not because she had done anything wrong," but because they feared she would spread the disease to the students.[49] She sued, claiming disability rights protection as a person with a contagious disease. By the time her case got to the Supreme Court, the AIDS epidemic was in its early and ferocious years and the focus of much public anxiety. Any legal protections for other infectious diseases would apply to people with AIDS, which was much more salient than tuberculosis. Solicitor General Charles Fried argued for the Reagan Administration in *Arline* against interpreting the statute to protect people with contagious diseases, explicitly claiming that discrimination against people with asymptomatic HIV should be permitted under the Rehabilitation Act because contagiousness is not the same as disablement.[50] The administration's argument was squarely rejected.

Instead, the first step the Court took was to individualize the personhood of each contagious person and to reject a population-level risk management approach. The Court held that contagiousness could not be separated from the concept of disability, but rather that the risk of infecting others with one's disease had to be subjected to an objective risk analysis, individualized inquiry, and accommodation on the job if possible. "Few aspects of a handicap give rise to the same level of public fear and misapprehension as contagiousness," Justice Brennan observed in his opinion for the majority.[51] "The fact that *some* persons who have contagious diseases may pose a serious health threat to others under certain circumstances," he wrote, "does not justify excluding from the coverage of the Act *all* persons with actual or perceived contagious diseases."[52] Lack of a careful and narrow exception would mean that contagious individuals may suffer several wrongs, according to Brennan's opinion: "[T]hose accused of being contagious would never have the opportunity to have their condition evaluated in light of medical evidence and a determination made as to whether they were 'otherwise qualified,'" and "they would be vulnerable to discrimination on the basis of mythology—precisely the type of injury Congress sought to prevent."[53] The second step after individualizing the person from the condition is to remove the judgment of risk from the realm of social norms and place it in the realm of medical and scientific expertise—employers, the Court directs, should base their employment decisions on the "reasonable medical judgments of public health officials."[54]

Congress has also recognized that conceptions of risk may often contribute to demonizing those who are different; therefore, the evidence that courts use to determine risk of disabled workers is statutorily required to be scientific, objective, and individualized. "The determination that an individual with a disability will pose a direct threat to others," legislators insisted when framing the ADA, "must not be based on generalizations, misperceptions, ignorance, irrational fears, patronizing attitudes, or pernicious mythologies."[55] Current federal regulations reiterate the requirement of "an individualized assessment, based on reasonable judgment that relies on current medical knowledge or on the best available objective evidence."[56] Brennan's formulation of the proper judicial response to managing risk of workers with disabilities combines functional individualism (the right to be evaluated as qualified) with deference to medical authority as the source of that "mythology"-free determination. The individualized assessment is understood as medical and therefore objective. There is no room for the possibility that medicalization and normalization may enforce inequality by defining some people as dysfunctional. The physicians who examined Arazella Manuel, Catherine McDermott, and Joyce English pronounced them dysfunctional despite their test results because of an *a priori* conviction that a woman that fat could not possibly be healthy. The easy opposition of mythology on the one hand and medical knowledge on the other evades the very problem that actuarial personhood exposes: that the logic and techniques of actuarial personhood can pose questions about difference and legal protection in a new way, but they cannot give us neutral or value-free ways of resolving them.

Balancing Risks in Disability Law

The ADA's "direct threat" or "significant risk" defense expressly invites conjectures about actuarial personhood into antidiscrimination law. It is a concession to the logic of actuarial personhood within legislation that otherwise sought to dispel fears that people with disabilities are dangerous to have in the workplace. The ADA permits employers to defend themselves against litigation by an employee with a disability who poses a "direct threat" within the workplace, defined in EEOC guidelines as "a significant risk of substantial harm to the health or safety of the individual or others that cannot be eliminated or reduced by reasonable accommodation."[57] The direct threat defense is the flip side of *Arline*-type cases: if someone cannot be reliably individualized and her dangerousness neutralized by medical interventions and precautions, the employer can fire her because of her disability. Regulations set out a four-part balancing test for courts to use in determining whether or not someone poses a direct threat: (1) the duration of the risk; (2) the nature and severity of the potential harm; (3) the likelihood that the potential harm will occur; and (4) the imminence of the potential harm.[58] The Supreme Court has stipulated that "[a]n employer . . . is not permitted to deny an employment opportunity to an individual with a disability merely because of a slightly increased risk. The risk can only be considered when it poses a significant risk, i.e., high probability of substantial harm; a speculative or remote risk is insufficient."[59] A publication directed at helping physicians to evaluate workers' risk cautions that "[a] doctor cannot declare an individual unfit to work if there is only a minimal chance of injury to himself or others or if the condition is a degenerative one and no harm is likely to occur for many years."[60] If the risk is significant and cannot be accommodated, then the disabled person does not meet the prong of the legal test that requires that she be "otherwise qualified" for the job: risk becomes the person's incapacity to perform.[61] The direct threat defense relies on a much more ad hoc application of actuarial personhood than an insurance company does when using its weight charts to screen out fat job applicants, of course. A supervisor has to make a judgment call about an employee's level of risk, often without any comparative data about how others with that same disability have functioned in that job. Use of the direct threat defense in practice is thus less professionalized (by actuaries) but more managerial (at the particular workplace, in which a compliance officer or supervisor decides whether the risk is too great).

Many deployments of the direct threat defense focus on the mental instability or contagiousness of the plaintiff, particularly where his conduct is hard to manage and predict, or where infection of others would bring about death. A mine blaster with migraine headaches and psychological problems was not a qualified individual under the ADA due to the threat he posed,[62] nor was a chlorine gas tank filler with insulin-dependent diabetes who had not monitored his insulin levels and would sometimes black out on the job,[63] nor a pump and engine mechanic in a refinery who sustained manic episodes.[64] These men and women were often dismissed from jobs that required physical exams as part of the regulation of their dangerous working conditions and as a guard against industrial accidents. Cases involving insulin-dependent diabetics seem to turn on expert testimony assessing the plaintiff's level of responsibility and control in managing insulin levels. The chlorine gas worker with insulin-dependent diabetes, for instance, showed "poor self-management of his condition," according to his doctor, who also noted that "as an unsupervised operator, he would be at serious risk of death and would be placing the surrounding community at risk of a catastrophic event."[65]

Even though courts willingly admit that there have been a miniscule number of cases in which HIV has been transmitted from a health care worker to a patient, the catastrophic outcome prompts some judges to permit the direct threat defense. An HIV-positive dental hygienist was legally fired because of his infected status upon the court's finding that "transmission theoretically could happen, even though the risk is small and such an event never before has occurred."[66] An HIV-positive medical resident was similarly barred from surgical practice,[67] and an HIV-positive surgical technician was found to be a direct threat to the safety of others.[68] In another kind of case, the risks posed are not as severe as death, but the disabling condition is a relatively newly named psychological problem that may still carry social stigma. In one First Circuit case, the court found that a health care worker with depression had been legitimately dismissed because of the risk that her depression would prevent her from correctly administering medications.[69] The Fifth Circuit protected a hospital's decision to fire a neurologist with attention deficit hyperactivity disorder (ADHD), which interfered with his memory, ability to complete charts, and ability to interpret tests.[70] A truck driver who was fired from his job transporting highly flammable gasses because he suffered from Post Traumatic Stress Disorder (PTSD) was not a qualified individual under the ADA because of the direct threat his condition posed.[71]

Interestingly, the cases in which courts have refused to permit the direct threat defense to excuse firing do not differ significantly in the facts presented from cases in which the defense has been permitted. Instead, judges simply display different attitudes toward risk. They place more emphasis on the unlikelihood of the dangerous event rather than upon its disastrous outcome. Employers have failed in attempts to establish that the same kinds of risks discussed above—HIV transmission, psychological instability, and so on—outweigh the employment rights of the disabled. A Maine dentist was unable to avail himself of the direct threat defense after he refused to fill the cavity of an HIV-positive woman. After several rounds of fact-finding and oral arguments, the trial court concluded, and the Supreme Court upheld, that the dentist should have simply used the universal precautionary methods recommended by the American Dental Association and that, had he done so, there would have been a very low risk of HIV transmission from the patient.[72] An Oregon ski resort attempted to fire one of its ski patrollers because his wife had AIDS and the company feared that he would contract the virus and pass it on to an injured skier while performing first aid. Even though the resort presented evidence that infection of a guest was "certainly possible," the judge found that it was only a "remote risk" since no first responder had ever been known to transmit the virus, and it was very unlikely that the employee would contract the virus from his wife in the first place.[73] Even though a skier would die if infected with HIV from the ski patroller, the court found insufficient "statistical significance of a ski patroller with HIV transmitting the virus to others."[74]

Other courts focus on the requirement to accommodate, since if the risk dissipates or becomes insignificant with accommodation, then the ADA protects the employee. Recall that the school district was required to go back and see if it could accommodate Ms. Arline, the teacher with tuberculosis, not just fire her. Wal-Mart could not use the defense against a fired cashier who suffered from occasional fainting spells on the job. That court found that Wal-Mart could have accommodated her fainting by restricting her lifting and carrying of heavy things, and that in any case she was very unlikely to hurt anyone else.[75] In a case brought under Title II of the ADA (prohibiting discrimination not in employment, but in places of public accommodation and in public services), a day care center was unsuccessful in defending their decision to dismiss an eight-year-old boy with autism from the care center.[76] The court noted that the day care center had not bothered to implement the most basic accommodations for the boy's disability, such as preparing a daily schedule for him, and thus the center could not then use his baseline behavior without the accommodations (erratic physical movements, screaming) to justify excluding him. Risk, then, is supposed to be combined with accommodations tailored for the individual's needs, not considered as a more abstract future projection in an unresponsive world.

In addition to differing attitudes toward risk and greater inclinations to demand accommodations, courts that render pro-plaintiff rulings in direct threat cases also go to some effort to protect groups of disabled people that are most likely to be vilified, such as drug addicts. In a case in which the Bay Area city of Antioch had passed a special zoning law to keep a methadone clinic from opening in order to treat heroin addiction, the Ninth Circuit directed the trial court on remand to bear in mind that one of the ADA's primary purposes was to shield disabled people from discrimination based on unfounded fears, and so the neighborhood's fear for its children had to be objectively established.[77] The Ninth Circuit was highly aware that members of the public may be easily worked up into a state of irrational fear by imagining threats to children, but it did not permit this highly emotionally charged topic to have extra weight in the decision-making process of the zoning board. The case itself does not resolve some of the factual issues (but rather sends them back to be retried), and thus there is no final judgment on the question of risk. The parties must have reached some sort of agreement, however, because the methadone clinic currently operates at the disputed site.[78]

A concern like PECO's or Xerox's (that a fat employee would be absent, underproductive, or costly) would not excuse a company's discrimination if the fat employee otherwise met the definition of a qualified person with a disability (a very big if). (The next chapter considers in more detail what it would mean to consider fatness or obesity a legal disability.) The proffered risk would have to be that the worker would have a sudden heart attack while driving, for example, and that would probably be too attenuated a risk under the current rules. Adopting a direct threat-type approach to fat workers would mean confronting their alleged riskiness head on rather than diverting it into the logic of functional individualism, as a perceived disability case would do. There, the employer's assessment of risk would be perception of disability as in the Xerox case, and the fat employee gets an individualized physical assessment to prove the employer wrong. But what if a fat worker is not exactly the picture of health and fitness but also does not have any health problems at the moment of the exam (say, a history of heart disease in the family, slightly elevated cholesterol and blood pressure, but nothing dramatic)? Allowing into antidiscrimination law a view of fat people's difference as health risk would be rather bold, since plaintiffs would still have all the threshold problems of establishing themselves as people with disabilities under the ADA in the first place, and they would risk further reifying the view of fatness as "a heart attack waiting to happen."

Summoning Actuarial Techniques to Combat Mortgage Lending Discrimination

Legal battles over the use of actuarial conjectures applied to racial groups or to certain neighborhoods have evolved in a rather choppy way. Though overtly discriminatory policies typically associated with blatant redlining faded after the 1970s, in the 1990s these "were replaced by subtle underwriting, marketing, and agent location practices whose purpose or effect was to avoid any significant business from minority areas."[79] The result is that many studies confirm that there are still significant differences in loan application outcomes at the aggregate level of racial groups, but it is difficult (though not impossible) to transform these results into successful litigation. The U.S. Department of Housing and Urban Development (HUD) recently disclosed results of an Urban Institute study showing that minorities are still less likely than whites to obtain mortgage financing and when they do, it is on less desirable terms (even taking different levels of creditworthiness into account).[80] One recent study estimates that discrimination in the home loan industry costs African American homeowners $10.5 billion in extra payments, depriving each homeowner of nearly $4,000 in higher interest rate payments.[81] The National Fair Housing Alliance (NFHA) conducted a two-year experiment in nine cities to test whether or not these kinds of insurance underwriting practices were racially discriminatory. The study matched test homes on relevant characteristics (size and type of structure for which insurance was sought, financial status of the applicant), but divided the testers who tried to obtain coverage by race and ethnicity (whites and African Americans/Latinos).[82] The results varied by city, but on average there was a discriminatory outcome (operationalized as higher cost, inferior policy, low agent responsiveness to calls, less information and discounts, unequal application of rules, imposition of extra requirements, and simple verbal discouragement) for the African American or Latino testers who tried to get loans more than half the time (ranging from a high of 83 percent of the time in Chicago for Latinos to a low of 32 percent in Memphis for African Americans).[83] The evidence suggests that racial discrimination and not simply different levels of financial success across racial groups is responsible.

The political and legal will to address racial discrimination in the financial industry has come and gone in waves, driven by varying levels of attention and resources within the Congress, the Attorney General's office (empowered to bring lawsuits under the Fair Housing Act, or FHA), administrative agencies, and private organizations. George Lipsitz, examining political trends in the politics of race and housing over many decades, observes that "[e]very judicial, legislative, and executive victory in the fight against housing discrimination fell victim to subterfuge and subversion by defenders of discrimination."[84] Congress enacted the Fair Housing Act (also known as Title VIII of the Civil Rights Act of 1968) under the powers of the 13th Amendment and in response to urban riots and racial tension, though, according to Lipsitz, the weak investigatory and enforcement powers it bestowed made it "virtually unenforceable."[85] The hope was that aiding African Americans in attaining home ownership would promote safe neighborhoods and prevent white flight. Amendments in 1976 to the 1974 Equal Credit Opportunity Act (EEOA) extended EEOA provisions to prohibit racial discrimination in credit transactions, and in 1975 Congress enacted the Home Mortgage Disclosure Act, which required lenders to report loan business by census tract.[86] In 1977, Congress passed the Community Reinvestment Act (CRA), which required financial institutions to supply credit and loans within the communities in which they operate.[87]

There were very few mortgage discrimination lawsuits filed based on the FHA until the late 1980s, and the few lawsuits filed prior to that time were isolated in the Chicago area and in the state of Ohio.[88] There was also an extended legal battle over whether or not the FHA covered the homeowner's insurance industry, finally resolved in favor of coverage. Legal uncertainty, weak enforcement provisions, and lax data collection combined with the realities of litigating on behalf of poor clients against wealthy financial institutions also meant few lawsuits and little change within the industry. Media publicity prompted more federal action in the 1990s, including establishing an Interagency Task Force on Fair Lending, publishing a report, and holding conferences on the problem.[89] A 1988 series in the *Atlanta Journal and Constitution* entitled "The Color of Money" had exposed the practices of many Atlanta-area banks that restricted their lending to white areas, and this exposé prompted Congress to include a provision in the Financial Institutions Reform, Recovery, and Enforcement Act of 1989 amending the HMDA to require reporting of home loans and applications grouped according to census tract, income level, racial characteristics, and gender.[90] The 1975 version of the Act had only required reporting by census tract, which had not provided sufficient data for litigating discrimination cases. As a direct result of the Atlanta reporting, the Justice Department investigated financial institutions in the area, and in 1992 brought suit against Decatur Federal Savings and Loan using the newly available data. The case was settled by consent decree soon after it was filed (though it took the Justice Department one year and $1 million in funds to set up the case).[91] In addition, the NFHA filed complaints based on the tests described above with HUD against Nationwide, Allstate, and State Farm. In 1996, they reached a settlement with State Farm which included a cessation of certain underwriting practices as well as a commitment to finance first mortgages in Toledo for African Americans and Latinos at reduced interest rates and to open offices in urban neighborhoods across the nation.

The litigation history of racial discrimination in mortgage insurance and of redlining is characterized by low rates of actual lawsuits filed, a high level of engagement with federal administrative agencies, which, depending on the inclination of the President, may be more or less determined to stop housing and lending discrimination[92]), extensive data collection and highly contested evidence in the form of experiments and statistical measurements, and settlements rather than final judgments on the merits. Thus the federal statute that authorizes data gathering about the practices of the financial industry—the Home Mortgage Disclosure Act—is just as important to legal strategies to combat these actuarial practices as the statute that forms and defines the legal wrong itself—the Fair Housing Act. Instead of greeting an actuarial characterization with a defense of the individual, the legal and political response to racial discrimination by mortgage lenders uses actuarial tools to combat actuarialism: assembling data based upon zip codes, census tracts, and so on, and filing lawsuits for the purpose of obtaining a consent decree in which entities like State Farm promise to insure more people in certain categories.

Conclusion: The Failures of Antidiscrimination Law to Grasp Actuarial Personhood

There is no coherent account in U.S. law about why it might be unjust in some cases to permit actuarial calculations to deprive certain individuals or groups of goods like access to insurance or jobs. That is because the dominant account of why it is wrong to consider a person's difference is that the difference does not matter for their individual functioning or performance.[93] This functional individualist logic maps very poorly onto what we have called statistical stereotypes because they are empirically relevant according to the standards of normal business practice in the insurance industry and in health care delivery. The scattershot approach to insurance discrimination in state law shows how a combination of political urges to protect salient groups and rent-seeking by certain professions and sports enthusiasts can gain protective cover from actuarial logics without really defeating actuarialism itself. Fat people, who have none of these state law protections and only the sympathetic view of a few judges here and there, are fully in the grasp of both actuarial logics (with their attendant tools of normalization and medicalization) as well as moral panic. They provide the clearest picture of how actuarial personhood determines what justice looks like on its own terms.

Actuarial personhood, because it deeply challenges the surface-level conceptions of justice for persons in antidiscrimination law, gets some challenge from disability law and from laws regulating racial discrimination in credit and lending. Disability law would be nonsensical if it did not query normal functioning on some level, and racial discrimination is sufficiently salient as an injustice in our society that challenges to actuarialism can be articulated in Justice Department policy, however sporadically or weakly. But even in disability rights law, we saw that the first option is to defend the functional individual like Ms. Arline, who must be presumed to be either exceptional, accommodatable, or both, even though infectious diseases are of course risky in general. The direct threat defense steps in if the accommodation seems unworkable from the employer's perspective, and there we saw that judges were supposed to defer to medical authorities. Medical authority is similar to legal authority, however; it supplies arguments for multiple courses of action but does not supply a meta-principle for choosing among them that everyone agrees upon. So the judges relied on narratives of risk and responsibility that, depending on where the emphasis about the risk was placed, either protected people with dangerous conditions or protected their co-workers and clients instead. Legal action against mortgage lending institutions leans toward a more fully social account of insurance, in which it is to be harnessed for the public good rather than in ways that push riskier purchasers out in order to increase profits. The Justice Department actions participate in a disparate impact-style logic of blame-shifting in which the number of loans and the service level to a certain population must simply be increased, and there is no concern for individuals having been stereotyped in a certain encounter, for example. The experiments with individual testers provide data that discrete acts of bias are occurring, but the remedy is not to sue those biased individuals but rather to mandate redistributions to a racially defined population.

Jonathan Simon predicts that the "success of actuarial methods in shaping a new ideological basis for the governance of social life will be marked by its ability to colonize legal discourse with its representations."[94] It is not so much that actuarial discourses are heavily colonizing antidiscrimination law (although he and Malcolm Feeley make a compelling case for their colonization of the criminal law and police practice),[95] but rather that antidiscrimination law's accounts of the person are deployed awkwardly and sporadically and without any grappling with the deep justice questions that they raise for the treatment of difference. Because of the easy access to these other logics of personhood—functional individualism and some blame-shifting where the political will exists—we seem to have answers to problems of costs, risk, health, suffering, and access to a secure and peaceful life when in fact we have not even been able to pose the right questions in the first place. The questions are not about inaccurate myths or stereotypes, but rather about who gets to live a life defined as safe, normal, and healthy and who does not, and the real suffering of those whose lives cannot be made safe, normal, and healthy under current distributions.

5

Accommodating Fatness

Introduction: The Difference of Disability

Disability rights law has been a refuge for many of the fat women who were able to win their lawsuits mentioned throughout this book: Ms. Nedder, the college teacher, Ms. Manuel, the airport bus driver, Ms. Cook, the nurse, and Ms. McDermott, the business systems specialist. They all successfully argued that their employers had misread their functional capacities by assuming that their weight disabled them when in fact it did not. This prong of disability rights law protects persons against false stereotypes. This "perceived disability" theory defends the functional individualism of agile and capable fat people, but as I pointed out, it cannot answer statistical stereotypes (when empirically verifiable differences appear). Ms. Webb, the would-be school bus driver, did not fit behind the wheel of the bus. Her functional capacities were indeed impaired by the construction of the work space. Even though she was protected by the only height and weight state-level anti-discrimination clause in the country, she still was not hired because of her size. How could this be? The answer is found in the way logics of personhood guide interpretation of the Michigan law. It protects functional individuals against animus based on a particular trait; it does not protect persons who have an insoluble difference that requires accommodation. It does not compel redistributions by shifting the blame for what appear to be dysfunctions to the systems that produced dysfunction in certain populations. So if disability law is to reach any further than conventional antidiscrimination statutes do, it must be able to draw upon logics that shift the blame from the disabled person's body to the conventions of the work environment. It must have a new answer to the problem of difference. Like the blame-shifting of the 1964 Civil Rights Act, the Americans with Disabilities Act (ADA) is an attempt to implement strategy (3), in which it must be conceded that members of a group function differently from the norm, but where defenders insist that the standards themselves are constructed in favor of the dominant group to naturalize and maintain its privilege.

Many scholars say the ADA actually does do something different: it recognizes substantive equality over formal equality. For Ruth Colker, the accommodationist provisions of the ADA require employers to expend resources to help a certain disadvantaged class of workers.[1] That obligation is of course what conservative legal theorists dislike about it.[2] Linda Krieger has called it a "transformative statute . . . requiring structural equality" and Pam Karlan and George Rutherglen applaud its "fundamentally different approach to . . . and remedy for invidious discrimination."[3] What is new is the turn to accommodations for difference and the acceptance that difference may be insoluble, and that ignoring it may be the height of oppression rather than the best hope for seeing past it.

Disability law implies a potentially very capacious view of the person. It represents a recent attempt at innovating and blending logics of personhood to better respond to changing ideas about difference. If we think of disabilities as differences that cannot be ignored but which require a response in the interests of justice, then they force us to reconsider our most basic impulses, such as the conflation of normality with functional capacity. Normal adult bodies are those that can walk, see, hear, and speak. They do not suddenly flail about, stutter, lurch, use machines for mobility, wear diapers, have prostheses in the place of limbs, or require assistance eating or keeping clean. Functional individualism left to its own devices would simply reinforce this classic divide between normal people and the afflicted. Once we decide that people with disabilities deserve integration into the community as full citizens, then we must move from measuring functional individualism according to the norm for non-disabled functioning into accommodating people with disabilities. They are still functional individuals—qualifications still matter for jobs—but the logic of functioning has been partially uprooted by a logic of blame-shifting. It is not that persons with disabilities do not fit the workplace and must be either cured or made objects of social welfare; the workplace does not fit persons with disabilities, and therefore must be altered.

This understanding of disability rights is what advocates and disability studies scholars call the social model of disability, in which the built environment and social norms are the focus of change, not the supposedly diseased or dysfunctional body. A person's bodily or mental difference marks the boundaries of tolerance and the limits of the normal. We should regard those bodies and minds marked as disabled as reflections back on the limits of our own imagination: why should the world be made so as to exclude them? What would it be to think of them as entitled to inclusion rather than as special, costly, or discomforting? The understanding this social model challenges is the classic medical model of disability, in which disabilities are medical problems and unfortunate afflictions that should be cured, rehabilitated, and pitied. They are different in the same way that genetic anomalies or so-called birth defects are different: rare, lamentable, unlucky, but explainable by medical science.

The scholars who celebrated the enactment of the ADA hoped that it would usher in substantive equality through accommodation and transformation of the built environment and perhaps even challenge the way we think about other categories like race and gender (as social rather than biological, and requiring substantive interventions rather than "blindness").[4] Disability studies scholars and activists hoped the social model of disability would dominate discussion of what would need to change to provide real opportunity for persons with disabilities. Modeling the alternatives of disability rights law along the social model/medical model continuum mischaracterizes what has actually become of disability and difference in the law, however. American disability law governs disabled identities in an individualized, accommodationist, and managed way through the logic of personhood I introduced in the Introduction as managerial individualism. It is both medical and social. Its focus on process eclipses that dichotomy as the most important lens through which to understand it. Many fat advocates who argue for fatness as a disability base their optimism upon the social model of disability, which imagines a civil rights-type group identity for fat people.[5] I argue here, however, that fatness as a disability would actually be governed under this managerial view of disability.

Who Is a Person with a Disability, Anyway?

Critically, the ADA does not simply list broad categories of disabilities that would surely be included. To be legally disabled under the employment discrimination section of the ADA, a person must have a physical or mental impairment that substantially limits one or more major life activity, have a record of such impairment, or be regarded as having such an impairment.[6] Major life activities are things like breathing, walking, and reproducing. A physical impairment is any physiological disorder, condition, cosmetic disfigurement, or anatomical loss affecting a body system: neurological, musculoskeletal, special sense organs, respiratory, cardiovascular, reproductive, digestive, genito-urinary, hemic and lymphatic, skin, and endocrine. A psychological impairment is a mental or emotional illness. Ordinary characteristics are explicitly not covered, like hair and eye color, left-handedness, or normal height and weight. The person must be otherwise qualified to perform the job and, as I discussed in the previous chapter, not pose excessive risk on the job. As I noted in chapter 3, some people are peremptorily disqualified from being disabled by amendment to the ADA, such as transsexuals, pedophiles, voyeurs, pyromaniacs, and people currently using illegal drugs and not seeking treatment. People who can establish that they are otherwise qualified persons with disabilities are entitled to reasonable accommodations on the job. "Reasonable" means not unduly burdensome to the employer in terms of cost, disruption, and so on.

"Unlike other civil rights categories, like race," Ruth O'Brien notes, "people with disabilities must prove they have one."[7] We have never before had an antidiscrimination law that insists on the complete indeterminacy of the line between who is covered under it and who is not. For better or worse, most antidiscrimination laws help describe and solidify certain stories of what it means to bear an identity marker such as race, and the first step in doing that is always to explicitly or implicitly define the boundaries of the group to whom the law is directed. Title I of the ADA, of course, protects qualified workers with disabilities, but nearly all the jurisprudential scuffling has been over whom that label actually covers. According to the Supreme Court, determining membership in the group is "an individualized inquiry," and regulations insist that disability is "not necessarily based on the name or diagnosis of the impairment the person has, but rather on the effect of that impairment on the life of the individual."[8]

When Congress deliberated on the ADA, members referred to the 43 million Americans with disabilities that the bill would help. The Supreme Court has seized upon the number as an upper bound, using it to reason that inclusion of people with extremely common conditions in the ADA would expand the population covered beyond 43 million and thus could not be what Congress intended. Justice O'Connor has advocated for a "demanding standard for qualifying as disabled."[9] Those who want a broader interpretation of the statute point out that 43 million surely captures more than just severely disabled people and that the "regarded as disabled" prong captures potentially anyone, and so Congress could not have intended such a pinched view of the population meant for protection. It is telling that a simple number has taken on such significance in ADA jurisprudence. Disabled identity as a legal idea does not on its own tell us anything about who is included, so arbitrary markers become significant. The judges worry that the identity group must be restrained by judicial definition or it will burst right open, and so many people will be included within it that businesses could be overwhelmed by their obligations. Given the reluctance with which many people, including some people with disabilities, claim formal legal rights to non-discrimination, these worries seem unfounded. Nonetheless, this judicial anxiety and gate-keeping has certainly kept the idea of who is disabled very unstable.

Many disability studies scholars have set out to highlight the person-to-person variations in functioning among disabled people rather than to emphasize them as a "like-race" subgroup, while others try to preserve some distinct meaning for disabled identity even across so many different kinds of disability.[10] As it turns out, the focus on individual variation among disabled people and socially situated accommodation constitutes the overlapping vocabulary between Congressional representatives, judges, a subset of disability scholars, and activists. The Supreme Court and those disability rights scholars who are not invested in group identity agree on at least two important things: that "the disabled" are in fact a heterogeneous group without any sustained connections or shared experiences, and that accommodations, when they are required, must be adapted to the individual and her working conditions. It is these two factors that I argue comprise the unique substantive account of disabled people's functional personhood.

Transforming disability using antidiscrimination tools has been extremely challenging because of the long-standing assumption that being disabled *means* not being able to work, and because of various gate-keeping mechanisms built into the ADA that make it very difficult for workers to qualify as legally disabled. In fact, plaintiffs in ADA cases lose nearly 90 percent of the time.[11] Most of these losses come on summary judgment motions before the case even gets to a jury, and the finding is that the plaintiff does not qualify as disabled under the ADA definition. Perhaps there is no underlying impairment, as with an otherwise healthy fat person who just needs an armless chair, or perhaps the impairment does not substantially limit a major life activity. Limiting a less-than-major life activity does not count, for example, even if the employer fired the person because of the limitation. Before there's any celebrating of the unique strategies enabled by the ADA, then, one should clearly understand that because of definitional gate-keeping, the law has had very little transformative effect.

Is Fatness a Disability?

As I noted in the last chapter's discussion of the medicalization of obesity, there are many professionals who hope fatness will become understood as a disability. Public health and anti-obesity researchers hope to direct more resources and attention to fatness by changing it from a character flaw to a medical problem understood as having complex environmental and individual causes. Pharmaceutical companies stand to gain financially from sales of new anti-obesity drugs, and bariatric surgeries are a growth industry for physicians. It seems that the most likely form of rights expansion for fat people would have to come through a gradual expansion of already-existing legal terms like disability, which, as I argued in chapter 3, has happened with transgender rights and discrimination on the basis of sex. In one telling development, Medicare policy recently changed to characterize obesity as a disease, making it possible for beneficiaries to apply for coverage for weight loss treatments.[12]

There is some confusion in the law about whether being fat can be a disability. "Except in rare circumstances," federal regulations currently state, "obesity is not considered a disabling impairment."[13] In other words, if someone is fat and disabled, there must be some underlying cause of the fatness, like a thyroid condition or a thrifty gene.[14] But there is legal precedent and wording in federal regulations to suggest that so-called morbid obesity, defined as body weight 100 percent above the norm, is per se disabling regardless of underlying conditions.[15] Currently many fat plaintiffs lose their cases because they are not able to point to an underlying impairment as a cause of their obesity. Much scholarly criticism of the ADA has focused upon its excessive attention to medicalized impairment and its crabbed treatment in the courts.[16] If fat people were to gain ADA protections, then, this critical perspective would predict that they would exchange moral condemnation for the typical personal tragedy story of people with disabilities, understood as unfortunate souls afflicted with a lamentable condition beyond their control. The focus would remain on their bodily or genetic impairments, because most people still think of disabilities in that way (and the ADA definition certainly promotes a medical impairment view). Fat people come in lots of different sizes, of course, and so there would also be the same problem of individualization versus group consciousness that bedevils the disability rights movement generally. An extremely fat person is much more likely to be seen as medically disabled but we know from extensive research on anti-fat bias that employment discrimination kicks in at much lower weights, especially for white women.[17] What counts as fat and what effects being fat has on a person's employment opportunities or enjoyment of public spaces will vary somewhat according to context (though I do not mean to toss up my hands here—"Everybody's different!"—and resort to individualization, because overwhelming evidence suggests broad and systemic stigmatization against fatness beginning at relatively modest levels).

As Abigail Saguy and Kevin Riley document, many fat activists would very much like to contest the language of "epidemic," "morbidity," and "disease" currently driving the American panic over fat, and see the move toward medicalization as a direct threat to a more affirmative identity-based politics.[18] Fat activists would want fatness to be named a disability, perhaps, but only if another model of disability were to eclipse the medicalized one that they understand the ADA to offer them. Rosemarie Garland-Thomson describes this view of socially disabled fat people quite succinctly: "The fat body is disabled because it is discriminated against in two ways: first, fat bodies are subordinated by a built environment that excludes them; second, fat bodies are seen as unfortunate and contemptible."[19] Rather than asking what's wrong with fat people, a legal regime built on the social model of disability would simply require that their bodily difference not stand in the way of work opportunities, travel, and enjoyment of public places. Fat people, in what Kathleen LeBesco calls the "will to innocence," would not have to assure everyone that they are in fact dedicatedly healthy and cannot in any way change their bodies, but perhaps could move away from those pitfalls toward figuring out what "an inhabitable subject position for fat people" might be in all its complexity.[20] The medical model of disability, focused on the disorder of the individual body as the site of transformation, would continue to aid those searching for the fat gene, the thyroid problem, the diet that actually works, the safer stomach-stapling technique, and so on.

So what would it be like to think of fat people as legally entitled to disability accommodations? To do so would mean drawing upon strategy (3), in which advocates turn the idea of a neutral standard on its head and decry it as actually serving to protect the privilege of the dominant group. Stairs and small chairs are not just the normal and natural way things ought to be; they are tools of exclusion and privilege for some bodies over others. Fat people require different spatial arrangements, different seating, and perhaps other changes to scheduling and movement within the work space. Disability rights law requires transformations of these supposedly neutral spaces in an attempt to balance and remake the privilege conferred upon so-called able bodies.

So how does this accommodations process work, and how does it construct the disabled identity persons may receive? What does it show us about the interaction between law, personhood and identity that is under appreciated? A disabled worker and her employer must engage in what is called the interactive process to find an accommodation that will make the worker fully functional in the job. Arguably, this moment of interaction proves the point that disability rights scholars maintain: that disabilities are socially created and can thus be socially dispelled. Ruth O'Brien argues that the interactive process has great potential to "undermine managerial prerogative power" and "undercut the standardization of the workplace."[21] In her view, this power of this moment can be expanded beyond those classically understood as disabled and used to feminize the workplace and to rearrange its power relations entirely.

A particular account of disabled personhood makes this straightforward rearrangement of power relations unlikely, however, and at best indeterminate. Socio-legal scholars already know, after all, that businesses and organizations mediate and reinterpret what antidiscrimination laws mean within their own organizational cultures.[22] What is waiting for fat plaintiffs is an individualized management of their functional capacities that must be discretely negotiated without the assistance of an overarching identity narrative. The creation of fat plaintiffs as recognizable legal subjects shows us a new path of legal recognition, in which medical individualization combines with managerial imperatives. The individualism of liberal legalism has a supple new form, made all the more powerful through consolidation with medical and managerial discourses of the person.

Before we take stock of what fat identity will gain with disability rights, let's recall the cases involving disability law that we've already discussed. Arazella Manuel, the first bus driver, successfully used a perceived disability argument in her case, which I characterized as really an instance of a court adopting what I call functional individualism, because it demanded that she be evaluated simply on her capacities and not on her doctor's prejudicial beliefs about what fat people could do. Likewise, Mary Nedder's teaching ability was held apart from her appearance as a fat professor, and the court demanded that the college treat her as a well-functioning teacher, not a teacher whose body could be allowed to be embedded within prejudicial social meanings (disrespect, lack of care for the self, and so on). These two cases showed what it would be like for fatness to be stripped of its negative connotations and stigma. In both cases, the courts required that the employer simply measure whether or not the person could perform her job without taking her fatness into account. As we saw, functional individualism requires ignoring fat people's difference, and it does not provide any reason to accommodate them. Stacey Webb, another bus driver, and Deborah Marks, the telemarketer, failed to get any accommodations either for the built environment or to transform prejudices. So while ignoring fatness and promoting functional individualism (and its de-stigmatizing properties) seems to grant fat advocates some of what they want, the shortcomings of the *Webb* case suggest that disability coverage is still necessary if changes to the built environment are to be part of the new world for fat workers. In my concluding thoughts, I consider an alternative antidiscrimination regime developed in San Francisco, which does not depend on the blindness versus accommodations trade-off that the federal laws set up.

Managed Functioning in Disability Law

What kind of social practices and stories of personhood await fat plaintiffs within our disability rights regime? The ADA recognized people with disabilities as a legally protected group, even, as Congress put it in the preamble to the law:

[A] *discrete and insular minority* who have been faced with restrictions and limitations, subjected to a history of purposeful unequal treatment, and relegated to a position of political powerlessness in our society, based on characteristics that are beyond the control of such individuals and resulting from stereotypic assumptions not truly indicative of the individual ability of such individuals to participate in, and contribute to, society.[23]

The language of discrete and insular minorities comes from the history of equal protection doctrine under the 14th Amendment (Louis Lusky's famous 1938 *Carolene Products* footnote 4, specifically). The preamble to the ADA therefore invokes a borrowed justification intended to link people with disabilities to the other prominently protected subjects of rights in the American civil rights pantheon. Notice also the invocation of stereotyping about abilities alongside political powerlessness and inequality. The preamble pulls in every evocative phrase available to characterize discrimination, in other words. The height of the language used is especially dramatic given the depths to which the law would quickly fall, with the Supreme Court severely reigning in its interpretation within a few years. But here we see the initial impulse: to retain the framework of functional capacities as the proper grounds for judgment and to vanquish stereotypes about ability.

Much of the political-legal-scholarly consensus about disabilities, as I noted, has emphasized the wide range of forms that disablement takes. This focus on individualism and variation dominates the contemporary judicial reception of disability cases, and, as Ruth O'Brien explains in her study of the evolution of disability policy since World War II, it also helps explain why the ADA has been remarkably ineffective and even punitive toward many of the people its preamble claims to protect.[24] The notion of a legal remedy for discrimination that is person-specific and contextually crafted provides the chance to produce and to manage functional personhood—that is, personhood imagined as primarily about how one moves about and accomplishes things in the world—on a minute level. This interaction of law with difference is regulatory. As Alan Hunt defines it, " '[r]egulation' refers to a specific style of purposive, instrumental, and policy-oriented mechanisms of control that avoid negative or prescriptive imposition of rules in favor of regulatory negotiation that makes the regulated agent play some part in the process of both the development and implementation of those processes of control."[25] That is, rather than looking for a certain suspect ratio that may trigger suspicion of disparate impact against disabled people (as EEOC regulations set out for marking suspicious ratios of minorities to whites or women to men, for instance), the ADA makes use of a process of negotiated accommodations for disabled people that the employee herself helps to develop and implement. In this section, I examine this interactive process for accommodating disabled workers, reading cases about it as the law's newest account of how to bring about just outcomes for differently functioning individuals.

Processing People, Producing Identity

Management of the individual person seems to be inherent in an accommodationist approach. Each disabled person enters into a collaboration with her employer in a discrete location—her building, her workstation, the assembly line, the bathrooms, the stairs—to produce and to manage an account of what changes to the environment her disability requires and what she should do in return to continue to perform her job. Both the worker and the employer must move through a legally mandated process and only then do the employer's obligations become clear: to accommodate disabled workers who can be reasonably accommodated and still do the job, but not to keep on those whose accommodations are either too expensive or who fail to participate properly in their own refashioning. This approach to managing functionality of persons in the law also links up to (and often seems directly derivative of) other important practices of governing the person, such as medical evaluations and bureaucratic determinations of eligibility for government benefits based on disability, for example.

The employer and the employee must undertake an interactive process in order to determine what precise accommodation will be made. The requirement for an interactive process does not occur within the language of the ADA itself. Interpretive regulations promulgated by the EEOC at the behest of Congress provide that in order

> to determine the appropriate reasonable accommodation it may be necessary for the [employer] to initiate an *informal, interactive process* with the [employee] in need of accommodation. This process should identify

the precise limitations resulting from the disability and the potential reasonable accommodations that could overcome those limitations.[26]

Not all federal courts have accepted that an interactive process is necessary, but in some jurisdictions it has been read into the jurisprudence of the ADA. The lead case from 1996, *Beck v. University of Wisconsin Board of Regents,* stipulates that "once an employer knows of an employee's disability and the employee has requested reasonable accommodations, the ADA and its implementing regulations require that the parties engage in an interactive process to determine what precise accommodations are necessary." [27] Indeed, some judges have been quite enthusiastic about the interactive process requirement as a tool of social justice. One judge has particularly high hopes:

[The process] may . . . not only lead to identifying a specific accommodation that will allow a disabled employee to continue to function as a dignified and valued employee, it may also help sensitize the employer to the needs and worth of the disabled person. It therefore furthers the interest of the employer, and the dignity and humanity of the disabled employee.[28]

Thinking more broadly about the liberating potential of processes for identities, Martha Minow has specifically proposed that we think of identity in the law not as a thing, but as a process of negotiation.[29] By proposing process over a fixed identity, Minow means to highlight the specific historical settings and interactions through which people live their identities, such that even subordinated people can "take advantage of the space between their assigned identities and their own aspirations and alternate conceptions for themselves."[30] This praise for process as dignifying, sensitizing, and liberating is quite strong from several directions.

So the implementation of the ADA turns on a conversation or series of interactions between workers and employers meant to bring to light the employee's different or lost functioning and to accommodate it. From published cases in which the interactive process was a primary feature of the dispute, we can glean some important details about how these interactions play out, and begin to form conclusions about the structural and personal power relations that produce judgments of managed functional personhood. Many cases address the duties of both parties to enter the interactive process in good faith, and turn on the question of who is responsible for a breakdown in the process. If the employee is responsible, he does not qualify for accommodation and job protection. He is then not covered under the ADA because he is not a legally disabled person. Watching how the process breaks down shows how it is supposed to build up the properly functioning worker. When courts assign blame for malfunctions in the interactive process, they are delineating what kind of persons deserved to be functionally reformed, and how that reformation should have proceeded. One case example— *Carter v. Northwest Airlines*—shows this process in action, as well as hints at what kinds of organizational cultures may be springing up to manage disabled identity.

Recall that Romell Carter worked for Northwest Airlines at Chicago O'Hare airport for several years, loading and unloading baggage until he crushed his foot between two forklifts in 1999. Upon his return in 2000, Northwest sent Margaret Sommers, a professional accommodations assessment advisor, to assess what type of work Carter could still do.[31] Initially, Ms. Sommers attempted to set up an evaluation with Mr. Carter at the job site, but he could not attend on the date she had set and was not able to notify her because he did not have a phone. When she subsequently conducted the evaluation with his supervisor present instead, she found that Mr. Carter would not be able to do his old job anymore. She began Northwest's "Alternative Duty Exploration" process, attempting to find a position that would not require Mr. Carter to stand on his foot, which caused him severe pain. For three months Ms. Sommers would send Mr. Carter abbreviated descriptions of open jobs and then answer his questions about what each job involved. Sedentary jobs were already filled by more senior employees, and the one job that was open to him required passing a typing test and moving to Florida. Mr. Carter did not know how to type (and failed the test). The ADA does not require bumping more senior employees to find an accommodation for a disabled employee, and so Northwest's insurance paid for Mr. Carter to take a keyboarding class at a local community college. Although he took the class, he never retook the test despite being invited to do so by Northwest on two occasions.

Because he was still not able to work, Carter sued under the ADA, claiming that Northwest had failed in their duty to accommodate him. In the *Beck* case, the court gave examples of what to look for in assigning blame: "A party that obstructs or delays the interactive process is not acting in good faith. A party that fails to communicate, by way of initiation or response, may also be acting in bad faith. In essence, courts should attempt to isolate the cause of the breakdown and then assign responsibility."[32] Mr. Carter was responsible for the breakdown, in the view of both the trial court and the court of appeals. Northwest succeeded in showing that their evaluation and attempts at job shifting were reasonable (and, under *Beck,* a reasonable effort is all that is required of employers).

Determining a person's functioning is a social and a legal process, and the varying resources the opposing parties bring to bear on that determination help produce the employee as one who functions suitably or as one who does not. One understanding of Ms. Sommers' job is that she was hired to monitor Mr. Carter and to make sure Northwest could prove that it tried to accommodate him. By hiring her, Northwest secured immunity from judgment under the ADA well before any lawsuit was even filed; indeed, it is difficult to imagine that Northwest would not be found reasonable if it devoted an entire position toward accommodating employees. Mr. Carter, on the other hand, had no context for realizing the full ramifications of the interactive process. He alleged that it was not fair that Ms. Sommers and his supervisor assessed his job without his presence, and that the job listings Ms. Sommers sent him were so abbreviated that he could not tell what the jobs required. There was no explanation for his failure to retake the typing test, however, and so it seems that he did not do everything he could have done to get another position. We cannot tell from the record what he thought was happening in the interactive process—did he realize he was ceding away his rights under the ADA by not responding in the proper way? Perhaps his skill level was not sufficient to transfer from a job based on physical labor to one based on technological skills and customer service. Perhaps he changed his mind about moving from Chicago to Florida.

The important things to notice about the *Carter* case, then, are the institutional context of the interactive process as well as the legal background, and the way they work together to determine the functioning of persons. Even with a smashed foot that left him unable to stand without pain for more than ten minutes, we simply cannot know in advance of the process whether Mr. Carter belongs in the class of 43 million disabled Americans. If Mr. Carter had mastered typing and had been willing to move from Chicago to Florida, then the legal obligations of Northwest Airlines would have redefined and reproduced him as a functioning worker. Then he would have been a qualified individual with a disability. This outcome depended upon the interactive process happening in a certain smooth way (to avoid "breakdown"). The meetings, phone calls, applications, evaluations, transfers, and so on should ideally fit together with the disabled worker's proper attitude and efforts. Once Northwest expended a reasonable effort and negotiated in good faith, however, its duties to Mr. Carter ended. Mr. Carter failed to reinvent himself as a functioning worker, and so he did not get ADA protection. There was no fixed identity script to justify the accommodation, but rather an indeterminate managerial process to hash it out, to be repeated over and over in contexts in which law emphasizes the uniqueness of the individual being managed.

O'Brien argues that the interactive process undercuts Weberian standardization and enables sites of resistance to dominant workplace norms. Identities as processes are indeed more fluid and perhaps able to muster resistance and take on new forms, as Minow also hoped they would be. But the question is, who is likely to have more power in the management of these accommodations? Legal identity is a process here, too, not a boundary enclosing a certain group of people. Laws can govern by categories ("No vehicles in the park") or processes ("Petition the park manager to see if you can bring your vehicle in the park"). We think that civil rights laws govern by categories ("disabled"), but we see that they can certainly operate as processes ("Did you emerge as someone who can be accommodated?"). While this new way of conceiving of law and identity certainly opens possibilities for social change (remaking the spaces in which we live and work), there is little reason to think that it is somehow intrinsically liberating.[33]

Fat Identity as a Process, Not a Status

When it was enacted, the ADA looked like it might fulfill advocates' hopes for accommodation of a group (a sufficiently coherent notion to attract the necessary political consensus) without suppressing individual variation and adaptation among disabled people. As theorists like Janet Halley have emphasized, civil rights campaigns on behalf of other groups such as women and gays have put up with a monolithic account of their groups' experience because individual variation within the group often counts as evidence against group subordination.[34] The obvious fact that disabilities can be of many kinds would seem to undermine such solidifying tendencies, and disability law's enthusiastic embrace of this individualist, inessentialist picture of disabled people alleviates this particular worry. If one is opposed to highly scripted identities, as Appiah calls them, then one might wish for more contingently defined legal categories.[35]

Should we be pleased that the ADA seems to represent a legal subject whose identity is inessential, protean, and available for recreation? Will such a conception help construct new practices that fat advocates describe, through which they hope to "revamp fat subjectivity, accord new usefulness to the signifier of fat, and to explore new linkages of affinity and action"?[36] Fatness is a fascinatingly unbounded trait, after all. Supposedly more and more of us are joining the category all the time; it seems to combine mutability (if overeating makes one fat) and immutability (if it is true, as much research suggests, that dieting is hopeless for many fat people);[37] it varies over the life span and with contingencies such as medications or injuries; its meanings change with racialization, sexualization, and gendering;[38] and its prevalence varies geographically, even if one focuses only on the contemporary United States. What does this openness of the class portend? What does it mean to try to construct a legal identity out of this group of people and to insert them into the managed processes I've described here?

People with disabilities, as we saw, emerge in a legal framework that acknowledges the social production of functional capacity but that nonetheless must work itself out on particular individuals. The high level of contestation over who fits under ADA coverage begins at the highest levels of its interpretation and carries all the way down to the level of the interactive process (as we saw with Mr. Carter). Because the identity group to be protected was understood as constituted socially and environmentally and not pre-fixed, the ADA adopted a threshold inquiry into membership into the group, then a negotiation of accommodation. These are its two most critical features. The ADA, I argued, regulates persons through its categorical elasticity and the practices of accommodation that it has produced within organizations. While other laws certainly do these things too, the ADA is unique for blending this regulation with a still-unstable identity category. Most commentators have been focused on the ADA's accommodations as yet-to-be-realized redistributive benefits, but my analysis troubles the linkage between justice and accommodation.

Principally, I find the trouble in the ways that the social practices of the ADA construct a regime of what I've termed managerial individualism. Nikolas Rose points out that in the current period, "regulatory practices seek to govern individuals in a way more tied to their 'selfhood' than ever before."[39] Identity is becoming a process in the law, not something that demarcates a class, as I also argued in chapter 2 has happened in the move to talk about diversity rather than intransigent patterns of racial inequality. Fat identity will not be assisted in a traditional civil rights-group emergence by gaining disability rights, because those rights will operate managerially on fat people one by one, destabilizing opportunities for collective accounts of fat oppression.

We cannot afford to consider the ways that law promotes certain social practices of identity without also noting the managerialization of law, which sociologists Lauren Edelman, Sally Riggs Fuller, and Iona Mara-Drita define as "the process by which conceptions of law may become progressively infused with managerial values as legal ideas move into managerial and organizational arenas."[40] In their study of the transformation of "diversity rhetoric" within organizations, Edelman, Fuller, and Mara-Drita suggest that "the managerialization of law has the potential to undermine legal ideals as managers shift the focus of attention from law to management."[41] Recall Margaret Sommers, the professional accommodations assessment advisor from the *Carter* case. Could she represent a contingent of knowledge workers who are currently constructing the social practices by which law intervenes into the meaning of disability? Is she part of the group that Eric Abrahamson calls "management fashion setters—consulting firms, management gurus, business mass-media publications, and business schools" that promote, as he puts it, "the appearance of rationality and progress"?[42] Her function was literally to manage Romell Carter's relationship to the legal protections offered under the ADA, after all. We must remember to give a critical place in our analysis of fat politics to those professionals who will actually do the work of managing fat employees in work spaces, employee benefits programs, health care, and in places of public accommodation, because when identity is a process then there must be processors.

Conclusion: *Navigating Individual Variation and Systemic Disadvantage*

When the context is the legal determination of functionality, emphasizing individualized assessments of disabled workers touches off powers of management within the organizations that the law regulates. Managed individualism may be the new legal individualism. Its main function is to preserve the functionalist account of what people deserve, even in the face of compelling group-based subordination and even where there is some political consensus that redistributions or accommodations are acceptable. Now the Supreme Court is strictly monitoring the boundaries of the protected category "disabled," *and* individual disabled people find their functioning "socially constructed"—through organizational practices and personal interactions—but without a sustained critique or shared agreement about the power dynamics of the workplace that delineate the functional from the dysfunctional. I intimated at the start of this essay that medicalization has often secured sympathy, of a certain pat-on-the-head sort, from the dominant culture. (Though certainly not always. Eugenics campaigns and the construction of homosexuality as pathology certainly stand as counter-examples to even the patronizing version of medicalized sympathy.)

Might we secure medicalization for fat citizens, but without a critique of the politics of disgust? Feelings of disgust often track delineations of subordinated groups, and disgust plays an important role in the law.[43] Tobin Siebers's analysis of disability and the culture wars reminds us that oppression "often takes the form of an aesthetic judgment, though a warped one, about [minority groups members'] bodies and the emotions elicited by them."[44] Paul Campos argues that disgust over fat people, especially over images like fat poor Mexican American women going into Wal-Mart, shows that they are the new target for an old process by which elites maintain their feelings of superiority over the lower classes.[45] Disability politics would seem to answer this disgust by calling forth discrete individuals with highly variable conditions and trying to talk about their rights to full participation in society. I noted earlier that if fat activists want political recognition of fat oppression, accommodations in the public sphere, and recognition in the law, they are faced with a dilemma. I argued that identification as disabled is the current route to accommodations, but also that such recognition may undercut the political solidarity they will need to forge a more positive group identity. If Campos is right at all about the operations of a large-scale politics of disgust that serves the interests of many elites, it is going to take a lot of work to generate this positive group identity for fatness no matter how strictly or contingently it is constituted. In addition, fatness will confront a new version of medicalization, in which pharmaceutical companies and their direct-to-consumer advertising transform all kinds of ordinary problems into medical diagnoses that require a pill ("Ask your doctor about . . .").[46] There are currently several weight-loss drugs either on the market or in development, and we will almost certainly see a concerted effort to promote this medicalized treatment of fatness. What fat identity looks like in the future, including what kinds of discourses and communities are possible for it (disgust, medicalized support group dialogues, pity?) is fairly undetermined right now, but I cannot imagine that it will evade the new medicalization.

The challenge, after all, is to find a politically appealing argument about why fat people should be protected from the negative consequences of being fat. If functional individualism will not do as a proposal because it leaves out too many differently functioning people, then the accommodationist features of disability laws seem appealing. (After all, none of the weight loss drugs have been able to safely bring about much weight loss, so even with medicalization by pharmaceuticals, there will likely still be plenty of fat people.) One particularly promising example is San Francisco's weight and height antidiscrimination ordinance, which blends the best of non-discrimination and disability accommodations without any need to claim a medicalized impairment. There does not have to be anything wrong with a fat person; she simply has a right to insist on access and equal treatment as a member of a named category. It exemplifies the common sense notion that accommodations must be part of equality when people differ in ways that cannot be ignored. (Imagine the ADA if everyone who interpreted and implemented it had used a social model of disability all along.) The Human Rights Commission Compliance Guidelines require reasonable accommodations in both employment and public accommodations, and give as examples larger seating in movie theaters, steps and handrails on swimming pools, and properly fitting hospital gowns, blood pressure cuffs, and uniforms.[47] The ordinance also prohibits harassment and covers housing discrimination as well. The enforcement powers are limited to mediation, however. The ordinance does not create identity through a managerial process, but rather constructs fat identity as simply different, and weaves accommodation requirements into the basic notion of non-discrimination.

How might producing fat people as disabled actually work, at least for everyone else who does not reside in San Francisco? Fat workers may be easier to accommodate under the ADA regime than workers with other kinds of disabilities, since they may only need armless chairs. Public accommodations may be as simple as creating a few larger-sized seats in airplanes, buses, and theaters, for instance. These accommodations are so obvious that they may not require much interaction and scrutiny. If obesity is considered a disease and if treatment compliance were also protected, workers would require time during the day for exercise and availability of lower-calorie food in cafeterias. Businesses may happily go along with such requirements because they are not very expensive (in the case of armless chairs), and they may please everyone, not just fat employees (in the case of better food and exercise time). We already know from the previous chapter that promoting a healthy lifestyle among employees is in a company's best interests because of the legal requirements to treat every person in the employee health plan the same regardless of actuarial risk. (Interestingly, we also know that such policies will likely improve employee health but will not bring about significant weight loss.) If the process goes something like this, then one version of fat identity will be produced in a way that undercuts the individualism I have criticized here. Their accommodations may be simple and common enough to undercut the relentless drumbeat of individual variation in disability law. The powerlessness of an individual in the interactive process would be assisted by the sheer obviousness (and non-individualized nature) of the accommodation. Emphasizing how a few simple changes in work space can provide equal opportunity will make the hegemony of thinness more and more untenable.

This story has a happy ending, in which recognizing fatness as a disability is transformative for disability law as I've critically described it. But fatness as disability might turn out to be part of managerial individualism rather than a challenge to it. After all, fatness varies widely by degree as well as by its impact on health and mobility. If talking about fatness always begins with a nod to the infinite variation of fatness in different people's lives, then it is on the same trajectory as other disabilities. This is a largely inescapable bind: I have to concede that there is indeed individual variation in the effects of a disability, but then I lose the critical force needed to describe group-level inequalities and give over each unique individual to managerial processes. Determining access to rights, therefore, will require scrutinizing individual bodies to determine where they will fit and what they can do. Fat also carries different meanings in intersections with race, ethnicity, gender, and sexuality, and these variations will make it difficult to describe uniform fat experiences with discrimination. And there is no reason to think that fat employees will not also be unruly and uncooperative in the interactive process. They may be loath to take on the label of disabled and to claim rights in a way that is recognizable to the employer, and if they do, they will face all the challenges of the power imbalance.[48]

Fat personhood in the law will be a fascinating site for study for years to come, and we will see a developing example of how a group of people come to be seen as deserving, on what terms, and by what methods. The ADA was supposed to mean a lot of things for a new approach to difference in the law: perhaps that people with disabilities were a discrete and insular minority, or perhaps that disability is a socially constructed idea that can be unmade through sympathetic accommodations. People with disabilities certainly did not turn out to be legally discrete in the sense of readily identifiable, marked, or set apart. Who is disabled as a matter of law is anything but clear. Nor does insularity play any part in legally defining disability. Where law gives up clear standards, it must have process instead. What disability laws actually come to mean for disabled personhood—and whether fat personhood will be interpellated as disability—can be understood through the social practices they establish.

Conclusion

What Is Worth Wanting in American Antidiscrimination Law?

The challenge of difference is to know which features of persons matter for justice and in what ways they matter. Antidiscrimination law in the contemporary United States offers a structure for making sense of difference: listing categories and greatly restricting reliance on them for decision making about what persons deserve. These lists of traits tell us which differences are likely to attract unjust treatment, but simultaneously should not matter for measuring a person's merit or desert. I have proposed in this book, however, that we should think of antidiscrimination laws not as a set of categories and instructions about how to think (or not to think) about difference, but as a complex and interwoven set of logics of personhood through which we learn to classify and interpret difference in the first place and which then determine what just treatment can look like. Logics of personhood are prior to any legal conclusion that some trait of difference is relevant, and they supply the most basic and pervasive discourses for talking about it. We can tell that logics of personhood are prior to political and legal outcomes because when one logic—say, functional individualism—outlives its usefulness or starts to look unjust, we simply bump about and revise our premises about persons, difference, and merit and come up with something else. The promise and limits of antidiscrimination law, therefore, are not found in the lists of protected traits (or what is missing from them), but rather in the ways that these polyvocal logics of personhood entice us to explain each other. They are the commonplace and widely accessible starting points of debates about what antidiscrimination protections should be and for whom. I have argued that the logics we use to explain each other are more plentiful than we may have first thought, but also that they each have very distinct boundaries beyond which they have trouble imagining difference in new ways.

Law is not, then, a closed professional field or a set of discrete doctrines, but rather a place of cultural convergence that, with its unique
powers and rigidities, enacts and resolves disputes among competing
logics of personhood. It is highly porous; terms and priorities from
other domains such as business and medicine seep in continuously. We
should think of the legal field as one site at which strongly salient ideas
and terms—diversity, stereotyping—are maintained and made useful
for resolving disputes. Thinking of antidiscrimination terms this way
helps us to see why "stereotyping" and "diversity" seem able to do so
much work in certain cases but without maintaining a consistent and
clear meaning. Their incoherence is not a defect; it is what makes them
useful. Our preference for individualized processes over bureaucratically
defined lists fits well in this picture of law, and it also sits well with the
American political project of decentralization, variation, and dispersion
in government.

Much of the description I've given here of the logics of personhood
we have to work with has stressed their limitations and inadequacy.
Functional individualism turned out to be useful for deflecting the most
bigoted responses to difference, such as ones that denied a fat person
even the opportunity to show she could drive a bus as well as anyone
else. It would be naïve to underestimate how many of our most narrow-
minded preconceptions could be dismissed with functional individualism alone; surely it can do a lot of good on behalf of a lot of folks. But
if antidiscrimination law limits its goals to defending functional individualism, it cannot address the possibility that norms of functioning
themselves are biased or that distributions in society (of goods like education and training, for example) are unfairly skewed so that some persons seem dysfunctional at the high-stakes moment when abilities are
assessed. Functional individualism suffers from whatever limitations are
imposed in defining functioning in the first place, and yet it also ob-
scures and naturalizes those limitations.

As a foil to functional individualism, embedded personhood and the
normative stereotypes that describe it could only look like prejudice,
except when a trait was not considered protected at all. Then antidiscrimination law stood back and let plaintiffs like Ms. Marks, the fat
telemarketer who wanted to do face-to-face sales, get mired down in
others' distaste. Embedded personhood, rather than richly describing a
meaningful self, becomes everything about a person that is not her bare

functional capacities, and thus irrelevant to the law (while remaining part of everyday judgments). I argued in chapter 1 that fat plaintiffs get bounced back and forth between being functional individuals in job contexts constructed for thinner bodies, or they are understood to be mired down in fatness and then dismissed from coverage in much antidiscrimination law. The result was unsatisfying because we never really had to challenge ourselves about what fatness means as an axis of difference: either it wasn't allowed to mean anything or it meant whatever the employer wanted it to mean. One could certainly dispute that laws should try to change meanings of traits of difference in the first place, but if we are going to have antidiscrimination laws in a democratic society, they must be centrally about altering stigmatized meanings of traits and they ought to do so forthrightly and richly, in a politically accountable way. As I argued again in chapter 3, this unsatisfying and incoherent path is not just laid out for traits that are peripheral to antidiscrimination law: gender discrimination is also decipherable through the competing logics of functional individualism, in which we're supposed to ignore gender, and embedded personhood, in which gender semiotics and appearance are deeply meaningful. It is no coincidence that "sex" in Title VII got there in a silly way and then had no story to go with it about why exactly sex discrimination was a bad thing. Because of the way that these two logics hold one another at a distance, judges could not talk about transgender identities in the law as something significant on their own terms, instead converting Jimmie Smith into a man who just started to look like a woman at work one day. Sometimes such instability can be productive, and of course lawmaking is often messy, but we should not fool ourselves that we have answered any difficult questions about the meaning of difference when we add a new trait to the law. The process may just be starting.

The blame-shifting logic of personhood was able to transform the presuppositions of functional individualism by querying the norms of functioning itself. As I argued in chapter 2, legacies of state-sponsored racial discrimination yielded fertile grounds for developing an account of persons as produced in part by structural inequalities rather than as functional individuals. Disability rights law also rests on this same critical impulse. Difference in the sense of deviation from the norm may not be personal failure, lack, or incapacity; it may be a reminder of how the world still needs to be refashioned. Interestingly, those antidiscrimination measures that have expressed a blame-shifting logic, such as disparate impact discrimination, affirmative action, or ADA accommodations, have also been the least effective in terms of plaintiffs' win rates. Invoking histories of discrimination to blame others is also politically unpopular, to say the least, particularly for race-conscious affirmative action-type policies or welfare policies with an explicitly redistributive bent. Characterizing people with disabilities as needy is a softer way of justifying redistributions that hold wider appeal, since if we are lucky to live long enough we will all experience disability. Even when the blame-shifting logic was embraced for racial identity in the passage of the 1964 Civil Rights Act, it was crucial that the problem was conceptualized as a straitjacket in which "the Negro" had been confined. So while some use of blame-shifting logic is necessary to push past functional individualism, we have yet to conceptualize it politically or legally as a complex interaction rather than as a straitjacket inhibiting people who are otherwise not different from the norm (such that, once it is removed, the problem has been addressed). If antidiscrimination law works as I say it does—as a site and language for general ideas with shifting meanings (not strongly articulated goals) to become easily absorbed into preexisting power relations, dissolving disputes without radical change—then blame-shifting logic seems extremely unlikely to sustain any program of redistributions and power sharing.

The deflection of affirmative action into diversity management is a perfect example. Diversity is cosmopolitanism and tolerance without a critique of power relations. The blame-shifting logic would have supplied a reason why, for example, positions of power and university spots should not be filled with all white people or all men. But without a sense that some persons have been enriched at the expense of others (or some similar formulation), it becomes harder to say why diversity is necessarily a good thing. It can easily become a nagging sense of aesthetic propriety ("We couldn't have a panel of all white males at the event because that would look bad, so let's invite a woman/minority/minority woman"), easily lampooned by conservatives. The diversity rationale, untethered from any concern with specifically historically burdened identities, has lost any means of distinguishing between worthwhile forms of diversity and silly, counter-productive, or simply less meaningful or apolitical ones. Perhaps it is useful because it really does help people work together to solve problems. Research showing that diverse groups solve problems better than homogeneous groups do is certainly promising, but it does not have any necessary link to injustice. On that defense of diversity, racial diversity is desirable insofar as it contributes to problem solving, but other much less politically salient variations (like mixing logicians with poets) may contribute just as much or more to the group dynamics. Again, such uses of diversity constitute admirable goals and worthwhile structures for group interactions, but they cannot sustain the kind of politics that we need to grapple with intransigent inequalities and the agonies of *not* understanding one another, of *not* arriving at the best answer in group interactions, and of never interacting *at all.*

Davina Cooper's analysis of inequality wrestles with the question of smokers as an oppressed group—by what account can we distinguish them from other groups, if we grant that they are scorned, segregated, and in some sense oppressed?[1] Cooper concludes that we must watch for organizing principles of inequality that distinguish some groups such as smokers, who are merely burdened and restricted, from other groups given gender or racial identities that drive cultural norms. We simply wouldn't talk about cultural practices being "smoked" in the same way we say some are "gendered," she quite rightly points out.[2] This kind of differentiation, and, more importantly, the *grounds* for such differentiations, has not yet appeared in our law's discussion of the value of diversity. It is as if everyone is assuming that of course we mean the usual suspects when we talk about diversity (more blacks, Latinos, and sometimes white women or low-income whites and Asians), but there is no longer any justification for that presumption. The idea that people need to learn from those who are different from themselves is a much richer idea well grounded in the realities of contemporary life, but it is so expansive (What kind of difference? Any difference?) that it should be regarded as a necessary part of a complete education on its own, but not necessarily tied to addressing unequal opportunities.

When, under diversity management, identity is just another feature of the functional person, there may still be reason to offer increased opportunities to members of minority groups. This understanding is very flattering to identity partisans because it roots educational and organization success on their participation. As Elizabeth Anderson has argued, it also includes some drive to integrate.[3] But its justification contains a deep tension. If identities are to be included because they are enhancement to functional personhood, then insofar as they are obstructionist, withdrawn, or unwilling to participate in the process of sharing in others' identities, then they lose their reason for being included. As many critics of identity politics have pointed out, however, identity-based attachments often function in exactly those ways. Identities fit into the diversity rationale only if they give themselves up, becoming a distant attachment to personhood that is contingent and negotiable with others. Liberals who insist that the best way to think of our identities is as fully considered, voluntarily adopted, somewhat contingent features of the self will be pleased. But it may be hard to consider the contingency of one's identity if others refuse to do so: the police officer who pulls over the black man in the nice car, for instance. In such a case, the driver's identity is being done *to* him. Emphasizing identity as individualized and process-produced makes it seem as though everyone has the same kind of control over what his or her identity will mean.

Within a framework focused upon understanding the person as a font of capacities that may be hindered or promoted in social life, there are more possibilities than just promoting functional individualism, engaging in blame-shifting, or diversifying. Capacities can be managed and thereby produced by a legally compelled set of interactions within institutions such as the workplace. Disability law monitors the boundaries of the category "disabled" by monitoring those interactions using a logic of personhood I called managerial individualism. I argued in chapter 5 that activists, scholars, and judges share an overlapping consensus that disablement is a highly variable, individualized, unstable category that depends upon physical spaces and norms of workplace functioning. The Supreme Court's role has been to restrict the category of "disabled" and to maintain its indeterminacy by borrowing heavily from logics of governance outside the civil rights context, namely the regulation of risk (the "direct threat" exception) and the techniques of human resource management (the "interactive process" to find an accommodation). It would be wrong to characterize these processes as the same as the outcome of successful disparate impact litigation, where the identity group to which the plaintiff belongs is simply granted resources, but not refashioned. If late modernity deals in governmentality rather than in protecting the sovereign individual, the disabled worker is its exemplary new subject. Civil rights laws were always administered in discrete contexts and within networks of power relations, but with the ADA we saw legal categories and requirements themselves building in a kind of indeterminacy that requires management of the person in a newly refined way.

I have also suggested that the legal defense against actuarial person-hood uses this same tool of individualization in many cases, which is not really able to address the group-level risk management, medicalization, or normalization produced by an actuarial approach. Once again, antidiscrimination law has a defense of the person available that shuttles our thinking off into the land of hypothetical variation of the individual (perhaps generally this disease is dangerous, but one cannot assume that this particular person will infect the schoolchildren). This way of thinking certainly can help preserve the plaintiff's dignity and prevent decision makers from behaving irrationally against the tide of medical evidence. Since many fat advocates interpret medical data to suggest that being fat per se is not unhealthy, perhaps the individualization and evidence-based critique of panic will be helpful. But what actuarial techniques offer are ways of governing populations through validly generalizable propositions about persons' health, behaviors, attitudes, life spans, and so on. Simply to dispute these generalizations plaintiff by plaintiff is to ignore the power and range of actuarial personhood, not to mention fatally ill-suited to our time.

It is fair then to ask, how *should* we try to think about difference in antidiscrimination law? My goal throughout the book has been to show how logics of personhood shape, extend, and limit our understandings of what persons deserve from antidiscrimination law and why. If the reader can no longer utter the phrase, "Well, as long as she can do the job" without pausing to consider her use of functional individualism and its effects, I am satisfied. In other words, I am primarily interested in making the seemingly obvious ways we think about difference more complicated and important to ourselves. My goal has not been to overthrow these understandings of difference and replace them, but to unsettle them and make living with them less automatic, less comfortable. But while normative prescription has not been the first aim of this book, it has surely crept in already and it is helpful to embrace it forthrightly at this point. The ways of talking about persons I've discussed here are logics fixed within both legal culture and ordinary life, but they are not eternal and unchangeable. They often contradict each other. They are inflected with a conservative political mood in the country these days, but that mood will also change with time. In these speculations that follow, I set myself the requirement to remain within the bounds of the kind of discursive changes that are possible given past evidence about the range of possibility.

Returning to Our Thought Experiment

At the beginning of this book I proposed that the usefulness of my interventions might be measured by whether they have helped the reader to work her way through the stakes of a thought experiment. I asked the reader to imagine that she is an advocate for a group that currently receives no legal recognition or protection. She wants to use both law and political rhetoric to gain the best kind of legal identity. I've used fat citizens as the group to imagine protecting throughout this book, but the analysis is portable. How should she talk about the persons she wants to defend? I have argued that the descriptions in American law of personhood and identity are multifarious, complex, and responsive to several conflicting intuitions. What among them would be worth wanting? We've seen the options play themselves out to their limits. In making a plea for some group or individual, one could: (1) argue that the group members can function just as well as everyone else and that their defining trait should be ignored in all cases; (2) acknowledge that statistical stereotypes about the group are often empirically true, but that they should not burden this particular individual plaintiff; (3) concede that the group members function differently or appear differently from the norm and insist that the standards being used are not neutral, but rather constructed in favor of the dominant group to naturalize and maintain its power; (4) analogize them to African Americans and stress historical patterns of exclusion, segregation, and subordination (similar to the previous blame-shifting argument but including the explicit analogy); and (5) name their difference "diversity" and describe it as an enriching and unique feature of some individuals that can be usefully integrated into the goal-oriented activities of groups.

Each option, as we saw, has its own set of difficulties in implementation, implications, or outcome. The strategies were not the same as logics of personhood, though they are tightly intertwined. It might seem that trait-blindness is our strongest formulation of equality (and the most necessary to make gains for one's group). Stressing that one functions the same as others means that there is no reason for accommodations if one turns out to be different. It also strips one's difference of much richly embedded experience, since the reason to ignore it is that it has no meaning in that context. Gaining accommodations means accepting difference (which can be stigmatizing) and having one's functioning organizationally managed under conditions of unequal power.

"Like-race" arguments only work for groups who can squeeze themselves into the analogy and keep the focus of the debate on the terms of the analogy and the group's traits. Even "women" have not convincingly made the analogy, and introduced intersectional stresses on political coalitions while doing so. The touchstone of the analogy for groups like fat people or gay, lesbian, bisexual, or trans people is immutability, but that argument turns out either to beg the question or to solidify and medicalize the identity. Opponents characterize the trait as deviance and bad character, and point out that LGBT people and fat people were never enslaved by our government. Inevitably, some African Americans find the analogizing offensive (as Jews often do, in the case of Holocaust analogies), and their annoyance is easy fodder for opponents to further denigrate the would-be protected groups. Thus, the politics of analogy-making lacks good footholds for new groups to describe their own stories. Maybe history is not so important, if oppression exists in the present. Fatness, for example, has had many cultural meanings in different times and places, but there is no argument that in our time and place it is heavily stigmatized (even relatively small amounts of it). Both body size and sexuality can change over time, though many people experience them as unchangeable. They are both linked to behaviors and "lifestyles," though that does not dictate that fat people and LBGT people are second class citizens. I would argue that the bumpy parts of these "like-race" analogies help form and promote opponents' arguments, and thus the politics of the analogy has done more harm than good. Advocates should resist invoking explicit comparisons to other groups, or at least do so only in carefully measured ways and in contexts that permit that nuance to be appreciated.

The critique that the dominant group's norms are not neutral, but rather constructed to maintain their power and to ensure dysfunction in the out-groups is critical for our would-be protected group. We saw in chapter 3 that our legal regime at one time absorbed this critique, prompted by the salience of school segregation and African American male disenfranchisement and unrest. This impulse brought disparate impact discrimination and affirmative action-type solutions. These solutions have largely been eclipsed by a racial individualism that understands identity to be a contingent feature of functional personhood, however. I argued that these were the strongest modifications to the idea of functional personhood, and although the critique has been largely blunted by the conservative turn in American politics over the last several decades, we ought not forget that it has worked a time or two. Advocates should invoke rich descriptions of the ways that their group's functional capacities have been structurally undermined, all the while resisting the push to individualize failures to measure up.

Obviously one's advocacy in our thought experiment would turn on exactly what kind of subordination the group encounters. I'm also assuming that the group can realistically be described as a group, even though doing so will efface some internal differences. Using conflicting accounts of one's personhood all at once can help ease the totalizing effects of calling them a social group, however. Their subordination is likely to be multi-dimensional, and since there is no requirement of consistency in either law or politics, the group would be well served by the use of many forms of defense. Legal battles occur case-by-case, plaintiff-by-plaintiff, so it would be convenient to tailor each case to the plaintiff's needs and abilities. Where the group's functional capacity is maligned, respond that they can function just as well as anyone else. Plaintiffs like Mary Nedder or Arazella Manuel, who do not need accommodations, are well served by "regarded as disabled" claims under the ADA. Able-bodied fat employees should use this ADA prong just as it is, and advocates for transgendered people should urge Congress to remove the exclusion of trans people from the ADA. If it were not for that amendment to the ADA, trans people could have leveraged their medicalization into antidiscrimination protections, while at the same time working to establish themselves as just another variation in human identity. And since many people who encounter a trans employee may assume they have a mental disability, "regarded as" lawsuits would also be highly effective.

The rest of the ADA should be amended to make it easier to qualify as legally disabled, perhaps by replacing the medical impairment and major life activity prongs with a more flexible test about the ways the plaintiff functions differently from the norm regardless of the cause. Retaining a requirement of qualification for the job plus the undue burden defense would protect employers sufficiently. Using both parts of the ADA (real disability versus perceived disability) generates conflict about whether some condition really is a disability, and this is a very good thing. Having both legal options advances individualism in a helpful way (because it allows for variation in whether or not the condition is actually disabling or just stigmatizing), and it would help reinforce the multiple ways that functioning differently can block people's life plans.

A broader and less medicalized ADA would shift the blame without defining what disability is for everyone, but also without giving in to a fetishistic individualism undone by managerial prerogatives. The trick would be to proliferate the strategies that rely on a conception of the group as coherent and stigmatized over time and not let them be drowned out by the relentless individualism that now dominates discourses of disability, diversity, and stereotyping. One would not have to revert to simplistic or essentialist group politics, however, and drawing on multiple logics would keep any one account of the group from solidifying too much.

Where the plaintiff does indeed function differently, it would be helpful to establish ADA coverage and then to change the power dynamics of the interactive process. The duty to avoid breakdown should fall squarely on the employer rather than the employee to compensate for the power differential. In many cases, the employee is simply not in a position to know what accommodations might be available, such as job transfer, and the law ought to be set up so that the more powerful and knowledgeable party bears the most responsibility. Standards of proper accommodation and suggested *a priori* reasonable solutions could be widely promulgated and advertised, easing the individualistic bent of the process. Some basic and commonly used accommodations—armless chairs, extra recovery time, and job preservation after sex reassignment surgery—could be regarded as per se reasonable accommodations, provided whether or not the employee cooperates in exactly the right way. We could introduce a disparate impact-type option under the ADA, so that if one plaintiff identifies a practice or structural feature that has the effect of keeping disabled people out of the job generally, she could sue to change the situation in addition to receiving her own particular accommodation. Greater empowerment and funding for the Equal Employment Opportunity Commission (EEOC) could ease the burdens on plaintiffs to activate the adversarial legal system if EEOC lawyers had more powers to monitor workplaces and demand compliance. Some kind of national health insurance program would remove the headache for employers of monitoring workers' health, which right now increases their vigilance against disability and leaves even middle-class employees highly vulnerable to the loss of job and health coverage. After all, most ADA cases are about a newly disabled employee trying to keep her job, not about bringing unemployed disabled people into new jobs (as lawmakers originally envisioned). These policy changes would reconstruct disability accommodations as more structural and less individualistic, since I have argued that managerial individualism is not the kind of individualism worth wanting. We should reconfigure legal representations of individualism so that they do not excuse massive power imbalances between people and institutions and so they do not advance an unrealistic exceptionalism that diverts attention from structural inequalities.

So to defend the difference of fatness in ordinary conversation, one could begin by stressing all the things that fat people can do just as well as everyone else. Then, without making a "like race" analogy, one could talk about how weight loss for the vast majority of people just isn't possible and how it would be better to accept people's bodies as they are. Adding accounts of how much fat hatred there is in our society and reminding the interlocutor that it affects everyone including the anxious thinner people trying to maintain their privileged status would help promote a positive vision of a world in which we devote our attentions to the joys of our bodies rather than to their discipline. Without invoking a medicalized notion of obesity, one could advocate for armless chairs and bigger seats in public spaces on the grounds that fat people should not be humiliated and excluded from the opportunities other people enjoy. In response to the actuarial objection that fat people are risky and cost a lot of money, one could initially sidestep individualization by pointing out that insurance is for sharing risk among us all because we cannot really know what might befall us. Then one could also add that plenty of individual fat people live a long time. Of course all these arguments fall back on logics of personhood I've spilled much ink to critique. But they are also largely inescapable: that is our situation. As a matter of law, if fatness were included in Title VII as well as considered a disability (in this more social way I've described), then all the legal tools to call upon functional individualism or blame-shifting would be available. Perhaps the unique status of fat as an identity—changeable but only with great difficulty, linked to behaviors sometimes but sometimes not, heritable in most cases but not all, the subject of moral panic as well as scientific study, sexualized and racialized in contingent ways —could help us to revisit the other categories of antidiscrimination law that we presume we already understand. I would not be opposed to invoking fatness as diversity or turning to managerial techniques in response to individual circumstances as long as those are not the only ways of talking and governing persons and as long as we remain vigilant about the effects of relentless individualism there.

Because now we understand first, that law frames personhood using several powerful but multifarious logics of interpretation, and second, that no single logic has been able to secure a consistent set of legal outcomes, we can see that it is strategically superior to defend and to prop up legal identities drawing on as many logics and strategies as possible, and to have descriptions of oneself ready and waiting when new opportunities arise. As Janet Halley observes about being caught in double binds in arguing for gay rights, it is sometimes best "not to ensure the ascendancy of one model or the other, but to inhabit their cross-cutting vulnerabilities more consciously."[4] "Inhabiting cross-cutting vulnerabilities more consciously" is hardly a call to the barricades. But we must remember that in a rights-driven, contentious culture such as ours, consistency is not nearly as important as imagination.

Notes

1. By antidiscrimination I primarily mean statutes that purport to ban discrimination in employment, housing, access to public services, and so on. This is not a book about constitutional principles, though many of the same issues will be treated. I focus mostly on employment discrimination here because the employment relationship is one of the more heavily regulated in our society, and it is the focus of much of what we call antidiscrimination law.

2. I prefer to use the terms "fat" and "fatness" more often than "obese" or "obesity" because I want to analyze the medicalized account of fat as a health affliction, not to assume it. I will use "trans" or "transgender" to refer to the broad category of people who do not understand themselves to fit well into their sex as assigned at birth, and who may or may not make use of surgery or hormone therapies to transition physically to the opposite sex. "Transsexual" is the narrower and more medicalized term for a person who has sought treatment for gender dysphoria and has made or is seeking to make a full physical and social transition to the other sex.

3. Voters could of course use the referendum process, where available, to add new traits to civil rights laws. More frequently, however, direct democracy takes away minority rights rather than adds to them. An obvious example are the successes of anti-gay-marriage ballot initiatives across the country, but these measures are just the current version of general voter antipathy. Barbara S. Gamble, "Putting Civil Rights to a Popular Vote," *American Journal of Political Science* 41 (1997).

4. Rogers Smith, "Political Jurisprudence, the 'New Institutionalism,' and the Future of Public Law," *American Political Science Review* 82 (1988): 91.

5. The insistence that the formal law and our ordinary ways of talking about it coexist is crucial to my approach. Law's formal pronouncements in case law and statutes are the realm of analysis because they allow me to show the dynamic exchange between ordinary sentiments and the law. "The most prominent feature of the judicial opinion," James Boyd White notes, "is that it is not an isolated exercise of power but part of a continuing and collective process of conversation and judgment." We do not have to take law's formal terms for

granted even as we take the texts seriously, as he shows. "Cases are often not neatly packaged in the categories established by legislative or judicial rules," according to White, "but exhibit surprising configurations of their own, bringing to the surface hitherto unseen tensions and contradictions in our social life and culture." James Boyd White, *When Words Lose Their Meaning: Constitutions and Reconstitutions of Language, Character, and Community* (Chicago: University of Chicago Press, 1984), 264–265.

6. Wendy Brown, *States of Injury: Power and Freedom in Late Modernity* (Princeton, N.J.: Princeton University Press, 1995).

7. Washington, D.C., San Francisco, and the state of Michigan have added weight or body size to their list of legally protected traits. Mich. Comp. Laws Ann. 37.2202(1)(a) (West Supp. 2001); Santa Cruz, Cal., Mun. Code 9.83.010 (1995); San Francisco, Cal., Compliance Guidelines to Prohibit Weight and Height Discrimination (July 26, 2001); D.C. Code Ann. 2-1401.01 (2001). The Massachusetts State Legislature is currently considering a bill to add height and weight to the state's civil rights law, and a hearing is expected in the fall of 2007. Some similarly liberal jurisdictions have added gender identity or gender expression to statutes and the Sixth Circuit includes transsexualism under the federal ban on sex discrimination in employment. Additionally, dozens of colleges and universities have added transgender non-discrimination clauses in recent years. See the continually updated website of the Transgender Law and Policy Institute for a complete list. Transgender Law and Policy Institute, http://www.transgenderlaw.org/.

8. Austin Sarat and Thomas R. Kearns, Editorial Introduction, in *Identities, Politics, and Rights,* ed. Austin Sarat and Thomas R. Kearns (Ann Arbor: University of Michigan Press, 1995), 3.

9. Lee Abbott, "People Should Not Judge Others on Their Looks," *Providence Journal,* Oct. 22, 1992, F2.

10. Steven Greenhouse, "Overweight, but Ready to Fight; Obese People Are Taking Their Bias Claims to Court," New York Region Section, *The New York Times,* August 4, 2003, B1.

11. Robert Post, with K. Anthony Appiah, Judith Butler, Thomas C. Grey, and Reva B. Siegel, *Prejudicial Appearances: The Logic of American Antidiscrimination Law* (Durham, N.C.: Duke University Press, 2001). Functional individualism is very close to what Post calls the "dominant conception" of American antidiscrimination law. Antidiscrimination law, he observes, sets itself the goal of "neutraliz[ing] widespread forms of prejudice that pervasively disadvantage persons based on inaccurate judgments about their worth or capacities." Ibid.,10. But this of course depends upon an understanding of the person as a "presocial individual" endowed with " 'context-free' functional capacities." Ibid., 30. That is, once law directs decision makers' attention away from salient traits of appearance such as gender or race, then the picture of justice that is left

is a bare, neutral measurement of true ability, undistorted by prejudices. Post discusses the practice in orchestra auditions of having men and women play behind a screen so that judges cannot tell who is who, even providing rugs for them to walk on so that the weight of their footsteps cannot give them away, and gender stereotypes don't interfere with choosing the best violin players. In this book I take Post's dominant conception and add all the other logics of personhood that also contribute to making contemporary antidiscrimination law what it is, and also insist that other logics like managerial personhood and actuarial personhood are actually much more dominant in the law than doctrine would suggest.

12. *Equal Employment Opportunity Commission v. Texas Bus Lines*, 923 F.Supp. 965 (S.D.TX 1996), 971.

13. *McDermott v. Xerox Corp.*, 102 A.D.2d 543 (1984), 544.

14. Ibid., 545.

15. *Marks v. National Communications Association, Inc.*, 72 F.Supp. 2d (S.D.N.Y. 1999), 322, 327.

16. Ibid., 326.

17. Her theory was a "sex plus" discrimination claim, alleging that the company did not promote fat women. Sex plus claims tie together some trait that is covered under Title VII with others that are not, but still may not be used to treat men and women differently. So if the company had indeed promoted fat men but not fat women, Ms. Marks would have had a viable claim. But since there were no fat salespeople at all, and in fact the company asserted that it did not want salespeople if they were fat, regardless of gender, there was no sex plus claim.

18. Personal injury law includes the duty to mitigate the effects of an injury. When a fat person is hurt in a slip-and-fall case, doctors order weight loss as part of the healing process, and often the patient does not lose much weight. The defendant then argues that the failure to mitigate (by not sticking to the diet) absolves him of tort liability. The point is that the juries in these cases simply have to decide whether the plaintiff acted reasonably in fulfilling his duty to mitigate, and that will depend upon their understandings of the embedded person.

19. The case is *Griggs v. Duke Power*, 401 U.S. 424 (1971), establishing the Title VII disparate impact theory of discrimination. A Democratic Congress later wrote (and reenforced) the disparate impact theory into statutory law in the Civil Rights Act of 1991 after a more conservative Supreme Court narrowed its application in the 1989 term. Civil Rights Act of 1991 §105, 42 U.S.C.A. § 2000e-2(k)(1) (West Supp. 1992).

20. Richard Allen Epstein, *Forbidden Grounds: The Case against Employment Discrimination Laws* (Cambridge, Mass.: Harvard University Press, 1992).

21. Erin Kelly and Frank Dobbin, "How Affirmative Action Became Diver-

sity Management: Employer Response to Antidiscrimination Law, 1961 to 1996," *American Behavioral Scientist* 41 (1998).

22. Lauren B. Edelman, Sally Riggs Fuller, and Iona Mara-Drita, "Diversity Rhetoric and the Managerialization of Law," *The American Journal of Sociology* 106 (2001); David B. Wilkins, "From 'Separate Is Inherently Unequal' to 'Diversity Is Good for Business': The Rise of Market-Based Diversity Arguments and the Fate of the Black Corporate Bar," *Harvard Law Review* 117 (2004).

23. Jacqueline A. Gilbert, Bette Ann Stead, and John M. Ivancevich, "Diversity Management: A New Organizational Paradigm," *Journal of Business Ethics* 21 (1999); Avery Gordon, "The Work of Corporate Culture: Diversity Management," *Social Text* 13 (1995). Education researchers set to work identifying the ways that diversity contributes to learning, which was the original idea behind Justice Lewis Powell's defense of it in the *Bakke* case. Sylvia Hurtado et al., "College Environments, Diversity, and Student Learning," *Higher Education: Handbook of Theory and Research* 18 (2003); Patricia Gurin et al., "How Does Racial/Ethnic Diversity Promote Education?" *The Western Journal of Black Studies* 27 (2003).

24. John David Skrentny, *The Minority Rights Revolution* (Cambridge, Mass.: Harvard University Press, 2002).

25. Post, *Prejudicial Appearances*, 39.

26. *Jespersen v. Harrah's*, U.S. App. LEXIS 9307 (9th Cir. 2006).

27. *United States v. Virginia*, 528 U.S. 515 (1996), 533.

28. K. Anthony Appiah, "Stereotypes and the Shaping of Identity," in *Prejudicial Appearances: The Logic of American Antidiscrimination Law*, Robert Post et al. (Durham, N.C.: Duke University Press, 2001), 63–65.

29. Ibid., 64.

30. Jonathan Simon, "The Ideological Effects of Actuarial Practices," *Law & Society Review* 22 (1988).

31. Nikolas Rose, "The Politics of Life Itself," *Theory, Culture & Society* 18 (2001); Nikolas Rose, *Inventing Our Selves: Psychology, Power, and Personhood* (New York: Cambridge University Press, 1996).

32. *School Board of Nassau County v. Arline*, 480 U.S. 273 (1987), 276.

33. Ibid., 285 (emphasis in original).

34. *Los Angeles Department of Water and Power v. Manhart*, 435 U.S. 702 (1978), 704.

35. Ibid., 707–708.

36. Ibid., 710.

37. Americans with Disabilities Act, 42 U.S.C. § 12101. The ADA includes several Titles addressing different societal obstacles for people with disabilities. Title I prohibits employment discrimination, Title II prohibits discrimination in access to governmental programs, and Title III provides for access to public

buildings. The ADA expanded upon and greatly relied upon its predecessor, Section 504 of the Rehabilitation Act of 1973.

38. *Carter v. Northwest Airlines,* 93 Fed. Appx. 944 (2003).

39. Lauren B. Edelman, "Legal Ambiguity and Symbolic Structures: Organizational Mediation of Civil Rights Law," *The American Journal of Sociology* 97 (1992).

40. Jonathan Simon, "Governing through Crime," in *The Crime Conundrum: Essays on Criminal Justice,* ed. Lawrence M. Friedman and George Fisher (Boulder, Colo.: Westview Press, 1997).

41. Catharine A. MacKinnon, "Reflections on Sex Equality under Law," *Yale Law Journal* 100 (1991); John Thomas Noonan, *Persons and Masks of the Law: Cardozo, Holmes, Jefferson, and Wythe as Makers of the Masks* (New York: Farrar, Straus and Giroux, 1976).

42. Martha C. Nussbaum, "Human Functioning and Social Justice: In Defense of Aristotelian Essentialism," *Political Theory* 20 (1992).

43. John Rawls, *A Theory of Justice* (Cambridge, Mass.: Harvard University Press, 1971). My approach bears a greater similarity to Barbara Cruikshank's study of the citizen/subject of the welfare state, in which she adopts a similar reluctance to pose a positive image (the empowered citizen) against a negative one (the subjugated welfare recipient), but rather to measure their interrelationships. She insists that "if power is not external to the state of being citizen or subject, if to be self-governing is to be both citizen and subject, both subject to and the subject of government, then a welfare recipient, for example, is not the antithesis of the active citizen." Separating "citizen" and "subject" "presum[es] in advance of any analysis that the categories of measurement are self-evident. . . [but if] we fail to scrutinize the ways citizens are made, we may completely overlook the constitutive discourses of citizenship that are characteristic of liberal democracies." Barbara Cruikshank, *The Will to Empower: Democratic Citizens and Other Subjects* (Ithaca, N.Y.: Cornell University Press, 1999), 23–24. Likewise I refuse to presume that recognizing someone's personhood is the antithesis of prejudicial treatment on the basis of an identity trait.

NOTES TO CHAPTER 1

1. Greg Critser, *Fat Land: How Americans Became the Fattest People in the World* (Boston: Houghton Mifflin, 2003); Marion Nestle, *Food Politics: How the Food Industry Influences Nutrition and Health* (Berkeley: University of California Press, 2002); Eric Schlosser, *Fast Food Nation: The Dark Side of the All-American Meal* (Boston: Houghton Mifflin, 2001).

2. Paul F. Campos, *The Obesity Myth: Why America's Obsession with Weight Is Hazardous to Your Health* (New York: Gotham Books, 2004).

3. J. Eric Oliver, *Fat Politics: The Real Story Behind America's Obesity Epidemic* (New York: Oxford University Press, 2006); Marilyn Wann, *Fat!So?: Because You Don't Have to Apologize for Your Size* (Berkeley, Calif.: Ten Speed Press, 1999).

4. Jana Evans Braziel and Kathleen LeBesco, *Bodies Out of Bounds: Fatness and Transgression* (Berkeley: University of California Press, 2001); Kathleen LeBesco, *Revolting Bodies?: The Struggle to Redefine Fat Identity* (Amherst: University of Massachusetts Press, 2004).

5. The fat acceptance side calls the medical researchers "the obesity mafia," and the medical researchers think of the fat advocates as deluded about the consequences of obesity. Overlaying their disputes is a media focus on obesity that keeps up a steady drumbeat of stories, mostly reflecting the views of obesity researchers. Abigail C. Saguy and Kevin W. Riley, "Weighing Both Sides: Morality, Mortality, and Framing Contests over Obesity," *Journal of Heath Politics, Policy and Law* 30 (2005).

6. 49 C.F.R. § 391.41.

7. *Equal Employment Opportunity Commission v. Texas Bus Lines*, 923 F.Supp. 965 (S.D.TX 1996), 971.

8. Americans with Disabilities Act, 42 U.S.C. § 12101(2)(C).

9. K. Anthony Appiah, "Stereotypes and the Shaping of Identity," in Robert Post et al., *Prejudicial Appearances: The Logic of American Antidiscrimination Law* (Durham, N.C.: Duke University Press, 2001), 64. Also K. Anthony Appiah, *The Ethics of Identity* (Princeton, N.J.: Princeton University Press, 2005), 195.

10. 29 C.F.R. § 1630.2(1)–(3).

11. International human rights law would be much more likely to talk about the inherent rights and dignity of every person, as the Universal Declarations of Human Rights do. Some rights can be parsed at such a level of generality that they describe universal entitlements, such as freedom from genocide or from torture. Even these are subject to disagreement: abortion is not considered genocide, though anti-abortion activists call it that, and the Bush administration has defined its prerogatives for dealing with terrorists so widely that many characterize its policies as involving torture. If this were a book about human rights discourses rather than contemporary American antidiscrimination laws, the logic of transcendental personhood and its strategy of advancing the dignity of every human being would require much more analysis; however, these logics are rarely more than window dressing for my purposes here.

12. Stanley Kurtz, "Fair Fight," *National Review*, August 9, 2002.

13. Elizabeth M. Adamitis, "Appearance Matters: A Proposal to Prohibit Appearance Discrimination in Employment," *Washington Law Review* 75 (2000): 195.

14. Lee Abbott, "People Should Not Judge Others on Their Looks," *Providence Journal*, Oct. 22, 1992, F2.

15. "Dirty Jobs: Panelists Reflect on Opportunities for Women, Minorities, Older Employees," *Pittsburgh Post-Gazette,* October 13, 2002, W-3.

16. Appiah, *The Ethics of Identity,* 195.

17. Appiah, "Stereotypes and the Shaping of Identity," 68.

18. *Mary Nedder v. Rivier College,* 944 F.Supp. 111, 119–120 (D.N.H. 1996).

19. Rivier College Mission Statement, http://www.rivier.edu/about/default .aspx?id=1489.

20. *Nedder,* 119–120.

21. Ibid., 119.

22. Elizabeth Fernandez, "Exercising Her Right to Work: Fitness Instructor Wins Weight-Bias Fight," *San Francisco Chronicle,* May 7, 2002, A-1.

23. Ibid.

24. *Marks v. National Communications Association, Inc.,* 72 F.Supp. 2d 322, 327 (S.D.N.Y. 1999).

25. Ibid., 326.

26. Strict weight requirements used to be part of jobs like flight attending, for example, but many of these rules were determined to be sex discrimination because the women were held to stricter standards than the men. Some airlines have now abandoned weight requirements entirely.

27. Ibid., 330.

28. Women of all races and Asian and Latino men tend to be disproportionately screened out by height requirements, for instance. Police departments argued that an imposing stature was part of being an effective officer, but Title VII disparate impact litigation forced them to abandon that job requirement. *Horace v. City of Pontiac,* 624 F.2d 765 (6th Cir. 1980) (invalidating the five foot eight inch minimum height requirement for patrol police officers); *Guardians Association v. Civil Service Commission,* 431 F.Supp. 526 (S.D.N.Y. 1977) (invalidating the five foot seven inch minimum height requirement for police officers); *Officers for Justice v. Civil Service Commission,* 395 F.Supp. 378 (N.D. Cal. 1975) (invalidating the five foot six inch minimum height requirement for patrol officers).

29. *Cook v. State of Rhode Island Department of Mental Health, Retardation, and Hospitals,* 10 F.3d 17 (1993), 27.

30. Ibid.

31. Ibid.

32. Ibid., 28.

33. *Webb v. Bowman,* 2001 Mich. App. LEXIS 742 (January 16, 2001) (unpublished opinion), 14.

34. *Penzato v. Continental Cablevision of Michigan, Inc.,* 1996 Mich. App. LEXIS 1067 (unpublished opinion), 6.

35. LexisNexis searches turn up only thirteen cases litigated and reported

under the "height and weight" provision of the Michigan Act as of January 2005. One plaintiff who was fired for being fat was awarded $284,000 by a Michigan jury in 2006, however, bringing the total published cases to fourteen. Paul Egan, "Bosses Want a Say in What We Weigh: Michigan Law Banning Discrimination Worries Employers Who Want to Curb Unhealthy Behavior," *The Detroit News,* October 9, 2006, 1A.

36. Janet Cawley, "Last Target of Legal Bigotry: Obesity," *Chicago Tribune,* May 12, 1993, 1.

37. If fatness were a legally recognized disability, she could have filed a federal ADA lawsuit that would have superseded the limitations of the Michigan law, as some of the other plaintiffs I discuss here did. But she is presumably applying to be a state employee, and the Supreme Court has held that the ADA does not apply to state governments. Even if she did file a claim that was permitted to go forward, the ADA contains defenses if the accommodation is an undue hardship for the employer or if the employee poses a direct threat to the safety of others. If modifying the bus did not create an unreasonable safety risk or cost too much money (and if the ADA otherwise applied to the district as an employer, and if Ms. Webb were able to prove she was a qualified person with a disability), the school district would have been required to undertake it and to hire Ms. Webb.

38. *Boyd v. Ozark Air Lines,* 419 F.Supp. 1061 (1976). The applicant was only five feet two inches, and so the change did not force the airline to hire her. The court agreed that flying airplanes is sufficiently dangerous that the company could be quite strict in defining what was necessary for the business to operate safely and five feet five inches was as low as Ozark could be required to go.

39. *Pelman v. McDonald's Corp.,* 396 F.3d 508 (2nd Cir. 2005). Some claims in the lawsuit have been dismissed, but others remain alive because of consumer protection laws making McDonald's possibly liable for deceptive advertising.

40. Interestingly, McDonald's depends upon keeping the interest of its most frequent diners. Seventy percent of its visitors each day are customers who dine there multiple times per week. This group, usually younger males, were also the target of the "super size" deals, now withdrawn from the market. Delroy Alexander, "Will They Buy It? McDonald's Plan to Eliminate Supersize Portions Could Anger Its Most Loyal and Biggest-Spending Customers," *Chicago Tribune,* March 4, 2004, C1.

41. *Tanberg v. Ackerman Investment Co.,* 473 N.W. 2d 193 (1991).

42. Ibid.

43. T. A. Wadden et al., "Treatment of Obesity by Very Low Calorie Diet, Behavior Therapy, and Their Combination: A Five-Year Perspective," *International Journal of Obesity* 13 (1989).

44. In another similar case involving worker's compensation, the judge

found the medical expert testimony much more convincing, and the injured woman was awarded disability payments even though she too had been unsuccessful at losing weight. Marilyn Christensen, the worker, testified that she was undergoing hypnosis and was considering a gastric stapling procedure, even though this treatment is sufficiently experimental that her insurance would not cover the cost. *Christensen v. Argonaut Insurance Company,* 72 Or. App. 110 (1985). Her efforts were held to be reasonable. The judge's or jury's attitude toward the medicalization of fatness ("Can she help it?") is what determines the level of sympathy to this embedded legal subject. This same division of opinion based on either a moralistic model or a medical model also explains much public opinion variation about obesity issues. Eric Oliver and Taeku Lee, "Public Opinion and the Politics of Obesity in America," *Journal of Health Politics, Policy and Law* 30 (2005).

45. John David Skrentny, *The Minority Rights Revolution* (Cambridge, Mass.: Harvard University Press, 2002).

46. And of course there would also have to be an extremely activist Supreme Court willing to create new rights within the three-tier system of equal protection. No new categories or "bump ups" have been created since the 1970s when the Court was more liberal than it is today. The Roberts Court is one of the most conservative Courts in many decades, so it is simply beyond imagining that plaintiffs—gay, fat, transgender, suspected of terrorism—will find a sympathetic ear for new rights claims.

47. Kelly D. Brownell et al., eds., *Weight Bias: Nature, Consequences, and Remedies* (New York: Guilford Press, 2005).

48. LeBesco, *Revolting Bodies?*

49. Janet Halley, "'Like-Race' Arguments," in *What's Left of Theory: New Work on the Politics of Literary Theory,* ed. Judith Butler, John Gillory, and Kendall Thomas (New York: Routledge, 2000).

50. Lauren B. Edelman, Sally Riggs Fuller, and Iona Mara-Drita, "Diversity Rhetoric and the Managerialization of Law," *The American Journal of Sociology* 106 (2001): 1617. See also Erin Kelly and Frank Dobbin, "How Affirmative Action Became Diversity Management: Employer Response to Antidiscrimination Law, 1961 to 1996," *American Behavioral Scientist* 41 (1998).

51. Jacqueline A. Gilbert, Bette Ann Stead, and John M. Ivancevich, "Diversity Management: A New Organizational Paradigm," *Journal of Business Ethics* 21 (1999); R. F. Pearse and D. A. Zrebiec, "Diversity Management in the Total Quality Organization," *Compensation & Benefits Management* 13 (1997).

52. Edelman, Fuller, and Mara-Drita, "Diversity Rhetoric and the Managerialization of Law," 1617–1618.

53. Derrick Bell, "Diversity's Distractions," *Columbia Law Review* 103 (2003); John Wrench, "Diversity Management Can Be Bad for You," *Race & Class* 46 (2005).

NOTES TO CHAPTER 2

1. I mean most important in the sense of having prompted the greatest upheavals, the greatest amount of attention, the severest conditions of oppression, and thus having a special place jurisprudentially. Admittedly, I dwell in this chapter almost entirely on blackness as part of the legal imaginary. The claim is that the logics of personhood that I discuss here are driven by representations of the black experience with Jim Crow and its effects. I am not normatively endorsing a black/white binary approach to racial and ethnic differences. Nor am I attempting to describe what the black experience with discrimination actually was, but rather what judges and legislators imagined it to be. Many theorists would argue that I still ought not use the binary in the way I do here. Linda Martín Alcoff, "Latino/as, Asian Americans, and the Black-White Binary," *The Journal of Ethics* 7 (2003); Juan F. Perea, "The Black/White Binary Paradigm of Race: The Normal Science of American Racial Thought," *California Law Review* 85 (1997). I insist that it is worth understanding how even a one-sided account came to influence the ways we can and cannot find to argue about difference today.

2. Voting rights law is an example of group consciousness in American law. Voting districts in which racial minorities comprise a majority of voters are encouraged, meaning that some concept of voters' interests as group representation is at work.

3. It could also be a wrong done to a group of whites or of men. Antidiscrimination laws cover whites as well as minorities and men as well as women. But since the Civil Rights Act was very clearly understood to have been passed to combat racial discrimination against African Americans first and foremost, many people think of these categories as protecting discrete oppressed groups: blacks, women, Latinos, or Jews, for instance. So antidiscrimination law contains a deep tension: theoretically applicable to anyone, but historically tied to easing and monitoring the social conditions of a few listed groups. African Americans were the paradigmatic group, and other groups thought to be similar to them came to be seen as proper targets of monitoring and affirmative action. John David Skrentny, *The Minority Rights Revolution* (Cambridge, Mass.: Harvard University Press, 2002).

4. *Griggs v. Duke Power,* 401 U.S. 424 (1971). The Civil Rights Act of 1991 §105, 42 U.S.C.A. § 2000e-2(k)(1) (West Supp. 1992), was enacted to overrule *Wards Cove v. Atonio,* in which the Supreme Court had attempted to shift the burden of proof for the business necessity defense to plaintiffs and to soften the requirements for proving that a rule or practice was a business necessity.

5. *Griggs,* 430.

6. The *Brown v. Board of Education* ruling in 1954 had declared racially segregated schools unconstitutional. There was widespread non-compliance,

however, and litigation went on for several decades in which the Court confronted dual school systems over and over again.

7. Ibid.

8. 110 Congressional Record 7220 (1964) (remarks of Senator Clark).

9. U.S. Code Cong. & Admin. News, 88th Cong., 2d Sess. (1964), 2516–2517.

10. I use "he" deliberately because I argue in the next chapter that black men were the imagined beneficiaries of the legislation, with the hope that they would secure good jobs, become heads of households, and anchor the public life of their communities.

11. 347 U.S. 483 (1954), 494.

12. Skrentny, *The Minority Rights Revolution*.

13. Ibid., 101–103.

14. *United Steel Workers of America v. Weber*, 443 U.S. 193 (1979), 204.

15. 29 C.F.R. 1607.4 (D).

16. *International Brotherhood of Teamsters v. United States*, 431 U.S. 324 (1977), 339. Notice that even though sex discrimination was eligible for disparate impact complaints, the Justices do not include it here. Imagine what a radical proposal it would have been to presume that women should be half of all construction workers!

17. Federal sentencing guidelines instruct judges that disadvantage in childhood is not a reason to lessen the severity of a sentence, however. 2005 Federal Sentencing Guideline Manual §5H1.12. Lack of Guidance as a Youth and Similar Circumstances (Policy Statement), http://www.ussc.gov/2005guid/tabcono5_1 .htm. In capital cases, however, mitigating circumstances like these must be considered before the death penalty can be imposed.

18. Roger Clegg, "The Future of Racial Quotas: The Bad Law of 'Disparate Impact,'" *The Public Interest* (2000).

19. Lauren B. Edelman, Steven E. Abraham, and Howard S. Erlanger, "Professional Construction of Law: The Inflated Threat of Wrongful Discharge," *Law & Society Review* 26 (1992).

20. Linda Hamilton Krieger, "The Content of Our Categories: A Cognitive Bias Approach to Discrimination and Equal Employment Opportunity," *Stanford Law Review* 47 (1995).

21. Laura Beth Nielsen and Robert L. Nelson, "Scaling the Pyramid: A Sociolegal Model of Employment Discrimination Litigation," in *Handbook of Employment Discrimination Research: Rights and Realities,* ed. Laura Beth Nielsen and Robert L. Nelson (Dorecht, The Netherlands: Springer, 2005).

22. John J. Donohue, "The Legal Response to Discrimination: How Does Law Matter?" in *How Does Law Matter?* ed. Bryant G. Garth and Austin Sarat (Evanston, IL: Northwestern University Press, 1998).

23. 539 U.S. 306 (2003); 539 U.S. 244 (2003). On November 7, 2006,

Michigan voters approved Proposal 2 by 58 to 42 percent, banning consideration of race, gender, or national origin in any state program including University admissions and hiring.

24. It turns out that there are conflicting jurisprudential grounds for these two wings of our American antidiscrimination regime, particularly as they describe the relationship between a person and her politically significant identity traits. Lower courts have evaded this conclusion, however, holding that Title VII is a valid exercise of Congress's powers under Section 5 of the 14th Amendment (and not out of line with the intent-based account in equal protection law) because both disparate impact and equal protection jurisprudence aim at detecting intentional discrimination. *In re Employment Discrimination Litigation against the State of Alabama*, 198 F.3d 1305 (11th Cir. 1999). Looking back on the language of *Griggs* (where the Court had the chance to say that and instead affirmed the *distinction* from intent-based cases), however, this seems implausible. In fact, constitutional equal protection jurisprudence and statutory antidiscrimination laws, insofar as they allow disparate impact cases, are thoroughly in conflict.

25. Justice O'Connor writing for the Court in *Adarand Constructors, Inc. v. Pena*, 515 U.S. 200 (1996), 227 (emphasis in original). Given the chance to read *Griggs* into the Constitution, the Court decided emphatically that it could not in the 1976 case of *Washington v. Davis*, a case involving a job test to become a police officer, which black applicants failed in greater numbers than white applicants. A lower court had followed the reasoning of *Griggs*, concluding that the equal protection clause should be interpreted in the same way as Title VII to permit disparate impacts to count as official discrimination. The Supreme Court overruled, refusing to allow Title VII principles of disparate impact to govern equal protection jurisprudence. *Washington v. Davis*, 426 U.S. 229 (1976).

26. *Massachusetts Personnel Administrator v. Feeney*, 442 U.S. 256 (1979), 279.

27. Allen David Freeman, "Legitimizing Racial Discrimination through Antidiscrimination Law: A Critical Review of Supreme Court Doctrine," in *Critical Race Theory: The Key Writings That Formed the Movement*, ed. Kimberlé Crenshaw, et al. (New York: New Press, 1995).

28. Stereotyping, by contrast, is not itself a logic of personhood but rather a tool deployed to defend the functional individual or the diverse person. (The next chapter delves into all the ways we talk about stereotypes and the ways they interact with logics of personhood.) Invoking stereotypes was also a strategy. "Tools" and "strategies" cannot be totally analytically separated, but I have used "strategy" to characterize a rhetorical framing and "tool" as one salient word or idea within that rhetorical framing.

29. 438 U.S. 265 (1978).

30. Elizabeth Anderson argues that this language demonstrates recognition that integration, not color blindness is the Court's concern, and that racial integration is itself a compelling interest. Elizabeth Anderson, "Racial Integration as a Compelling Interest," *Constitutional Commentary* 21 (2004): 101–127.

31. University of Michigan News Service Archives, "New U-M undergraduate admissions process to involve more information, individual review," August 28, 2003, http://www.umich.edu/news/index.html?Releases/2003/Aug03/admissions.

32. Personal communication with Julie Peterson at the University of Michigan undergraduate admissions office, December 2004 (on file with the author).

33. Lino A. Graglia, "*Grutter* and *Gratz*: Race Preference to Increase Racial Representation Held 'Patently Unconstitutional' Unless Done Subtly Enough in the Name of Pursuing 'Diversity,'" *Tulane Law Review* 78 (2004).

34. Derrick Bell, "Diversity's Distractions," *Columbia Law Review* 103 (2003).

35. Patricia Gurin, Jeffrey S. Lehman, and Earl Lewis, *Defending Diversity: Affirmative Action at the University of Michigan* (Ann Arbor: University of Michigan Press, 2004); Scott Page, *The Difference: How the Power of Diversity Creates Better Groups, Firms, Schools and Societies* (Princeton, N.J.: Princeton University Press, 2006).

36. Tom R. Tyler, *Why People Obey the Law* (New Haven: Yale University Press, 1990).

37. R. Shep Melnick, "Separation of Powers and the Strategy of Rights: The Expansion of Special Education," in *The New Politics of Public Policy,* ed. Marc Karnis Landy and Martin A. Levin (Baltimore: Johns Hopkins University Press, 1995).

38. Gurin, Lehman, and Lewis, *Defending Diversity.*

39. Erin Kelly and Frank Dobbin, "How Affirmative Action Became Diversity Management: Employer Response to Antidiscrimination Law, 1961 to 1996," *American Behavioral Scientist* 41 (1998); Lauren B. Edelman, Sally Riggs Fuller, and Iona Mara-Drita, "Diversity Rhetoric and the Managerialization of Law," *The American Journal of Sociology* 106 (2001).

40. "In the 1960s and 1970s, the stark disparity between the racial composition of the rank and file and that of the officer corps fueled a breakdown of order that endangered the military's ability to fulfill its mission. That threat was so dangerous and unacceptable that it resulted in immediate and drastic changes intended to restore minority enlisted ranks' confidence in the fairness and integrity of the institution." Consolidated Amicus Brief of Lt. Gen. Julius W. Becton, et al., in *Grutter v. Bollinger* and *Gratz v. Bollinger,* 28–29.

41. Brief of General Motors Corporation as Amicus Curiae in Support of Respondents in *Grutter v. Bollinger* and *Gratz v. Bollinger,* 2.

42. Edelman, Fuller, and Mara-Drita, "Diversity Rhetoric and the Managerialization of Law," 1617 (quoting from diversity policies of Hallmark and Westinghouse).

43. Robert Crawford, "Healthism and the Medicalization of Everyday Life," *International Journal of Health Services* 10 (1980).

NOTES TO CHAPTER 3

1. Appiah argues that "collective identities are a resource for . . . self-creation and not just a hindrance." K. Anthony Appiah, "Stereotypes and the Shaping of Identity," in Robert Post, with K. Anthony Appiah, Judith Butler, Thomas C. Grey, and Reva B. Siegel, *Prejudicial Appearances: The Logic of American Antidiscrimination Law* (Durham, N.C.: Duke University Press, 2001), 68. Concern over the gender of a prospective sexual partner is not only a version of normative stereotyping, he points out, but it is also a critical part of most people's sexuality. Therefore "we must accept the existence of normative stereotypes," particularly ones that are "configured in such a way as to serve as potential instruments in the construction of a dignified individuality." Ibid.

2. K. Anthony Appiah, "But Would That Still Be Me? Notes on Gender, 'Race,' and Ethnicity as Sources of 'Identity,'" *Journal of Philosophy* 87 (1990).

3. David O'Brien, "Ironies and Unanticipated Consequences of Legislation: Title VII of the 1964 Civil Rights Act," in *Congress and the Politics of Emerging Rights,* ed. Colton C. Campbell and John F. Stack, Jr. (Lanham, Md.: Rowman & Littlefield, 2002), 29.

4. Ibid., 29–30.

5. Ibid., 30.

6. There is scholarly disagreement on just how disingenuous Rep. Smith's amendment was, and over the degree to which it had anything to do with combating sex discrimination versus simply killing the bill (because it would seem so ridiculous). For a discussion of Rep. Smith's strategy and support of the ERA, see Katherine M. Franke, "The Central Mistake of Sex Discrimination Law: The Disaggregation of Sex from Gender," *University of Pennsylvania Law Review* 144 (1995); John David Skrentny, *The Minority Rights Revolution* (Cambridge, Mass.: Harvard University Press, 2002), 96–100.

7. Charles Whalen and Barbara Whalen, *The Longest Debate: A Legislative History of the 1964 Civil Rights Act* (New York: Mentor, 1985).

8. O'Brien, "Ironies and Unanticipated Consequences," 30–31.

9. Skrentny, *The Minority Rights Revolution,* 98.

10. O'Brien, "Ironies and Unanticipated Consequences of Legislation," 31.

11. Skrentny, *The Minority Rights Revolution,* 96.

12. Kimberlé Crenshaw's well-known essay on the intersectionality problem explains the erasure of black women as plaintiffs in Title VII cases in which no

black men or white women received negative treatment. The court in the case she analyzes, *DeGaffenreid v. General Motors*, reasons sequentially: first, the discrimination could not have been "because of race" because it did not happen to the black men, and second, it could not have been "because of sex" because it did not happen to all the women. Significantly, the court inveighs against "combin[ing] statutory remedies to create a new 'super-remedy' " for black women workers. Kimberlé Crenshaw, "Demarginalizing the Intersection of Race and Sex: A Black Feminist Critique of Antidiscrimination Doctrine, Feminist Theory and Antiracist Politics," in *Feminist Legal Theory: Foundations*, ed. D. Kelly Weisberg (Philadelphia: Temple University Press, 1993), 384. In this view, the black woman literally has two selves: the black self, to which the "race" protection attaches, and the woman self, to which the "sex" protection attaches. The remedy would be "super" because it would apply doubly to both selves, while white women and black men have only the singular self. The black woman is a person who could easily get more than she deserves, the court worries. Other cases since *DeGaffenreid* have grappled with intersectional identity in somewhat more helpful ways that permit minority women to be considered as a discriminated-against group even where minority men or white women did not receive the treatment as well. For example, *Jefferies v. Harris County Community Action Association*, 615 F.2d 1025 (5th Cir. 1980). Yet, the problem presents itself in the first place because of the way persons were inscribed into the future of Title VII jurisprudence.

13. *Sprogis v. United Air Lines, Inc.*, 444 F.2d 1194 (7th Cir. 1971), 1198.

14. *Reed v. Reed*, 404 U.S. 71 (1971).

15. *Frontiero v. Richardson*, 411 U.S. 677 (1973).

16. *United States v. Virginia*, 518 U.S. 515 (1996).

17. 435 U.S. 702, 704–705.

18. Ibid., 707–708.

19. Ibid., 710.

20. Ibid., 709.

21. Jonathan Simon notes that actuarial categories can be ideologically pernicious "because they demoralize—treat as morally neutral—differences that carry highly-charged political and social significance (such as race and gender), they threaten to obscure the historical effects of domination and conflict with modern efforts to remedy discrimination." Jonathan Simon, "The Ideological Effects of Actuarial Practices," *Law & Society Review* 22 (1988): 776. In his analysis, the *Manhart* case papers over the ideological effects of actuarial practices by promoting the decision along the familiar lines of individualism versus group rights. "*Manhart*," Simon writes, "stretches [the conception of invidious stereotypes] in order to fit actuarial representation into the mold of devaluing moral attributions (blacks are violent, Mexicans are lazy, Jews are cheap, women live longer.)" Ibid., 778.

22. *Phillips v. Martin Marietta*, 400 U.S. 542 (1971). The case is usually cited as a classic "sex-plus" discrimination case: sex discrimination applied to a subset of women, namely women with the "plus" factor of having young children.

23. Arlie Russell Hochschild, *The Second Shift: Working Parents and the Revolution at Home* (New York: Viking, 1989).

24. *Nguyen v. INS*, 533 U.S. 53 (2001).

25. Ibid., 68.

26. Ibid.

27. Justice O'Connor's dissenting opinion makes this exact argument. It also seems like the Court may have been worried about men leaving the country in wartime and impregnating women whose children could have claims to citizenship without ever knowing their fathers or their fathers' homeland. A single U.S. soldier could impregnate a large number of women, and even do so for a fee. The Court does not come out and refer to this possibility explicitly (though Justice Kennedy does list numbers of men serving overseas and show concern for them fathering children there), only anchoring their decision in the different birth roles of men and women. But perhaps it helped the majority to see the rule as rooted in biological reality rather than socially created stereotypes.

28. *Price Waterhouse v. Hopkins*, 490 U.S. 228 (1989), 278.

29. Ibid., 278.

30. Ibid., 251.

31. *Smith v. City of Salem*, 378 F.3d 566 (6th Cir. 2004). The action began early in Smith's transition period, during what is known as the "real life experience" of dressing as the sex one is in therapy to become. Smith had not yet changed his first name and considered himself to be pre-transition, and so I use the pronoun Smith used at the time. A transgendered police officer has since used the *Smith* ruling to win a $320,500 judgment plus $527,888 in attorney's fees against the city of Cincinnati for discriminating against her. *Barnes v. City of Cincinnati*, 401 F.3d 729 (6th Cir. 2005).

32. Ibid., 571.

33. Ibid., 574 (emphasis mine).

34. Rachel Toker, "Multiple Masculinities: A New Vision for Same-Sex Harassment Law," in *Feminist Legal Theory: An Anti-Essentialist Reader*, eds. Nancy E. Dowd and Michelle S. Jacobs (New York: New York University Press, 2003).

35. *Smith*, 574 (emphasis mine).

36. Ibid., 575.

37. *Jespersen v. Harrah's*, 444 F.3d 1104 (9th Cir. 2006); also *Willingham v. Macon Telegraph*, 507 F.2d 1084 (1975); *Devine v. Lonschein*, 621 F.Supp. 894 (1985).

38. *Jespersen*, 4123.

39. Ibid., 4127.

40. Ibid., 4132.

41. This situation is somewhat similar to Reva Siegel's account of preservation through transformation, in which courts adapt new kinds of justifications in light of changing social norms but rarely disrupt basic power relations in society. Reva B. Siegel, " 'The Rule of Love': Wife Beating as Prerogative and Privacy," *The Yale Law Journal* 105 (1996).

42. Currently Title VII permits an employer to employ an individual "on the basis of his religion, sex, or national origin in those certain instances where religion, sex, or national origin is a bona fide occupational qualification reasonably necessary to the normal operation of that particular business or enterprise." Age is also permissible grounds for a BFOQ under another federal statute, the Age Discrimination in Employment Act (ADEA), 29 U.S.C.A. § 623.

43. *E.E.O.C. v. Kamehameha Schools/Bishop Estate*, 990 F.2d 458 (9th Cir. 1993), 465.

44. As Robert Post has noted, "Title VII does not simply displace gender practices, but rather interacts with them in a selective manner." Post, *Prejudicial Appearances*, 34.

45. 110 Cong. Rec. 7213 (1964).

46. *Piatti v. Jewish Community Centers of Greater Boston*, 1993 Mass. Super. LEXIS 328 (1993).

47. *Pime v. Loyola University of Chicago*, 803 F.2d 351 (7th Cir. 1986).

48. *Kern v. Dynalectron Corporation*, 577 F.Supp. 1196 (N.D. Tex. 1983).

49. *Dothard v. Rawlinson*, 433 U.S. 321 (1977), 333. Equal Employment Opportunity Commission Guidelines on Discrimination Because of Sex explain that "[w]here it is necessary for the purpose of authenticity or genuineness, the Commission will consider sex to be a bona fide occupational qualification, e.g., an actor or actress." Equal Employment Opportunity Commission Guidelines on Discrimination Because of Sex, 29 C.F.R. 1604.2(a)(2) (1998).

50. *Levendos v. Stern Entertainment, Inc.*, (1989, WD Pa) 723 F.Supp. 1104.

51. *Fernandez v. Wynn Oil Company*, 653 F.2d 1273 (9th Cir. 1981).

52. *UAW v. Johnson Controls*, 499 U.S. 187, 192.

53. *Fesel v. Masonic Home of Delaware, Inc.*, 447 F.Supp. 1346 (3d Cir. 1979), 1352.

54. *EEOC v. Mercy Health Ctr.*, 1982 U.S. Dist. LEXIS 12256 (W.D. Okla. 1982); *Backus v. Baptist Med. Ctr.*, 510 F.Supp. 1191 (E.D. Ark. 1981).

55. *Healey v. Southwood Psychiatric Hospital*, 78 F.3d 128, 134 (3d Cir. 1996); *Jennings v. N.Y. State Office of Mental Health*, 786 F.Supp. 376 (S.D.N.Y 1992).

56. *Brooks v. ACF Indus.*, 537 F.Supp. 1122 (S.D.W.Va. 1982).

57. 110 Cong. Rec. 2550–2563 (1964).

58. Ibid., 2559.

59. Ibid. In the Senate, Senator John McClellan, a Democrat from Arkansas, introduced an amendment that would have effectively read back into the Civil Rights Act all communal norms regarding race. It would have permitted race-based hiring if "the employer believes, on the basis of substantial evidence, that the hiring of such an individual . . . will be more beneficial to the normal operation of the particular business or enterprise involved or to the good will thereof than the hiring of an individual without consideration of his race." 110 Cong. Rec. 13,825 (1964). Not surprisingly, this amendment also failed because supporters of the Act realized that deference to employers' beliefs about how race-based hiring contributed to the "good will" of their businesses would completely eviscerate the Act. The social norms of whites (and their economic behavior) were the focus of transformation in the first place. In response to the objection that it would be ridiculous not to allow a movie director to advertise for actors based on race if the movie featured African slaves, for example, Senators stipulated that there was *still* no need for a BFOQ based on race because "a director of a play or movie who wished to cast an actor in the role of a Negro, could specify that he wished to hire someone with the physical appearance of a Negro—but such a person might actually be a non-Negro." 110 Cong. Rec. 7217 (1964). This rather remarkable statement demonstrates the rhetorical lengths Congress was willing to go to at the time to keep the bigotry of embedded personhood from taking over the goals of the new law.

NOTES TO CHAPTER 4

1. *Philadelphia Electric Company v. Pennsylvania Human Relations Commission and Joyce A. English*, 68 Pa. Commw. 212 (1982). The court insisted that Ms. English's race was "totally irrelevant" to her case.

2. *Philadelphia Electric Company*, 223.

3. Ibid., 228.

4. This is the situation Marilyn Wann, a prominent fat activist, found herself in after she was no longer able to get health coverage through a freelance writers association she had joined. She was rejected for coverage because of her weight and could not obtain any health insurance at all despite being able to pay. Personal communication with the author, June 2005.

5. Deborah A. Stone, "The Struggle for the Soul of Health Insurance," *Journal of Health Politics, Policy and Law* 18 (1992).

6. Alaska Code Ann. § 21.36.460(d)(4) and § 21.36.430(a) (2005).

7. Miss. Code Ann. § 83-5-35(g) (2005); Deborah A. Stone, "The Rhetoric of Insurance Law: The Debate over AIDS Testing," *Law & Social Inquiry* 15 (1990): 392.

8. Col. Rev. St. Ann. § 10-3-1104(1)(f)(IV) (2006).

9. Mary Crossley, "Discrimination against the Unhealthy in Health Insur-

ance," *University of Kansas Law Review* 54 (2005): 88–89. As Crossley explains, the Age Discrimination in Employment Act and the Americans with Disabilities Act each provide very little protection against employers' use of age and disability respectively in reducing or eliminating benefits.

10. Ibid., 113–116. Crossley points out that because HIPAA does not require any certain level of coverage for any particular benefit, but rather that the coverage offered to everyone in the group be the same, there has been an unfortunate side effect: companies can simply set low limits for all, so that chronically ill employees wind up quickly exhausting their coverage.

11. American Management Association 2004 Workplace Testing Survey: Medical Testing, http://www.amanet.org/research/pdfs/Medical_testing_04.pdf. Drug screening is the most common reason for pre-employment tests. "Fitness for duty" was the second most common reason.

12. Shelly Reese, "New Concepts in Health Benefits: Employee Incentives," *Business & Health* 18 (2000).

13. Trisha Greenhalgh and Simon Wessely, " 'Health for Me': A Sociocultural Analysis of Healthism in the Middle Classes," *British Medical Bulletin* 69 (2004); Robert Crawford, "Healthism and the Medicalization of Everyday Life," *International Journal of Health Services* 10 (1980).

14. There are data to suggest that fat workers do indeed have more health problems that affect their work. R. P. Hertz et al., "The Impact of Obesity on Work Limitations and Cardiovascular Risk Factors in the U.S. Workforce," *Journal of Occupational and Environmental Medicine* 46 (2004). However, the Hertz study was funded by Pfizer, the drug manufacturer, and no doubt fat rights advocates would criticize its ties to a company that profits from the medicalization of obesity and from the sale of its weight loss treatments. Disability rights laws exist to protect people whose bodies function differently from the norm, however, so the study's conclusions nonetheless beg the question of whether it is just to fire or to fail to hire fat people even if they do exhibit more health problems. The Hertz et al. findings seem to be in tension with research showing that people with BMIs of 25–30 (overweight) actually live longer than either thin people or very fat people (those with a BMI over 35, about 8 percent of the population). Paul Campos et al., "The Epidemiology of Overweight and Obesity: Public Health Crisis or Moral Panic?" *International Journal of Epidemiology* 35 (2006). Morbidity and reasons for missing work are very different things, however.

15. *McDermott v. Xerox Corp,* 547–548. The Rehabilitation Act, the precursor to the ADA, would have been in effect at the time.

16. Ibid., 543.

17. Regina Austin offers one typically critical account of the insurers' view of the person as an actuarial subject of analysis: "Insurance companies do not view any insured as a whole person. Rather, every insured is compartmental-

ized. He is the sum of the many roles he plays as a result of being a member of many status groups. To an insurance company, the same individual may be an adult, a female, a divorcee, a parent, a lover, an executive, a debtor, a homeowner, a citizen, an urbanite, a commuter, a teetotaler, a lawbreaker, and a klutz. She is not a plenary, monolithic person. The company does not know her; it knows only the roles she plays." Regina Austin, "The Insurance Classification Controversy," *University of Pennsylvania Law Review* 131 (1983), 547. Her account presupposes a normative view that law *ought* to know the real person and that there is something wrong when law only knows "roles." My view is not that there is true personhood that the law should know and that actuarial personhood is a distorted version of that; rather I'm highlighting the stakes and consequences of thinking of persons in one way or another.

18. Abigail C. Saguy and Rene Almeling, "Fat in the Fire?: Science, the News Media, and the Obesity Crisis," *Sociological Forum* 23 (forthcoming 2008).

19. Christian Crandall and Monica Biernat, "The Ideology of Anti-Fat Attitudes," *Journal of Applied Social Psychology* 20 (1990); Christian Crandall, "Prejudice against Fat People: Ideology and Self-Interest," *Journal of Personality and Social Psychology* 66 (1994).

20. Paul Campos makes this exact argument: disgust at fat people (often brown or black fat people) and their eating is the new way for the upper classes to show their disgust at the lower sort. "The disgust the thin upper classes feel for the fat lower classes has nothing to do with mortality statistics, and everything to do with the moral superiority engendered in thin people by the sight of fat people," he argues. Paul F. Campos, *The Obesity Myth: Why America's Obsession with Weight Is Hazardous to Your Health* (New York: Gotham Books, 2004), 68.

21. Brian J. Glenn, "Postmodernism: The Basis of Insurance," *Risk Management & Insurance Review* 6 (2003): 134.

22. Brian J. Glenn, "The Shifting Rhetoric of Insurance Denial," *Law & Society Review* 34 (2000).

23. Jonathan Simon, "The Ideological Effects of Actuarial Practices," *Law & Society Review* 22 (1988): 794.

24. This is certainly not to say that boundaries around groups are essential or fixed. It is only to say that we experience them as real, and they have real consequences.

25. Peter Conrad, "Medicalization and Social Control," *Annual Review of Sociology* 18 (1992); Peter Conrad and Deborah Potter, "From Hyperactive Children to ADHD Adults: Observations on the Expansion of Medical Categories," *Social Problems* 47 (2000).

26. Mariana Valverde, *Diseases of the Will: Alcohol and the Dilemmas of Freedom* (New York: Cambridge University Press, 1998).

27. Abigail C. Saguy and Kevin W. Riley, "Weighing Both Sides: Morality, Mortality, and Framing Contests over Obesity," *Journal of Heath Politics, Policy and Law* 30 (2005).

28. Jeffery Sobal, "The Medicalization and Demedicalization of Obesity," in *Eating Agendas: Food and Nutrition as Social Problems,* eds. Donna Maurer and Jeffery Sobal (New York: Aldine de Gruyter, 1995).

29. International Obesity Task Force, http://www.iotf.org/intro/whatisiotf .htm.

30. Ray Moynihan, "Obesity Task Force Linked to WHO Takes 'Millions' from Drug Firms," *British Medical Journal* 332 (2006).

31. Eric Oliver and Taeku Lee, "Public Opinion and the Politics of Obesity in America," *Journal of Health Politics, Policy and Law* 30 (2005): 933.

32. Rogan Kersh and James Morone, "How the Personal Becomes Political: Prohibitions, Public Health, and Obesity," *Studies in American Political Development* 16 (2002).

33. Kersh and Morone postulate that lawsuits against so-called "Big Food" may mean that the courts will be the most important policy-making venue for obesity. Rogan Kersh and James A. Morone, "Obesity, Courts, and the New Politics of Public Health," *Journal of Health Politics, Policy and Law* 30 (2005). Lawsuits may be successful on the tobacco model if attention can be focused on advertising to children or deceptive advertising. The first McDonald's lawsuit, which made these arguments, is still being kicked around in the courts. State legislatures and the House of Representatives have responded with industry protection bills drawing on a rhetoric of personal consumer responsibility. If there is to be policy making in the courts, it seems to be far off. Polling done in 2001 suggested that most Americans are not very concerned about obesity and do not favor aggressive public health interventions by the government.

34. A 2002 lawsuit by Bronx teens alleging that fast food restaurants made them fat and affected their health was initially thrown out, but parts of the youths' claims have made it back into court. The House of Representatives passed a so-called "cheeseburger bill" in 2005 protecting the industry against such lawsuits, but the Senate has not acted on it.

35. The European Union does not allow advertisements for weight loss products to make claims about weight loss or alleviation of hunger, for example (while U.S. consumers are bombarded with such ads, with the asterisk note reading "Results not typical" in infinitesimal print). Harry L. Greene, Tessa Prior, and Hank I. Frier, "Foods, Health Claims, and the Law: Comparisons of the United States and Europe," *Obesity Research* 9 (2001). Other policies being considered in Europe include banning vending machines in schools, improving food labeling, putting health warnings on certain foods, restricting TV advertising of junk foods, and shifting taxation to support healthy foods (also suggested in Australia). "Ireland to Follow Neighbors' Initiatives," http://www

.nutraingredients.com/news/news-ng.asp?id=60194-ireland-to-follow. There is also greater emphasis on the way the environment contributes to the way citizens eat and move, and very little moral criticism of overweight people (in government reports, at least). An Irish taskforce report on obesity emphasizes that "factors outside the individual's immediate, conscious discretion are at play here." Report of the National Task Force on Obesity 2005 (Ireland), http:// www.healthpromotion.ie/uploaded_docs/Report_of_the_National_Taskforce_on _Obesity.pdf, 82. The European approach shares the assumption that more fat people, especially children, would be a bad thing. The main difference is greater willingness to limit business interests and greater emphasis on environmental changes to increase opportunities for exercise.

36. The two dueling studies were Katherine M. Flegal et al., "Excess Deaths Associated with Underweight, Overweight, and Obesity," *JAMA: The Journal of the American Medical Association* 293 (2005) and A. H. Mokdad et al., "Actual Causes of Death in the United States, 2000," *JAMA: The Journal of the American Medical Association* 291 (2004).

37. Campos et al., "The Epidemiology of Overweight and Obesity."

38. J. Eric Oliver, Fat Politics: *The Real Story Behind America's Obesity Epidemic* (New York: Oxford University Press, 2006), 22–23; Campos et al., "The Epidemiology of Overweight and Obesity," 56.

39. Soowon Kim and Barry M. Popkin, "Commentary: Understanding the Epidemiology of Overweight and Obesity—a Real Global Public Health Concern," *International Journal of Epidemiology* 35 (2006); Neville Rigby, "Commentary: Counterpoint to Campos et al.," *International Journal of Epidemiology* 35 (2006). Rigby's response also included criticisms of social scientists daring to evaluate epidemiological research, as well as a jab at their "curiously narrow American perspective, spun in rhetoric more redolent of a courtroom contest than serious academic discourse." Rigby, "Commentary: Counterpoint to Campos et al.," 79. I invite readers to read the entire debate themselves, but it seems clear that the only person engaged in ad hominem attacks or rhetorical excesses was Rigby himself.

40. Simon, "The Ideological Effects of Actuarial Practices," 771.

41. Peter N. Stearns, Fat History: *Bodies and Beauty in the Modern West* (New York: New York University Press, 1997).

42. J. Eric Oliver, Fat Politics: *The Real Story Behind America's Obesity Epidemic* (New York: Oxford University Press, 2006), 96–97.

43. Adolphe Quetelet, *Du Système Social et des Lois Qui Il Régissent* (Paris: Guillaumin et cie, 1848.)

44. Adolphe Quetelet, *Sur l'homme et le Développement de ses Facultés, ou Essai de Physique Sociale.* Volume 1. Bruxelles, 1836.

45. François Ewald, "Norms, Discipline, and the Law," *Representations* 30 (1990): 146.

46. "No society can exist without something akin to this common standard, a common language that binds individuals together, making exchange and communication possible," Ewald writes. Ibid., 159. Normalization is not perfection, but rather a way of gaining adequacy and predicting unusual or unusable pieces. It is also highly equitable in that every piece can be placed somewhere on the normal curve (just perhaps off on the tail). Ewald also notes that it is democratic in the sense of resting upon "the creation of associations where all interested participants—producers, consumers, engineers, scientists—can negotiate the common standard according to their respective requirements." Ibid., 152. Think of the push from the left to have nationwide standards for what constitutes organic food, or even of the now-defunct hope that Esperanto as a universal language would bring world peace.

47. Oliver, *Fat Politics*, 22.

48. Ibid.

49. *School Board of Nassau County v. Arline*, 480 U.S. 273 (1987), 276.

50. Ibid, 282 n.7.

51. Ibid., 284.

52. Ibid., 285 (emphasis in original).

53. Ibid.

54. Ibid., 288. The Court draws its four-point test for risk assessment (now a federal regulation cited below) directly from the amicus brief of the American Medical Association in *Arline*.

55. S. Rep. No. 116, 101st Cong., 1st Sess. 27 (1989); H.R. Rep No. 485, 101st Cong. 2d Sess. pt. 2, at 56 (1990) (Committee on Education and Labor).

56. 28 C.F.R. 36.208(c).

57. 29 C.F.R. 1630.2(r).

58. Ibid.

59. *Arline*, 287 n.16.

60. Sharona Hoffman and Glenn Pransky, "Pre-Employment Examinations and the Americans with Disabilities Act: How Best to Avoid Liabilities under Federal Law," *Journal of Occupational Rehabilitation* 8 (December 1998): 260.

61. The statute itself mentions only threats to others, the EEOC regulations expand direct threat to include threats to the disabled person herself, and federal circuit courts are split on that issue. *Kohnke v. Delta Airlines*, 932 F.Supp. 1110 (N.D. Ill. 1996) held that since the ADA mentions only threats to others, it should not be judicially expanded, but *Moses v. American Nonwovens, Inc.*, 97 F.3d 446 (11th Cir. 1996) expanded the concept to include threats to the self. The federal circuits are also split on the question of who bears the burden of proof on the threat question: the employee, who must prove she is not a threat, or the employer, who must prove she is. *Hutton v. Elf Atochem North America*, 273 F.3d 884 (9th Cir. 2001) held that the employer had the burden of proof since the direct threat defense is an affirmative defense, but the First and

Eleventh Circuits have held that the plaintiff must prove she is not a risk on the job [*EEOC v. Amego, Inc.*, 110 F.3d 135 (1st Cir. 1997); *Moses*].

62. *Borgialli v. Thunder Basin Coal Company*, 235 F.3d 1284 (10th Cir. 2000).

63. *Hutton.*

64. *Wilson v. Phillips Petroleum*, 1998 U.S. Dist. LEXIS 19784 (N.D. Texas, 1998).

65. *Hutton*, 889.

66. *Waddell v. Valley Forge Dental Associates*, 276 F.3d 1275 (11th Cir. 2001).

67. *Doe v. University of Maryland Medical System*, 50 F.3d 1261 (4th Cir. 1995).

68. *Estate of Mauro v. Borgess Medical Center*, 137 F.3d 398 (6th Cir. 1998).

69. *EEOC v. Amego, Inc.*, 110 F.3d 135 (1st Cir. 1997).

70. *Robertson v. Neuromedical Center*, 161 F.3d 292 (5th Cir. 1998).

71. *Newman v. Chevron U.S.A.*, 979 F.Supp. 1085 (S.D. Tex. 1997).

72. *Abbott v. Bragdon*, 524 U.S. 624 (1998).

73. *Doe v. An Oregon Ski Resort*, 2001 U.S. Dist. LEXIS 17449 (2001), 21.

74. Ibid.

75. *Nunes v. Wal-Mart*, 164 F.3d 1243 (9th Cir. 1999). The court refused to consider expanding the defense to include threat to the employee because the issue had not been adequately stated on appeal.

76. Americans with Disabilities Act, 42 U.S.C. § 12182 (a); *Burriola v. Greater Toledo YMCA*, 133 F.Supp. 2d 1034 (N.D. Ohio 2001).

77. *Bay Area Addiction Research and Treatment, Inc. v. City of Antioch*, 179 F.3d 725 (9th Cir. 1999), 737.

78. Bay Area Addiction Research and Treatment: Clinic Sites, http://www .baartcdp.com/clinic_sites.htm. A clinic address on Sunset Lane in Antioch, California appears. There is no record of a subsequent ruling in the case on remand, so perhaps the parties settled the case soon after the Ninth Circuit's ruling. Parties frequently settle after major rulings of this type that, though not final judgments on the merits, clearly establish that it is better to settle than to continue to litigate.

79. Richard J. Ritter, "Racial Justice and the Role of the U.S. Department of Justice in Combating Insurance Redlining," in *Insurance Redlining: Disinvestment, Reinvestment, and the Evolving Role of Financial Institutions*, ed. Gregory D. Squires (Washington, D.C.: The Urban Institute Press, 1997), 188–189.

80. Margery Austin Turner and Felicity Skidmore, "Mortgage Lending Discrimination: A Review of Existing Evidence," (Washington, D.C.: The Urban Institute, 1999).

81. Melvin L. Oliver and Tom Shapiro, *Black Wealth/White Wealth* (New York: Routledge, 1995), 142.

82. Shanna L. Smith and Cathy Cloud, "Documenting Discrimination by Homeowner's Insurance Companies through Testing," in *Insurance Redlining*, ed. Squires, 97–100.

83. Ibid., 108–109.

84. George Lipsitz, "Civil Rights Rhetoric and White Identity Politics," in *Cultural Pluralism, Identity Politics, and the Law*, ed. Austin Sarat and Thomas R. Kearns (Ann Arbor: University of Michigan Press, 2002), 116.

85. 42 U.S.C. §§ 3601–3619 (1992); Lipsitz, "Civil Rights Rhetoric and White Identity Politics," 115.

86. 15 U.S.C. section 1691(a)–(f) (1992); 12 U.S.C. §§ 2801–2810 (1992). According to economist Paul Huck, however, reporting under the HMDA may be skewed by the fact that some applicants do not self-report their race in mail and phone applications, making it likely that the racial disparities, though quite apparent, are under-reported, especially in refinancing and home improvement applications in low to moderate income areas. Lenders are required to state the race of anyone they meet in person, but they are not required to do so for phone or mail applicants. Paul F. Huck, "Home Mortgage Lending by Applicant Race/Ethnicity: Do HMDA Figures Provide a Distorted Picture?" *Policy Studies* (Consumer Issues Research Series, Federal Reserve Bank of Chicago) (October 2000): 1–32.

87. 12 U.S.C. sections 2901–2905 (1992). Like disparate impact discrimination, there is no search for a prejudicial loan officer, just a practice out of balance with the racial composition of the area. "[I]f [a financial lending institution's] failure to comply is correlated with the race of the underserved neighborhoods, intentional discrimination, in violation of the Fair Housing Act and the Equal Credit Opportunity Act, can be inferred." Hearings Before the Senate Comm. on Banking, Housing and Urban Affairs Concerning Mortgage Lending Discrimination, 103d Congress, 1st Session 534 (1993) (statement of Acting Assistant Attorney General James P. Turner, Civil Rights Division, U.S. Department of Justice).

88. Robert G. Schwemm, "Introduction to Mortgage Lending Discrimination Law," *John Marshall Law Review* 28 (1995): 318 n. 4. Schwemm speculates that private organizations in those areas were able to mobilize around housing litigation in ways that other groups were not able to replicate. Varying levels of interest in insurance discrimination can be increased by outside activism or drastic events, and factors including urban unrest and media reporting have been the main causes of bursts of social change in this area. Ibid., 320–321.

89. "Policy Statement on Discrimination in Lending," 59 Fed. Reg. 18, 266–274 (1994).

90. Financial Institutions Reform, Recovery, and Enforcement Act, Pub. L. No. 101-73, 103 Stat. 183 (1989); 12 U.S.C. section 2803(b)(4).

91. Schwemm, "Introduction to Mortgage Lending Discrimination Law," 322.

92. In contrast to the Decatur Federal Savings and Loan investigation, the Reagan Justice Department only filed two housing discrimination cases in the first two years of the administration and actively thwarted efforts elsewhere. Lipsitz, "Civil Rights Rhetoric and White Identity Politics," 118–119.

93. Much scholarly critique of insurance practices takes this line, arguing that if bias would stop distorting actuarial calculations, stigmatized populations would be better served. Deborah Stone also argues that actuarial practices "have all the trappings of scientific objectivity—medical terminology, elaborate matrices of diseases and point values, and numbers—but they often seem to be based as much on social prejudices and stereotypes as on empirical knowledge." Deborah Stone, "The Struggle for the Soul of Health Care," *Journal of Health Politics, Policy & Law* 18 (1993), 296. Brian Glenn presumes that "[u]nderwriting decisions based on stereotypes or prejudice would eventually be challenged by the lack of data to support them, just as they were a century ago under the previous underwriting era, when biases and stereotypes were openly stated." Glenn, "The Shifting Rhetoric of Insurance Denial," 805. Treating racial prejudice in insurance as a tumor that can be lifted out while preserving the integrity of the surrounding practices papers over the larger context of social and economic vulnerability in which large numbers of racially marked people in this country live. Race and risk seem to have a dialectical relationship that is best understood not as the distortion of some truths by "myths," but rather as a social process that produces and reproduces inequality in racialized terms, by which some people are kept in risky circumstances of financial instability, poverty, crime, and ill health, which in turn reproduce fears of that risk in other populations.

94. Simon, "The Ideological Effects of Actuarial Practices," 775.

95. Malcolm M. Feeley and Jonathan Simon, "The New Penology: Notes on the Emerging Strategy of Corrections and Its Implications," *Criminology* 30 (1992).

NOTES TO CHAPTER 5

1. Ruth Colker, *American Law in the Age of Hypercapitalism: The Worker, the Family, and the State* (New York: New York University Press, 1998), 65.

2. Richard Allen Epstein, *Forbidden Grounds: The Case against Employment Discrimination Laws* (Cambridge, Mass.: Harvard University Press, 1992).

3. Linda Hamilton Krieger, "Backlash against the ADA: Interdisciplinary Perspectives and Implications for Social Justice Strategies," *Berkeley Journal of*

Employment and Labor Law 21 (2000): 2; Pamela S. Karlan and George Rutherglen, "Disabilities, Discrimination, and Reasonable Accommodation," *Duke Law Journal* 46 (1996): 2.

4. The trope of blindness in antidiscrimination jurisprudence sounds entirely different when the context shifts to disability and to considering actual blind people. It no longer describes an abstractly virtuous trait of all just citizens, but a feature of some people, which operates to exclude them from many spaces and activities in a very real way.

5. Sondra Solovay, *Tipping the Scales of Justice: Fighting Weight-Based Discrimination* (Amherst, N.Y.: Prometheus Books, 2000); Charlotte Cooper, "Can a Fat Woman Call Herself Disabled?" *Disability and Society* 12 (1997); April Herndon, "Disparate but Disabled: Fat Embodiment and Disability Studies," *NWSA Journal* 14 (2002).

6. Americans with Disabilities Act, 42 U.S.C. 12102(2)(A)–(C).

7. Ruth O'Brien, *Crippled Justice: The History of Modern Disability Policy in the Workplace* (Chicago: University of Chicago Press, 2001), 14.

8. *Sutton v. United Airlines*, 527 U.S. 471 (1999), p. 483; Interpretive Guidance on Title I of the Americans with Disabilities Act, 351–352.

9. *Sutton*, 483.

10. Anita Silvers argues against collectivizing disability perspectives into one political identity, because to do so would impose fealty to a certain banner-carrying way of being disabled, undermining the individualized inventions that disabled people develop in order to function in new ways. Anita Silvers, "Double Consciousness, Triple Difference: Disability, Race, Gender and the Politics of Recognition," in *Disability, Divers-Ability, and Legal Change*, ed. Melinda Jones and Lee Ann Basser Marks (The Hague: Martinus Nijhoff, 1999). But Rosemarie Garland-Thomson emphasizes the "complex ways that the particularities of human variation are imbued with social meanings [that] justify discriminatory practices," in a mode of analysis that highlights how group-based oppression can create an identity even in the presence of variation among the group members. Rosemarie Garland-Thomson, "Feminist Disability Studies," *Signs: Journal of Women in Culture and Society* 30 (2005): 1582.

11. Ruth Colker, *The Disability Pendulum: The First Decade of the Americans with Disabilities Act* (New York: New York University Press, 2005).

12. Ceci Connolly and Rob Stein, "Medicare Changes Policy on Obesity: Some Treatments May Be Covered," *The Washington Post*, July 14 2004.

13. Interpretive Guidance on Title I of the Americans with Disabilities Act, 29 C.F.R. 1630 (1991). Appendix to Part 1630, p. 352.

14. *EEOC v. Watkins Motor Lines*, 6th Cir., No. 05-3218, 9/12/06.

15. *Cook v. State of Rhode Island Department of Mental Health, Retardation, and Hospitals,* a 1993 case discussed in chapter 1, is a rare example of a federal case in which a fat person won a disability rights case. Ms. Cook was

five feet two inches tall and weighed 320 pounds and was fired from her job as a nurse because of concerns about the effects of her size. Although it could be read as a perceived disability case like the others I discuss, the court actually held that either theory (perceived disability or actual impairment) was supported by the evidence. The case is widely cited for the idea that fat people can win cases as persons with disabilities if they are extremely large.

16. Linda Hamilton Krieger, ed., *Backlash against the ADA: Reinterpreting Disability Rights* (Ann Arbor: The University of Michigan Press, 2003).

17. Kelly D. Brownell et al., eds., *Weight Bias: Nature, Consequences, and Remedies* (New York: Guilford Press, 2005).

18. Abigail C. Saguy and Kevin W. Riley, "Weighing Both Sides: Morality, Mortality, and Framing Contests over Obesity," *Journal of Heath Politics, Policy and Law* 30 (2005).

19. Garland-Thomson, "Feminist Disability Studies," 1582.

20. Kathleen LeBesco, *Revolting Bodies?: The Struggle to Redefine Fat Identity* (Amherst: University of Massachusetts Press, 2004), 124.

21. Ruth O'Brien, "Other Voices at the Workplace: Gender, Disability, and an Alternative Ethic of Care," *Signs: Journal of Women in Culture and Society* 30 (2005): 1530.

22. Lauren B. Edelman, "Legal Ambiguity and Symbolic Structures: Organizational Mediation of Civil Rights Law," *The American Journal of Sociology* 97 (1992).

23. Americans with Disabilities Act (Preamble), 42 U.S.C. § 12101(a)(7) (1999).

24. O'Brien, *Crippled Justice*.

25. Alan Hunt, *Explorations in Law and Society: Toward a Constitutive Theory of Law* (New York: Routledge, 1993), 315.

26. Interpretive Guidance on Title I of the Americans with Disabilities Act, p. 343.

27. 75 F.3d 1130 (7th Cir. 1996), p. 1137.

28. *Conneen v. MBNA America Bank,* 2003 U.S. App. LEXIS 13181 (3d Cir. 2003), p. 30.

29. Martha Minow, *Not Only for Myself: Identity, Politics, and the Law* (New York: New Press, 1997), 50.

30. Ibid., 51.

31. *Carter v. Northwest Airlines,* 93 Fed. Appx. 944 (2003), p. 945.

32. *Beck,* p. 1135.

33. Shep Melnick's work on the Education for All Handicapped Children Act shows how creating processes honored the individualism of every child but also created an unwieldy system that conveniently helped politicians seem responsive to the diversity of needs while moving the burden of enforcing the law onto parents and guardians. R. Shep Melnick, "Separation of Powers and the

Strategy of Rights: The Expansion of Special Education," in *The New Politics of Public Policy,* eds. Marc Karnis Landy and Martin A. Levin (Baltimore: Johns Hopkins University Press, 1995).

34. Janet Halley, " 'Like-Race' Arguments," in *What's Left of Theory: New Work on the Politics of Literary Theory,* eds. Judith Butler, John Gillory, and Kendall Thomas (New York: Routledge, 2000).

35. K. Anthony Appiah and Amy Gutmann, *Color Conscious: The Political Morality of Race* (Princeton, N.J.: Princeton University Press, 1996), 99.

36. LeBesco, *Revolting Bodies?* 123.

37. T. A. Wadden et al., "Treatment of Obesity by Very Low Calorie Diet, Behavior Therapy, and Their Combination: A Five-Year Perspective," *International Journal of Obesity* 13 (1989).

38. Sander L. Gilman, "Fat as Disability: The Case of the Jews," *Literature and Medicine* 23 (2004).

39. Nikolas Rose, *Inventing Our Selves: Psychology, Power, and Personhood* (New York: Cambridge University Press, 1996), 196.

40. Lauren B. Edelman, Sally Riggs Fuller, and Iona Mara-Drita, "Diversity Rhetoric and the Managerialization of Law," *The American Journal of Sociology* 106 (2001): 1592.

41. Ibid.

42. Eric Abrahamson, "Management Fashion," *The Academy of Management Review* 21 (1996): 255, 259.

43. Martha Craven Nussbaum, *Hiding from Humanity: Disgust, Shame, and the Law* (Princeton, NJ: Princeton University Press, 2004).

44. Tobin Siebers, "What Can Disability Studies Learn from the Culture Wars?" *Cultural Critique* 55 (2003): 185.

45. Paul F. Campos, *The Obesity Myth: Why America's Obsession with Weight Is Hazardous to Your Health* (New York: Gotham Books, 2004), 68.

46. Jonathan M. Metzl and Rebecca M. Herzig, "Medicalisation in the 21st Century: Introduction," *Lancet* 369 (2007).

47. Compliance Guidelines to Prohibit Weight and Height Discrimination, City of San Francisco Human Rights Commission, San Francisco Administrative Code Chapters 12A, 12B, and 12C, and San Francisco Municipal/Police Code Article 33, http://www.sfgov.org/site/sfhumanrights_page.asp?id=5911.

48. Anna Kirkland, "Think of the Hippopotamus: Rights Consciousness in the Fat Acceptance Movement," *Law & Society Review* 42 (forthcoming June 2008).

NOTES TO THE CONCLUSION

1. Davina Cooper, *Challenging Diversity: Rethinking Equality and the Value of Difference* (New York: Cambridge University Press, 2004), 60–64.

2. Ibid., 63.

3. Elizabeth Anderson, "Racial Integration as a Compelling Interest," *Constitutional Commentary* 21 (2004).

4. Janet Halley, " 'Like-Race' Arguments," in *What's Left of Theory: New Work on the Politics of Literary Theory,* ed. Judith Butler, John Gillory, and Kendall Thomas (New York: Routledge, 2000), 53. For example, gay rights opponents seem to know that to govern someone as a named identity is to step along the road to recognition and the extension of rights. The federal Hate Crimes Statistics Act is a fascinating example of governmental tracking of identities that includes sexual orientation as a vector of hate crime, even though there are no federal-level civil rights laws that protect people against discrimination based on sexual orientation. The Act directs the U.S. Attorney General to gather and report statistics each year "about crimes that manifest evidence of prejudice based on race, religion, disability, sexual orientation, or ethnicity, including where appropriate the crimes of murder, non-negligent manslaughter; forcible rape; aggravated assault, simple assault, intimidation; arson; and destruction, damage or vandalism of property." Read along with the other traits, it is clear that the underlying idea is that violence against gays and lesbians exists, is morally reprehensible, and ought to be tabulated (the first step toward governance). Congressional conservatives added that "[n]othing in this Act shall be construed, nor shall any funds appropriated to carry out the purpose of the Act be used, to promote or encourage homosexuality" because they were afraid that it would do precisely that. Hate Crimes Statistics Act, P.L. 104-155 (1996), 28 U.S.C.S. § 534.

Index

Ability. *See* Functional individualism

Accommodation: for fat workers, 43–45, 133–134, 140–146, 168n37; as managerial process, 23, 133, 136–140; as required by the Americans with Disabilities Act, 22–23, 118–119, 136–137. *See also* Disability; Interactive process; Managerial individualism

Actuarial personhood: concept introduced and explained, 19–22, 102–109; of fat people, 97–98, 102–114, 119–120, 153; as handled in credit and lending discrimination cases, 120–123; as handled in disability rights law, 114–119; law's incoherent response to, 123–125. *See also* Logics of personhood; Risk

Adarand Constructors v. Pena, 172n25

Adolphe Quetelet, 112–113

Advocacy strategies, 25–26, 154–159

Affirmative action, 14, 61–62, 64–65, 70, 171n23. *See also* Blame-shifting; Diversity

African Americans: and masculine entitlement to jobs, 79, 171n10; and school segregation, 58–60, 170n6; as unique focus in American antidiscrimination law, 61–63, 71–73, 78–79, 92–93, 170n1, 170n3. *See also* Race discrimination

Age Discrimination in Employment Act (ADEA), 1, 177n42

Americans with Disabilities Act (ADA): definition of disability under, 22–24, 128–130; direct threat defense to obligations under, 116–120, 183n61; enactment of, 129–130, 134–135, 164n37; ineffectiveness of, 130. *See also* Disability; Managerial individualism

Amicus curiae briefs in support of diversity, 66, 70–71, 173n40

Antidiscrimination ordinances on the basis of weight. *See* Weight discrimination

Appearance: and compliance with workplace grooming policies, 17–18, 87–89, 94–95; contrasted to functional ability, 7–9, 35; and diversity, 51–52, 71; and embedded personhood, 9–11; and role modeling, 36–41

Ballot initiatives, 161n3, 171n23

Barnes v. City of Cincinnati, 176n31. See also *Smith v. City of Salem*; Transgender discrimination

Blame-shifting: concept introduced and explained, 12–14, 55–60; in context of disability discrimination law, 127–128; in context of race discrimination law, 55–64; as a fat rights strategy, 49–50. *See also* "Like-race" analogies; Race discrimination; Straitjacket metaphor

Body Mass Index (BMI), 112–113

Bona fide occupational qualification (BFOQ), 90–94, 177n42, 177n49, 178n59

Boyd v. Ozark Air Lines, 46, 168n14

Brown v. Board of Education, 58–60, 170n6

Carter v. Northwest Airlines, 23–24, 138–140

Center for Consumer Freedom (CCF), 111

"Cheeseburger bill." *See* Personal Responsibility in Food Consumption Act

Civil Rights Act of 1964: historical background of, 12–13, 56–59, 78–79; protected categories included in, 56, 170n3. *See also* Race discrimination; Sex discrimination

Civil Rights Act of 1991, 170n4

Color blindness, 12, 187n4

Common sense reasoning, 32–34, 47
Community, 46–49
Community Reinvestment Act (CRA), 121
Congress: and Americans with Disabilities Act, 129–131; and Civil Rights Act of 1964, 78–79; and housing and lending discrimination legislation, 121–122; powers of under Section 5 of the 14th Amendment, 172n24
Cook v. State of Rhode Island Department of Mental Health, Retardation, and Hospitals, 42–43
"Critical mass," 66, 68
Customer preferences in employment discrimination law, 10. *See also* Embedded personhood; Role modeling

DeGaffenreid v. General Motors, 175n12
Dieting, 47–48
Difference: accommodating, 22–24, 127–128; logics of personhood as stories about, 1–4, 147–153; as actuarial prediction, 19–22, 153; as differing capabilities, 7–9, 148; as diversity, 14–16, 64–71, 150–152; managing, 22–24, 152; as produced by unequal conditions between groups, 12–14, 55–60, 149–150; strategies for talking about, 25–27,154–159; as subject of stereotype, 16–19; as socially meaningful, 9–11, 148–149. *See also* Actuarial personhood; Blameshifting; Diverse personhood; Embedded personhood; Functional individualism; Logics of personhood; Managerial individualism
Dignity, 34
Disability: individualization of, 114–115; as a legally protected category, 23, 33, 128–131; medical model of, 128; obesity as, 131–134, 140–146; "regarded as" claims of, 33, 38; required accommodations for, 22–23, 118–119, 136–137; and risk, 114–120; social model of, 127–128. *See also* Accommodation; Americans with Disabilities Act (ADA); Managerial individualism
"Discrete and insular minority," 135
Disgust, 143–144, 180n20
Disparate impact discrimination, 13, 41–42, 46, 57–58, 61–63, 167n28, 172n25. *See also* Civil Rights Act of 1964; *Griggs v. Duke Power*; Intent to discriminate
Disparate treatment discrimination, 57

Diverse personhood: concept introduced and explained, 14–16. *See also* Diversity
Diversity: and person's appearance, 51–52, 71; benefits of, 150–151, 164n23; in corporate management, 15, 51–52, 66, 70–71; critiques of, 68, 150–152; fatness and, 51–52, 56; individualization within, 64–73, 107; legal concept under 14th Amendment equal protection, 15, 64–71; in the military, 66, 70–71; and racial and ethnic minorities, 51, 67–71, 151–152; as strategy for establishing rights, 26, 49–52. *See also* Affirmative action
Duty to mitigate injury by losing weight, 47–48, 163n18, 168n44

Education for All Handicapped Children Act, 188n33
Elliott-Larsen Civil Rights Act, 44, 126, 162n7, 167n35
Embedded personhood: concept introduced and explained, 9–11, 36–41; of fat people, 46–49; and preservation of gender in antidiscrimination law, 11, 17–19, 75–77, 89–96, 149; as vehicle for prejudice, 10–11, 148–149, 178n59. *See also* Appearance; Logics of personhood; Normative stereotype; Role modeling; Sex discrimination
Employment discrimination. *See* Civil Rights Act of 1964
Equal Credit Opportunity Act (ECOA), 121
Equal Employment Opportunity Commission (EEOC), 60–61
Equal Employment Opportunity Commission v. Texas Bus Lines, 7–8, 32–34. *See also* Functional individualism
Equal protection clause, 49–50, 64–65, 89, 169n46, 172n24
Equal Rights Amendment (ERA), 78, 174n6

Fair Housing Act (FHA), 121–122
False stereotype, definition of, 18–19, 76. *See also* Stereotypes
Fat: disgust at, 143–144, 180n20; evidence of discrimination on the basis of, 50; and diversity, 51–52, 56; as a legally protected trait, 31–54, 131–134, 140–146; and logics of personhood, 31–54; moral panic over, ix, 30, 110–111, 113, 132, 143, 180n20; as queer, 50; social meanings of, 9–10; use of term, ix, 161n2. *See also* Obesity; Weight discrimination

Foucault, Michel, 5
"Four-fifths rule," 61–62
Fourteenth Amendment. *See* Equal protection clause
Functional individualism: altered in disability law, 127–128; concept introduced and explained, 7–9, 34–36, 162n11; as strategy for establishing rights, 26, 32–36, 40–41; as unjust given structural disadvantage, 57–60, 148–150. See also *Equal Employment Opportunity Commission v. Texas Bus Lines*; Logics of personhood; *Mary Nedder v. Rivier College*

Gender discrimination. *See* Sex discrimination
Governmentality, 5, 152
Gratz v. Bollinger, 64–71
Grooming requirements, 17–18, 87–89, 94–95. *See also* Appearance
Griggs v. Duke Power, 13, 57–60, 163n19, 172n24, 172n25
Grutter v. Bollinger, 64–71

Hate Crimes Statistics Act, 190n4
Health: actuarial projections about, 21–22; and disability discrimination claims, 20–21; and weight, 110–112, 179n14
Health at Every Size (HAES), 110
Health Insurance Portability and Accountability Act (HIPAA), 101, 179n10
Healthism, 74
Height requirements, 168n38. See also *Boyd v. Ozark Air Lines*; Disparate impact discrimination
Home Mortgage Disclosure Act (HMDA), 121–122, 185n86
Housing and Urban Development, U.S. Department of, 120–122
Human rights, 166n11

Identity: indeterminacy under disability law, 140–143; indeterminacy under diversity management, 68–71; produced through legal process, 136–142; relation to personhood, 24–25
Individualism. *See* Functional individualism; Individualization; Managerial individualism
Individualization: to combat stereotyping, 41–43; in disability law, 114–115, 129–130, 143–146; in diversity rhetoric, 64–73, 107; and fatness, 43, 145; and risk,

114–115; in sex stereotyping, 21–22, 81–82. *See also* Functional individualism; Managerial individualism
In re Employment Discrimination Litigation against the State of Alabama, 172n24
Insurance discrimination, 99–101, 106, 120–123, 178n4, 186n93. *See also* Actuarial personhood; Risk
Integration, 173n30
Intent to discriminate, 13, 57–58, 172n24, 172n25
Interactive process, 133, 136–140. *See also* Accommodation; Process
Interagency Task Force on Fair Lending, 122
International Obesity Task Force (IOTF), 109
Intersectionality, 77–79, 92–93, 171n10, 174n12

Jazzercise weight discrimination case. See Portnick, Jennifer
Jefferies v. Harris County Community Action Association, 175n12
Jespersen v. Harrah's, 17–18, 87–89, 94–95
Jim Crow, 170n1

Legal process. *See* Process
"Like-race" analogy, 26, 49–51, 155
Logics of personhood: applied to fatness, 31–54; concept introduced and explained, 2–5, 34; limitations of each, 148–153; philosophical roots of, 5–6. *See also* Actuarial personhood; Blameshifting; Diverse personhood; Embedded personhood; Functional individualism; Managerial individualism; Personhood; Transcendental personhood
Los Angeles Department of Water and Power v. Manhart, 21–22, 81, 94, 175n21. *See also* Actuarial personhood; Risk; Sex discrimination

Managerial individualism: and accommodations for fat people, 143–146; concept introduced and explained, 22–24; and disability, 22–24, 134–146; and identity production, 140–142. *See also* Accommodations; *Carter v. Northwest Airlines*; Interactive process; Process
Managerialization of law, 142

Marks v. National Communications Association, 9–10, 39–40, 163n17
Mary Nedder v. Rivier College, 38–39
McDermott v. Xerox, 8, 19–20
McDonald's: customer base of, 168n40; obesity litigation against, 47, 110, 168n39, 181n33. See also *Pelman v. McDonald's*; Personal Responsibility in Food Consumption Act
Medicalization of fat, 105, 108–112, 143–144
Medical model of disability, 128
Michigan height and weight antidiscrimination law. See Elliott-Larsen Civil Rights Act; *Webb v. Bowman*; Weight discrimination
Moral panic, ix, 30, 110–111, 113, 132, 143, 180n20
Mortgage lending discrimination, 120–123, 185n86, 185n87, 185n88

National Association to Advance Fat Acceptance (NAAFA), 7
National Fair Housing Alliance (NFHA), 120–121
Nguyen v. INS, 83–84, 95, 176n27
Normalization, 104, 112–114, 183n46
Normative stereotype, definition of, 19, 36–37, 76–77. See also Stereotypes

Obesity: as contested terminology, ix, 161n2, 166n5; as a disability, 131–134, 140–146, 187n15; and employment discrimination, 32–34; as epidemic, ix, 30, 109; government guidelines defining, 112–113; and health, 109–112, 115, 179n14; and moral panic, ix, 30, 110–111, 113, 132, 143, 180n20; public opinion about, 110–111,169n44; regulations to reduce, 110, 181n35. See also Fat; Weight discrimination

Pelman v. McDonald's, 168n39, 181n33, 181n34
Perceived disability. See "Regarded as" disabled
Personal injury. See Duty to mitigate injury by losing weight
Personal Responsibility in Food Consumption Act, 47, 181n34
Personhood: concept introduced and explained, 3–7, 25, 165n43. See also Actuarial personhood; Blame-shifting; Diverse personhood; Embedded personhood; Functional individualism; Logics of personhood; Managerial individualism; Transcendental personhood
Phillips v. Martin Marietta, 82
Policy recommendations, 156–159
Portnick, Jennifer, 39–40
Price Waterhouse v. Hopkins, 84–88, 93–95
Process: contrasted with legal entitlement, 69; and disability accommodations, 22–24, 136–142; and identity, 69–70, 140–142, 152; university admissions, 66–67. See also Interactive process; Managerial individualism
Proposal 2 (Michigan anti-affirmative action ballot initiative), 171n23
Public opinion on obesity, 169n44

Race discrimination: conceptualized as structural, 56–60, 63, 72–73; and diversity, 51, 56, 64–71; and ethno-racial categorization, 61–62; and intersections with sex discrimination, 16, 77–79, 92–93; in lending, 120–123, 185n86, 185n87, 186n93; and masculinity, 171n10; as unique focus in American legal development, 12, 49–50, 55, 61–63, 170n1, 170n2. See also African Americans; Blame-shifting; Civil Rights Act of 1964; *Gratz v. Bollinger*; *Griggs v. Duke Power*; *Grutter v. Bollinger*; *Washington v. Davis*
Recommendations. See Policy recommendations
Redlining, 120–123, 185n86, 185n87
"Regarded as" disabled, 33, 38, 156. See also Disability; *Equal Employment Opportunity Commission v. Texas Bus Lines*; *Mary Nedder v. Rivier College*
Regents of the University of California v. Bakke, 15–16, 65–66
Risk: and construction of the person, 98–99, 101–109, 179n17; and disability, 114–120; and fat employees, 119–120; and individualization, 114–115; and insurance underwriting, 99–101, 186n93; judicial interpretations of, 116–119; of medical problems on the job, 97, 103–104, 114–118; and race, 105–106,120–123, 186n93; and stigmatization of groups, 105–107, 114–115, 175n21, 186n93. See also Actuarial personhood

Role modeling, 36–41. *See also* Appearance; Embedded personhood; *Marks v. National Communications Association*; *Mary Nedder v. Rivier College*; Portnick, Jennifer

San Francisco "height and weight" antidiscrimination ordinance, 39, 144–145
School Board of Nassau County v. Arline, 20–21, 114
Segregation, 58–60, 170n6
Sentencing guidelines, 171n17
Sex discrimination: amendment to Civil Rights Act of 1964, 78–79; and appearance, 84–89; bona fide occupational qualification (BFOQ) as excuse for, 90–94, 177n42, 177n49, 178n59; and intersections with race discrimination, 77–79, 92–93, 171n10; plus weight discrimination, 39–40; and stereotyping, 17–18, 75–96; transgender discrimination as, 85–89. *See also Jespersen v. Harrah's*; *Los Angeles Department of Water and Power v. Manhart*; *Nguyen v. INS*; *Phillips v. Martin Marietta*; *Price Waterhouse v. Hopkins*; *Smith v. City of Salem*; *United States v. Virginia*
"Sex plus" discrimination, 39–40, 163n17, 176n22. See also *Marks v. National Communications Association*; *Phillips v. Martin Marietta*
Sex stereotyping. See *Price Waterhouse v. Hopkins*; Stereotypes
Smith v. City of Salem, 85–89, 93–94. *See also* Transgender discrimination
Social model of disability, 127–128
Statistical stereotype, definition of, 18, 76. *See also* Stereotypes
Stereotypes: and construction of identity, 36–37; different conceptions of within antidiscrimination law, 18–19, 36–37, 76–77; and empirically valid generalizations, 41–43; and legal strategy, 26,

95–96; in sex discrimination law, 17–18; 75–96. *See also* False stereotype; Normative stereotype; Statistical stereotype
Straitjacket metaphor, 59–60, 150

Tanberg v. Ackerman Investment Company, 47–48. *See also* Duty to mitigate injury by losing weight
Thought experiment, 25–27, 154–159
Title VII. See Civil Rights Act of 1964
Tort law. See Duty to mitigate injury by losing weight
Transcendental personhood, 34, 166n11
Transgender discrimination, 85–89, 156, 162n7

Unfair Trade Practices Act (UTPA), 100
United States v. Virginia, 82
Universal Declaration of Human Rights, 166n11

Voting rights, 170n2

Washington v. Davis, 64, 172n25. *See also* Disparate impact discrimination; *Griggs v. Duke Power*; Intent to discriminate
Webb v. Bowman, 44–45, 168n37
Weber, Max, 5
Weight charts, 98. *See also* Body Mass Index (BMI); Normalization
Weight discrimination: in insurance, 100; laws prohibiting, 39, 44, 162n7; strategies to combat, 25–27, 154–159; weight requirements as, 44, 167n28. *See also* Elliott Larsen Civil Rights Act; *Equal Employment Opportunity Commission v. Texas Bus Lines*; *Marks v. National Communications Association*; *Mary Nedder v. Rivier College*; Portnick, Jennifer; San Francisco "height and weight" antidiscrimination ordinance; *Webb v. Bowman*
Workforce 2000, 15–16. *See also* Diversity

About the Author

Anna Kirkland is Assistant Professor of Women's Studies and Political Science at the University of Michigan.

Printed in the United States
138293LV00001B/17/P